EXAM✓CRAM

CompTIA®
Cloud+
CV0-003
Exam Cram

William "Bo" Rothwell

T0100645

Pearson

CompTIA® Cloud+ CV0-003 Exam Cram

Copyright © 2022 by Pearson Education, Inc.

All rights reserved. This publication is protected by copyright, and permission must be obtained from the publisher prior to any prohibited reproduction, storage in a retrieval system, or transmission in any form or by any means, electronic, mechanical, photocopying, recording, or likewise. For information regarding permissions, request forms, and the appropriate contacts within the Pearson Education Global Rights & Permissions Department, please visit www.pearson.com/permissions.

No patent liability is assumed with respect to the use of the information contained herein. Although every precaution has been taken in the preparation of this book, the publisher and author assume no responsibility for errors or omissions. Nor is any liability assumed for damages resulting from the use of the information contained herein.

ISBN-13: 978-0-13-739325-1

ISBN-10: 0-13-739325-3

Library of Congress Control Number: 2021916057

1 2021

Trademarks

All terms mentioned in this book that are known to be trademarks or service marks have been appropriately capitalized. Pearson IT Certification cannot attest to the accuracy of this information. Use of a term in this book should not be regarded as affecting the validity of any trademark or service mark.

Warning and Disclaimer

Every effort has been made to make this book as complete and as accurate as possible, but no warranty or fitness is implied. The information provided is on an "as is" basis. The author and the publisher shall have neither liability nor responsibility to any person or entity with respect to any loss or damages arising from the information contained in this book or from the use of the supplementary online content.

Special Sales

For information about buying this title in bulk quantities, or for special sales opportunities (which may include electronic versions; custom cover designs; and content particular to your business, training goals, marketing focus, or branding interests), please contact our corporate sales department at corpsales@pearsoned.com or (800) 382-3419.

For government sales inquiries, please contact governmentsales@pearsoned.com.

For questions about sales outside the U.S., please contact intlcs@pearson.com.

Editor-in-Chief
Mark Taub

Director, ITP Product Management
Brett Bartow

Executive Editor
Nancy Davis

Managing Editor
Sandra Schroeder

Project Editor
Mandie Frank

Copy Editor
Chuck Hutchinson

Indexer
Ken Johnson

Proofreader
Abigail Manheim

Technical Editor
Akhil Behl

Publishing Coordinator
Cindy Teeters

Designer
Chuti Prasertsith

Compositor
codeMantra

Pearson's Commitment to Diversity, Equity, and Inclusion

Pearson is dedicated to creating bias-free content that reflects the diversity of all learners. We embrace the many dimensions of diversity, including but not limited to race, ethnicity, gender, socioeconomic status, ability, age, sexual orientation, and religious or political beliefs.

Education is a powerful force for equity and change in our world. It has the potential to deliver opportunities that improve lives and enable economic mobility. As we work with authors to create content for every product and service, we acknowledge our responsibility to demonstrate inclusivity and incorporate diverse scholarship so that everyone can achieve their potential through learning. As the world's leading learning company, we have a duty to help drive change and live up to our purpose to help more people create a better life for themselves and to create a better world.

Our ambition is to purposefully contribute to a world where:

- Everyone has an equitable and lifelong opportunity to succeed through learning.

- Our educational products and services are inclusive and represent the rich diversity of learners.

- Our educational content accurately reflects the histories and experiences of the learners we serve.

- Our educational content prompts deeper discussions with learners and motivates them to expand their own learning (and worldview).

While we work hard to present unbiased content, we want to hear from you about any concerns or needs with this Pearson product so that we can investigate and address them.

- Please contact us with concerns about any potential bias at https://www.pearson.com/report-bias.html.

Credits

Figure 3-1   Screenshot of CPU Compute Options © 2021, Amazon Web Services, Inc.

Figure 3-2   Screenshot of Database Class © 2021, Amazon Web Services, Inc.

Figure 3-3   Screenshot of Microsoft Azure Regions © Microsoft 2020

Figure 4-1   Screenshot of AWS EC2 Instance Types © 2021, Amazon Web Services, Inc.

Figure 5-1   Screenshot of Federation login example © Copyright 2021 Cisco DevNet

Figure 5-2   Screenshot of Invalid certificate warning © Google

Figure 5-3   Screenshot of List of CAs on a Google Chrome browser © Google

Figure 7-1   Screenshot of AWS Password Policy © 2021, Amazon Web Services, Inc.

Figure 7-2   Screenshot of Changing the permissions of a file in Windows © 2021, Amazon Web Services, Inc.

Figure 8-1   Screenshot of AWS Tags © 2021, Amazon Web Services, Inc.

Figure 10-1   © DZone, Inc.

Figure 10-2   © 1994 - 2018 Micro Focus

Figure 11-1   Screenshot of AWS instance details © 2021, Amazon Web Services, Inc.

Figure 12-1   © 2021, Amazon Web Services, Inc.

Figure 12-2   © 2021, Amazon Web Services, Inc.

Figure 14-3   Screenshot of Type 3 hypervisor © 2021, Amazon Web Services, Inc.

Figure 14-4   Screenshot of CPU Clock Speed value © 2021, Amazon Web Services, Inc.

Figure 15-1   Screenshot of Exporting a virtual machine in OVF format © 2021 Oracle

Figure 17-1   Screenshot of AWS Cloudwatch dashboard data representations © 2021, Amazon Web Services, Inc.

Figure 17-2   Screenshot of AWS Service Health Dashboard © 2021, Amazon Web Services, Inc.

Figure 17-3   Screenshot of AWS Personal Health Dashboard © 2021, Amazon Web Services, Inc.

Figure 18-1   Screenshot of AWS database instance bandwidth © 2021, Amazon Web Services, Inc.

Figure 21-1   Screenshot of Network diagram from Lucidchart tool © 2021 Lucid Software Inc

Figure 24-1   Screenshot of AWS Service Health Dashboard © 2021, Amazon Web Services, Inc.

Figure 25-1   Screenshot of The Wireshark command © Wireshark

Contents at a Glance

Contents

About the Author

At the impressionable age of 14, **William "Bo" Rothwell** crossed paths with a TRS-80 Micro Computer System (affectionately known as a "Trash 80"). Soon after, the adults responsible for Bo made the mistake of leaving him alone with the TSR-80. He immediately dismantled it and held his first computer class, showing his friends what made this "computer thing" work. Since that experience, Bo's passion for understanding how computers work and sharing this knowledge with others has resulted in a rewarding career in IT training. His experience includes cloud, Linux, UNIX, IT security, DevOps, and programming languages such as Perl, Python, Tcl, and BASH. He is the founder and lead instructor of One Course Source, an IT training organization.

Dedication

To my sister, Betsy, who I tormented so much growing up. I'm glad that now we are adults you have either forgotten or forgiven my misdeeds.

To my parents: 99.7 percent of the time Betsy confessed and got in trouble, it was really me.

To my childhood dog, Hansel, thank you for always being there, under the dining room table, when I needed vegetables to disappear from my plate. You learned to chew silently, and for that, I was grateful.

To my seventh-grade homeroom teacher, you know who you are. You said I was lazy and would never amount to anything. If you are reading this now, you have concrete proof in your hands that you were mistaken.

Acknowledgments

I always worry when I write this section that I will miss someone who has helped me with this book. It takes a team to write a book, but often the author gets all of the credit. For all of the editors and support staff who have helped make this book possible, thank you very much.

About the Technical Reviewer

Akhil Behl, CCIE Emeritus No. 19564, is a passionate IT executive with a key focus on the cloud and security. He has 18+ years of experience in the IT industry working across several leadership, advisory, consultancy, and business development profiles with various organizations. His technology and business specializations include cloud, security, infrastructure, data center, and business communication technologies. Currently, he leads business development for the cloud for a global systems integrator.

Akhil has written multiple titles on security and business communication technologies. In addition, he has contributed as technical editor for more than a dozen books on security, networking, and information technology. He also has published four books with Pearson Education/Cisco Press.

He has published several research papers in national and international journals, including *IEEE Xplore*, and presented at various IEEE conferences, as well as other prominent ICT, security, and telecom events. Writing and mentoring are his passion and a part of his life.

He holds CCIE Emeritus (Collaboration and Security), Azure Solutions Architect Expert, Google Professional Cloud Architect, Azure AI Certified Associate, Azure Data Fundamentals, CCSK, CHFI, PMP, ITIL, VCP, TOGAF, CEH, ISM, CCDP, and many other industry certifications. He has a bachelor's degree in technology and a master's of business administration degree.

We Want to Hear from You!

As the reader of this book, you are our most important critic and commentator. We value your opinion and want to know what we're doing right, what we could do better, what areas you'd like to see us publish in, and any other words of wisdom you're willing to pass our way.

We welcome your comments. You can email or write to let us know what you did or didn't like about this book—as well as what we can do to make our books better.

Please note that we cannot help you with technical problems related to the topic of this book.

When you write, please be sure to include this book's title and author as well as your name and email address. We will carefully review your comments and share them with the author and editors who worked on the book.

Email: community@informit.com

Reader Services

Register your copy of *CompTIA Cloud+ CV0-003 Exam Cram* at www.pearsonitcertification.com for convenient access to downloads, updates, and corrections as they become available. To start the registration process, go to www.pearsonitcertification.com/register and log in or create an account.* Enter the product ISBN 9780137393251 and click **Submit**. When the process is complete, you will find any available bonus content under Registered Products.

*Be sure to check the box that you would like to hear from us to receive exclusive discounts on future editions of this product.

Introduction

Welcome to *CompTIA Cloud+ CV0-003 Exam Cram*. This book will help you get ready to take and pass the CompTIA Cloud+ exam CV0-003.

This book is designed to remind you of everything you need to know to pass the CV0-003 certification exam. Each chapter includes a number of practice questions that should give you a reasonably accurate assessment of your knowledge, and, yes, we've provided the answers and their explanations for these questions. Read this book, understand the material, and you'll stand a very good chance of passing the real test.

Exam Cram books help you understand and appreciate the subjects and materials you need to know to pass CompTIA certification exams. *Exam Cram* books are aimed strictly at test preparation and review. They do not teach you everything you need to know about a subject. Instead, the authors streamline and highlight the pertinent information by presenting and dissecting the questions and problems they've discovered that you're likely to encounter on a CompTIA test.

Let's begin by looking at preparation for the exam.

How to Prepare for the Exam

This text follows the official exam objectives closely to help ensure your success. The CompTIA exam covers 5 domains and 27 objectives, and this book is aligned with those domains and objectives. These official objectives from CompTIA can be found here:

https://www.comptia.org/training/resources/exam-objectives

As you examine the numerous exam topics now covered in Cloud+, resist the urge to panic! This book you are holding will provide you with the knowledge (and confidence) that you need to succeed. You just need to make sure you read it and follow the guidance it provides throughout your Cloud+ journey.

Practice Tests

This book is filled with practice exam questions to get you ready!

▶ **CramSaver questions at the beginning of each chapter:** These difficult, open-ended questions ensure you really know the material. Some readers use these questions to "test out" of a particular topic.

▶ **CramQuizzes at the end of each chapter:** These quizzes provide another chance to demonstrate your knowledge after completing a chapter.

In addition, the book includes two full practice tests in the Pearson Test Prep software available to you either online or as an offline Windows application. To access the practice exams, please see the instructions in the card inserted in the sleeve in the back of the book. This card includes a unique access code that enables you to activate your exams in the Pearson Test Prep software.

If you are interested in more practice exams than are provided with this book, Pearson IT Certification publishes a Premium Edition eBook and Practice Test product. In addition to providing you with three eBook files (EPUB, PDF, and Kindle), this product provides you with two additional exams' worth of questions. The Premium Edition version also offers you a link to the specific section in the book that presents an overview of the topic covered in the question, allowing you to easily refresh your knowledge. The insert card in the back of the book includes a special offer for an 80 percent discount off this Premium Edition eBook and Practice Test product, which is an incredible deal.

Taking a Certification Exam

After you prepare for your exam, you need to register with a testing center. At the time of this writing, the cost to take the Cloud+ exam is $338 USD for individuals. Students in the United States are eligible for a significant discount. Additionally, check with your employer because many workplaces provide reimbursement programs for certification exams. For more information about these discounts, you can contact a local CompTIA sales representative, who can answer any questions you might have. If you don't pass, you can take the exam again for the same cost as the first attempt until you pass. The test is administered by Pearson VUE testing centers with locations globally. In addition, the CompTIA Cloud+ certification might fulfill requirements for many within the U.S. military, and testing centers are available on some military bases.

You will have 90 minutes to complete the exam. The exam consists of a maximum of 90 questions. If you have prepared, you should find that this is plenty of time to properly pace yourself and review the exam before submission.

Arriving at the Exam Location

As with any examination, arrive at the testing center early (at least 15 minutes). Be prepared! You need to bring two forms of identification (one with a picture). The testing center staff requires proof that you are who you say you are and that someone else is not taking the test for you. Arrive early, because if you are late, you will be barred from entry and will not receive a refund for the cost of the exam.

> **ExamAlert**
>
> You'll be spending a lot of time in the exam room. Plan on using the full 90 minutes allotted for your exam and surveys. Policies differ from location to location regarding bathroom breaks. Check with the testing center before beginning the exam.

In the Testing Center

You will not be allowed to take into the examination room study materials or anything else that could raise suspicion that you're cheating. This includes practice test material, books, exam prep guides, or other test aids. The Testing Center will provide you with scratch paper and a pen or pencil. These days, this often comes in the form of an erasable whiteboard.

Examination results are available after the exam. After submitting the exam, you will be notified whether you have passed or failed. The test administrator will also provide you with a printout of your results.

About This Book

The ideal reader for an *Exam Cram* book is someone seeking certification. However, it should be noted that an *Exam Cram* book is a very easily readable, rapid presentation of facts. Therefore, an *Exam Cram* book is also extremely useful as a quick reference manual.

You can read this book cover to cover, or you may jump across chapters as needed. Because the book chapters align with the exam objectives, some chapters may have overlap on topics. Where required, references to the other chapters are provided for you. If you need to brush up on a topic, you can use the index, table of contents, or Table I.1 to find the topics and go to the questions that you need to study. Beyond helping you prepare for the test, we think you'll find this book useful as a tightly focused reference on some of the most important aspects of the Cloud+ certification.

This book includes other helpful elements in addition to the actual logical, step-by-step learning progression of the chapters themselves. *Exam Cram* books use elements such as ExamAlerts, tips, notes, and practice questions to make information easier to read and absorb. This text also includes a very helpful glossary to assist you.

> **Note**
>
> Reading this book from start to finish is not necessary; this book is set up so that you can quickly jump back and forth to find sections you need to study.

Use the *CramSheet* found in the front of the book to remember last-minute facts immediately before the exam. Use the practice questions to test your knowledge. You can always brush up on specific topics in detail by referring to the table of contents and the index. Even after you achieve certification, you can use this book as a rapid-access reference manual.

Exam Objectives

Table I.1 lists the skills the CV0-003 exam measures and the chapter in which the objective is discussed.

TABLE I.1

Exam Domain	Objective	Chapter in Book That Covers It
1.0 Cloud Architecture and Design	1.1 Compare and contrast the different types of cloud models.	Chapter 1
1.0 Cloud Architecture and Design	1.2 Explain the factors that contribute to capacity planning.	Chapter 2
1.0 Cloud Architecture and Design	1.3 Explain the importance of high availability and scaling in cloud environments.	Chapter 3
1.0 Cloud Architecture and Design	1.4 Given a scenario, analyze the solution design in support of the business requirements.	Chapter 4
2.0 Security	2.1 Given a scenario, configure identity and access management.	Chapter 5
2.0 Security	2.2 Given a scenario, secure a network in a cloud environment.	Chapter 6

Exam Domain	Objective	Chapter in Book That Covers It
2.0 Security	2.3 Given a scenario, apply the appropriate OS and application security controls.	Chapter 7
2.0 Security	2.4 Given a scenario, apply data security and compliance controls in cloud environments.	Chapter 8
2.0 Security	2.5 Given a scenario, implement measures to meet security requirements.	Chapter 9
2.0 Security	2.6 Explain the importance of incident response procedures.	Chapter 10
3.0 Deployment	3.1 Given a scenario, integrate components into a cloud solution.	Chapter 11
3.0 Deployment	3.2 Given a scenario, provision storage in cloud environments.	Chapter 12
3.0 Deployment	3.3 Given a scenario, deploy cloud networking solutions.	Chapter 13
3.0 Deployment	3.4 Given a scenario, configure the appropriate compute sizing for a deployment.	Chapter 14
3.0 Deployment	3.5 Given a scenario, perform cloud migrations.	Chapter 15
4.0 Operations and Support	4.1 Given a scenario, configure logging, monitoring, and alerting to maintain operational status.	Chapter 16
4.0 Operations and Support	4.2 Given a scenario, maintain efficient operation of a cloud environment.	Chapter 17
4.0 Operations and Support	4.3 Given a scenario, optimize cloud environments.	Chapter 18
4.0 Operations and Support	4.4 Given a scenario, apply proper automation and orchestration techniques.	Chapter 19
4.0 Operations and Support	4.5 Given a scenario, perform appropriate backup and restore operations.	Chapter 20
4.0 Operations and Support	4.6 Given a scenario, perform disaster recovery tasks.	Chapter 21
5.0 Troubleshooting	5.1 Given a scenario, use the troubleshooting methodology to resolve cloud-related issues.	Chapter 22
5.0 Troubleshooting	5.2 Given a scenario, troubleshoot security issues.	Chapter 23

Exam Domain	Objective	Chapter in Book That Covers It
5.0 Troubleshooting	5.3 Given a scenario, troubleshoot deployment issues.	Chapter 24
	5.6 Given a scenario, troubleshoot automation or orchestration issues.	
5.0 Troubleshooting	5.4 Given a scenario, troubleshoot connectivity issues.	Chapter 25
	5.5 Given a scenario, troubleshoot common performance issues.	

The Chapter Elements

Each *Exam Cram* book has chapters that follow a predefined structure. This structure makes *Exam Cram* books easy to read and provides a familiar format for all *Exam Cram* books. The following elements typically are used:

▶ Chapter topics

▶ Essential Terms and Components

▶ CramSavers

▶ CramQuizzes

▶ Notes

▶ Available exam preparation software practice questions and answers

> **Note**
>
> Bulleted lists, numbered lists, tables, and graphics are also used where appropriate. A picture can paint a thousand words sometimes, and tables can help to associate different elements with each other visually.

Now let's look at each of the elements in detail.

▶ **Chapter topics**—Each chapter contains details of all subject matter listed in the table of contents for that particular chapter. The objective of an *Exam Cram* book is to cover all the important facts without giving too much detail; it is an exam cram.

▶ **CramSavers**—Each chapter kicks off with a short-answer quiz to help you assess your knowledge of the chapter topic. This chapter element is designed to help you determine whether you need to read the whole chapter in detail or merely skim the material and skip ahead to the CramQuiz at the end of the chapter.

▶ **CramQuizzes**—Each chapter concludes with a multiple-choice quiz to help ensure that you have gained familiarity with the chapter content.

▶ **ExamAlerts**—ExamAlerts address exam-specific, exam-related information. An ExamAlert addresses content that is particularly important, tricky, or likely to appear on the exam. An ExamAlert looks like this:

ExamAlert

Make sure you remember the different ways in which you can access a router remotely. Know which methods are secure and which are not.

▶ **Notes**—Notes typically contain useful information that is not directly related to the current topic under consideration. To avoid breaking up the flow of the text, they are set off from the regular text.

Note

This is a note. You have already seen several notes.

Other Book Elements

Most of this *Exam Cram* book on Cloud+ follows the consistent chapter structure already described. However, various important elements are not part of the standard chapter format. These elements apply to the book as a whole.

▶ **Glossary**—The glossary contains a listing of important terms used in this book with explanations.

▶ **CramSheet**—The CramSheet is a quick-reference, tear-out cardboard sheet of important facts useful for last-minute preparation. CramSheets often include a simple summary of the facts that are most difficult to remember.

▶ **Companion website**—The companion website for your book allows you to access several digital assets that come with your book, including

  ▶ Pearson Test Prep software (both online and Windows desktop versions)

  ▶ Key Terms Flash Cards application

  ▶ A PDF version of the CramSheet

To access the book's companion website, simply follow these steps:

1. Register your book by going to: PearsonITCertification.com/register and entering the ISBN: 9780137393251.

2. Respond to the challenge questions.

3. Go to your account page and select the **Registered Products** tab.

4. Click the **Access Bonus Content** link under the product listing.

Pearson Test Prep Practice Test Software

As noted previously, this book comes complete with the Pearson Test Prep practice test software containing two full exams. These practice tests are available to you either online or as an offline Windows application. To access the practice exams that were developed with this book, please see the instructions in the card inserted in the sleeve in the back of the book. This card includes a unique access code that enables you to activate your exams in the Pearson Test Prep software.

Accessing the Pearson Test Prep Software Online

The online version of this software can be used on any device with a browser and connectivity to the Internet, including desktop machines, tablets, and smartphones. To start using your practice exams online, simply follow these steps:

1. Go to http://www.PearsonTestPrep.com.

2. Select **Pearson IT Certification** as your product group.

3. Enter your email/password for your account. If you don't have an account on PearsonITCertification.com or CiscoPress.com, you will need to establish one by going to PearsonITCertification.com/join.

4. In the **My Products** tab, click the **Activate New Product** button.

5. Enter the access code printed on the insert card in the back of your book to activate your product.

6. The product will now be listed in your My Products page. Click the **Exams** button to launch the exam settings screen and start your exam.

Accessing the Pearson Test Prep Software Offline

If you wish to study offline, you can download and install the Windows version of the Pearson Test Prep software. There is a download link for this software on the book's companion website, or you can just enter this link in your browser:

http://www.pearsonitcertification.com/content/downloads/pcpt/engine.zip

To access the book's companion website and the software, simply follow these steps:

1. Register your book by going to PearsonITCertification.com/register and entering the ISBN: 9780137393251.

2. Respond to the challenge questions.

3. Go to your account page and select the **Registered Products** tab.

4. Click the **Access Bonus Content** link under the product listing.

5. Click the **Install Pearson Test Prep Desktop Version** link under the Practice Exams section of the page to download the software.

6. After the software finishes downloading, unzip all the files on your computer.

7. Double-click the application file to start the installation, and follow the on-screen instructions to complete the registration.

8. When the installation is complete, launch the application and select the **Activate Exam** button on the My Products tab.

9. Click the **Activate a Product** button in the Activate Product Wizard.

10. Enter the unique access code found on the card in the sleeve in the back of your book and click the **Activate** button.

11. Click **Next** and then the **Finish** button to download the exam data to your application.

12. You can now start using the practice exams by selecting the product and clicking the **Open Exam** button to open the exam settings screen.

Note that the offline and online versions will synch together, so saved exams and grade results recorded on one version will be available to you on the other as well.

Customizing Your Exams

Once you are in the exam settings screen, you can choose to take exams in one of three modes:

▶ Study Mode

▶ Practice Exam Mode

▶ Flash Card Mode

Study Mode allows you to fully customize your exams and review answers as you are taking the exam. This is typically the mode you would use first to assess your knowledge and identify information gaps. Practice Exam Mode locks certain customization options because it is presenting a realistic exam experience. Use this mode when you are preparing to test your exam readiness. Flash Card Mode strips out the answers and presents you with only the question stem. This mode is great for late stage preparation when you really want to challenge yourself to provide answers without the benefit of seeing multiple-choice options. This mode will not provide the detailed score reports that the other two modes will, so it should not be used if you are trying to identify knowledge gaps.

In addition to these three modes, you will be able to select the source of your questions. You can choose to take exams that cover all of the chapters, or you can narrow your selection to just a single chapter or the chapters that make up specific parts in the book. All chapters are selected by default. If you want to narrow your focus to individual chapters, simply deselect all the chapters and then select only those on which you wish to focus in the Objectives area.

There are several other customizations you can make to your exam from the exam settings screen, such as the time of the exam, the number of questions served up, whether to randomize questions and answers, whether to show the number of correct answers for multiple-answer questions, or whether to serve up only specific types of questions. You can also create custom test banks by selecting only questions that you have marked or questions on which you have added notes.

Updating Your Exams

If you are using the online version of the Pearson Test Prep software, you should always have access to the latest version of the software as well as the exam data. If you are using the Windows desktop version, every time you launch the software, it will check to see if there are any updates to your exam data and automatically download any changes that were made since the last time you used the software. This requires that you are connected to the Internet at the time you launch the software.

Sometimes, due to many factors, the exam data may not fully download when you activate your exam. If you find that figures or exhibits are missing, you may need to manually update your exams.

To update a particular exam you have already activated and downloaded, simply select the **Tools** tab and select the **Update Products** button. Again, this is an issue only with the Windows desktop application.

If you wish to check for updates to the Pearson Test Prep exam engine software, Windows desktop version, simply select the **Tools** tab and select the **Update Application** button. This will ensure you are running the latest version of the software engine.

Contacting the Author

Hopefully, this book provides you with the tools you need to pass the Cloud+ exam. Feedback is appreciated. You can follow and contact the author on LinkedIn: https://www.linkedin.com/in/bo-rothwell/.

CHAPTER 1

Different Types of Cloud Models

This chapter covers the following official CompTIA Cloud+ exam objective:

▶ 1.1 Compare and contrast the different types of cloud models.

(For more information on the official CompTIA Cloud+ exam topics, see the Introduction.)

In this chapter you will learn about the different types of cloud deployment models. You will explore the differences between public, private, hybrid, and community cloud environments.

You will also learn how cloud providers offer a variety of features that relate to one of three service models: Infrastructure as a Service (IaaS), Platform as a Service (PaaS), and Software as a Service (SaaS). An important aspect of these service models, the shared responsibility model, is also covered at the end of this chapter.

Toward the end of this chapter, you will explore different advanced cloud services, including the Internet of Things (IoT), serverless applications, machine learning (ML), and artificial intelligence (AI).

CramSaver

If you can correctly answer these questions before going through this chapter, save time by skimming the ExamAlerts in this chapter and then completing the CramQuiz at the end of the chapter.

1. What are some of the advantages of a public cloud versus a private cloud?
2. What are some of the advantages of a private cloud versus a public cloud?
3. Describe the main features of an IaaS model.
4. Describe the main features of a PaaS model.
5. What are the main components of an IoT device?
6. What are some advantages of serverless applications versus applications that are deployed in an IaaS or a PaaS environment?

Answers

1. A public cloud tends to be more flexible and affordable than a private cloud.
2. A private cloud is typically more secure than a public cloud. Also, private clouds can more easier to adhere to strict regulatory requirements.
3. With an IaaS model, the customer is provided access to the underlying hardware.
4. With a PaaS model, the customer is provided access to a cloud-based application but is not required to maintain any part of the application.
5. The main components of an IoT device are that it has some computing power (a processor) and the capability to communicate over the Internet.
6. The advantage of creating serverless applications is that they are much more cost effective. An application runs only when needed (typically an action called a trigger starts the application), and the customer pays only when the application is running. After the application completes its tasks, it stops, and the customer isn't charged until the application starts again. In a PaaS scenario, the customer pays for the platform, regardless of whether the application is performing any tasks.

Cloud Deployment Models

For many organizations, moving their applications and services to the cloud is not a simple decision. For example, an organization must consider what applications or services can be candidates to migrate to the cloud, who is responsible for the migration, and who is responsible for administering these services after they are deployed in the cloud.

Another consideration is what sort of cloud deployment model to leverage. There are four primary cloud types:

- ▶ Public

- ▶ Private

- ▶ Hybrid

- ▶ Community

In addition, a few terms (*multicloud* and *multitenancy*) are related to deployment models and are important to understand when considering which deployment model to utilize.

Public Cloud

When most people think about "The Cloud," they are likely thinking of a public cloud. A *public cloud* is a shared platform that can be leveraged for cloud computing needs by anyone. This way, consumers (cloud customers) can scale their cloud deployments while leveraging economies of scale. The advantage of using a public cloud is that you typically pay only for what you use by the minute or hour (or you can have upfront commitments to bring ongoing costs down provided you know the organization's minimum compute, storage, bandwidth, and consumption for the next one to three years). For example, if you create a virtual machine (VM) in a public cloud, you typically pay for when it is active, and if you decommission it, you don't need to pay for that service any longer (there are exceptions, like reservations, which will be covered later in this book). This is better known as a pay-as-you-go (or PAYG) or subscription-based service.

There are several well-known public cloud platform providers, including

- ▶ Amazon Web Services (AWS)

- ▶ Microsoft Azure

- ▶ Google Cloud Platform (GCP)

Although public clouds are a more affordable solution, they may not always be a viable solution for an organization. Because the hardware resources are shared, there is a high chance that services "live" in the same environment as services from other organizations (shared infrastructure or resource pooling). This is called *multitenancy* (think "multiple tenants"). For compliance and security reasons, this setup might not be ideal or even permitted for some organizations—for example, defense and research.

Public cloud providers attempt to address this concern in many ways. For example, many public cloud providers allow an organization to reserve an entire server for their use only. This is better known as *dedicated hosting*. However, there can still be concerns (for example, the system will be on the same physical network as another organization).

A public cloud may not address the needs of all organizations—for example, defense or public utilities, where possession of and access to the data is of paramount importance. Another solution that these and other similar organizations should consider is a private cloud.

Private Cloud

When an organization needs a high level of security and needs to adhere to very strict regulatory, governance, or compliance requirements, a *private cloud* might be a better solution than a public cloud. In a private cloud, all physical resources—for example, the servers, the storage devices, and the network—are reserved for the organization that hosts these services. Think about the U.S. Department of Defense (DoD) hosting all its services in its private cloud; in this case, everything belongs to the DoD, and it has full control of resources and data in the private cloud.

While this solution sounds great, it comes with some disadvantages. For example, a private cloud tends to be much more expensive (compared to a public cloud deployment) because the organization must pay for all of the hardware resources up front, regardless of whether they are being used currently. This is known as *capital expense* or *capex*. Another disadvantage is that it may not be possible to quickly scale up (leverage overprovisioned or large amounts of unused hardware resources) because private clouds typically don't have as many hardware resources available that public cloud environments have. As a result, you will rarely see an organization move all of its services to a private cloud, but rather make use of a hybrid cloud. This is, of course, outside of an organization such as the DoD.

Hybrid Cloud

A *hybrid cloud* is a construct that exists when both public cloud and private clouds are used concurrently. With a true hybrid cloud, the merging of the private and public cloud should be as seamless as possible.

An organization that utilizes a hybrid cloud is able to take advantage of the best of both public and private clouds. In this case, resources that need a high level of security or that must follow strict regulatory compliance requirements are hosted in the private cloud. Rules are put into place as to which resources are "private" and which are "public." This allows for more flexibility at an overall lower cost. Applications that need "bursting" can be hosted on a public cloud (see the "Cloud Bursting" section in Chapter 3, "High Availability and Scaling in Cloud Environments, for details on this topic,").

Community Cloud

Consider a situation in which several medical research organizations are working together on a project. These organizations need to be able to share resources, but because each organization also has its own projects, it needs to keep the details private. So, using the cloud environment of any of these organizations isn't a good solution for security reasons.

In this case, a *community cloud* should be used. With a community cloud, multitenancy is handled differently than in a typical public cloud. The goal of multitenancy on a public cloud is to completely separate resources between tenants. On a community cloud, multitenancy allows for the sharing of resources or applications. A community cloud allows for greater collaboration between these organizations while still allowing each organization a measure of control over its users, resources, and services.

Cloud Within a Cloud

Recall that on a public cloud, multitenancy means that different organizations are utilizing the same hardware resources concurrently. Public cloud providers want to ensure that these organizations can't see each other's resources, so they make use of a virtual private cloud (VPC). Note in some environments, like Azure, a VPC is the same as a virtual network (VNet).

A VPC has features that permit an organization to see only its own resources, even if other organizations have resources on the same hardware. For example, two organizations could be sharing a physical network, but they can only see traffic that is being sent from or to their own resources.

The concept of VPC is referred to as a "cloud within a cloud."

Multicloud

While it isn't considered one of the four standard cloud deployment models, a *multicloud* is a solution that some organizations may leverage. A multicloud is a heterogenous construct that is born when an organization leverages more than one cloud platform, private or public, to host its services. For example, an organization can host its IaaS workloads in AWS, its PaaS workloads in Azure, and data-focused workloads in GCP. The databases can still be on-premises.

Multiclouds can be very complex and may require specialized software to integrate the different public cloud environments. Often this specialized software isn't readily available, meaning it needs to be created by the organization that is utilizing the multicloud.

Why use a multicloud? Different cloud vendors provide different solutions and in different geographic regions. In large organizations, the solutions provided by one cloud vendor might not meet the needs of one department in the organization but might be a great fit for the needs of another department in the organization. Using a multicloud also helps mitigate contractual and unavailability risks, such as vendor lock-in.

Multitenancy

Note that this exam objective is covered in the "Public Cloud" section in this chapter.

> **ExamAlert**
>
> You are likely to be given a scenario on the exam that outlines the needs of an organization and then be asked which cloud deployment solution would best fit the organization's requirements. Be aware of the advantages and disadvantages of public (flexible, low cost, easy to use), private (higher cost, more secure, and more likely to adhere to regulatory compliance requirements), and hybrid cloud deployment models.

Cloud Service Models

A cloud service model is a way of categorizing cloud features into one of three categories:

- ▶ Infrastructure as a Service (IaaS)

▶ Platform as a Service (PaaS)

▶ Software as a Service (SaaS)

There are some advantages to categorizing services into one of these service models.

One of the primary advantages is to get an idea of what components of the service are the responsibility of the cloud provider and which components of the service are the responsibility of the customer. This is referred to as the *shared responsibility model*. The key advantage is to understand the type of workload as it would exist in a cloud as opposed to on-premises. For example, a virtual machine on-premises can be modernized to a container architecture natively hosted as a PaaS service in the cloud platform of your choice. The patching process and underlying infrastructure specifics are no longer relevant because the underlying operating system and hardware are now a responsibility of the cloud provider.

Infrastructure as a Service (IaaS)

Suppose you want to deploy a service that has access to the hardware that is provided by the cloud platform. For example, you might want to deploy a virtual machine in the cloud. This service would be referred to as Infrastructure as a Service (IaaS). With IaaS, the service requires some sort of access to the underlying hardware.

Examples of IaaS include

▶ Azure Compute

▶ Google Compute Engine

▶ AWS EC2

With an IaaS solution, most of the responsibility of the service lies with the customer. See the "Cloud Shared Responsibility Model" section in this chapter for more details.

Note

Any virtual machine hosted in the cloud is better known as an *instance*.

Platform as a Service (PaaS)

In a PaaS service model, the cloud platform provider delivers a platform to clients, thereby enabling them to develop, run, and manage applications without worrying about the need to build and maintain the underlying infrastructure. A PaaS model allows developers to create software without having to worry about maintaining an operating system or the underlying hardware—for example, patching the OS or updating disk drives. The developers can focus on installing and running their development environments.

Examples of PaaS services include

▶ AWS Elastic Beanstalk

▶ Azure App Service

▶ Google App Engine

With a PaaS solution, more of the responsibility is shifted to the cloud provider (compared to IaaS). See the "Cloud Shared Responsibility Model" section in this chapter for more details.

Software as a Service (SaaS)

Odds are you have used a SaaS, in fact probably more than one. If you have leveraged any of the following, you have used SaaS:

▶ Microsoft Office 365

▶ Google Apps (like Google Docs and Google Mail)

▶ DocuSign

▶ Dropbox

▶ Zoom

▶ Salesforce

You might be thinking "these are just applications that run via my web browser" and that is exactly the point. With SaaS, the customer uses software that is hosted remotely (typically in the cloud).

With an SaaS solution, all of the responsibility is shifted to the cloud provider. See the "Cloud Shared Responsibility Model" section in this chapter for more details.

Advanced Cloud Services

Several cloud-based services can be considered advanced. For the Cloud+ exam, you should know at least the following: Internet of Things, serverless, machine learning, and artificial intelligence.

Internet of Things (IoT)

The IoT market has exploded in recent years, with many commercial products now readily available. They include "controller" devices like Amazon Echo, smart doorbells, smart light bulbs, smart appliances (washing machines, refrigerators, and the like), and many more.

> **Note**
>
> The industry that creates these devices often uses the term *smart* to distinguish regular devices from IoT devices.

What does it mean that a device is an IoT device? The main components of an IoT device are that it has localized compute and the capability to communicate over the Internet to a hub, where it can send the data collected and receive further instructions on the next set of activities.

IoT devices are not limited to home appliances. In fact, IoT originated as part of the manufacturing industry leveraging automation and remote machine-to-machine communications. IoT devices are used to monitor automobile traffic, determine the effectiveness of factories that produce products, and manage shipping from large shipping containers to millions of individual packages daily.

Serverless

Recall from the "Platform as a Service (PaaS)" section earlier in this chapter that a cloud provider provides a platform (the cloud-based operating system) and a developer creates an application that runs on the platform. In some cases an application may be complicated enough to need a full platform, but for smaller applications this might not be necessary. Instead, the application could be run as a "serverless" application, which uses less resources and is more cost effective.

In a sense, the term *serverless* is a bit misleading. The application still runs on a server/hardware. A serverless application is packaged code that can run on hardware, abstracting the hardware and any underlying dependencies from the user, typically a developer. For example, a Java developer may not know what hardware and operating system (Windows or Linux) are being used to run the Java environment and can focus only on development.

The advantage of creating a serverless application is that it is much more cost effective. The application runs only when needed (typically an action called a *trigger* starts the application), and the customer pays only when the application is running. After the application completes its tasks, it stops, and the customer isn't charged until the application starts again. In a PaaS scenario, the customer pays for the platform, regardless of whether the application is performing any tasks.

Examples of serverless products include the following:

▶ Azure Functions

▶ Google Cloud Functions

▶ AWS Lambda

ExamAlert

For the Cloud+ exam, know the differences between running a serverless application versus running an application in a PaaS model.

Machine Learning/Artificial Intelligence (AI)

Mat Velloso famously tweeted: "Difference between machine learning and AI: If it is written in Python, it's probably machine learning. If it is written in PowerPoint, it's probably AI." This joke plays on the machine intelligence community's dismay for how the term *artificial intelligence* has been diluted recently. The joke also attempts to address the difference between machine learning and AI in a humorous manner.

The preceding tweet makes it seem as if machine learning and AI are different things, but in reality, machine learning is a component of AI.

The goal of AI is to create software that can reason in a manner similar to how a human can reason. This topic is potentially very complex, but the concept is to move software beyond "follow these directions" to a point where software can make decisions on its own.

Machine learning is an important component of AI. For software to be able to make independent decisions, the software needs to be able to learn new information and concepts without having to be explicitly programmed to learn these things. Consider how you can learn something new (a new language, how to play a musical instrument) without someone telling you to learn that topic or even *how* to learn the topic. Yes, you can take a class on how to play the piano, but depending on your natural abilities, you might be able to just figure it out on your own. Machine learning attempts to have software programs learn in a similar manner to the way we humans learn. These are known as *learning models*, and ML leverages new models to learn about possible inputs, events, actions,
and outputs.

You may wonder why AI and machine learning are included in the objectives of the Cloud+ exam. AI and machine learning require massive amounts of computing power, which is available largely in cloud environments. As a result, cloud technologies are very important to the advancement of AI.

Cloud Shared Responsibility Model

Cloud platform providers want customers to realize what parts of a cloud service the customer is responsible for maintaining and what parts the cloud provider is responsible for. Table 1.1 provides a typical summary of these responsibilities.

TABLE 1.1 **Shared Responsibility Model by Service Model**

On-Prem	IaaS	PaaS	SaaS
Data	Data	Data	Data
Application	Application	Application	Application
Application Security	Application Security	Application Security	Application Security
Runtime	Runtime	Runtime	Runtime
Middleware	Middleware	Middleware	Middleware
OS	OS	OS	OS

On-Prem	IaaS	PaaS	SaaS
Virtualization	Virtualization	Virtualization	Virtualization
Server Hardware	Server Hardware	Server Hardware	Server Hardware
Storage	Storage	Storage	Storage
Networking	Networking	Networking	Networking
Physical Security	Physical Security	Physical Security	Physical Security

Note that *On-Prem* means "hosted on premises, or physically in the customer's environment." While customers may create their own private cloud in their server rooms, on-prem means "not hosted by a cloud provider."

In Table 1.1, the boxes with gray background indicate the responsibility of the cloud provider, and the boxes with white background indicate the responsibility of the customer. The following examples are designed to provide further clarity:

▶ A customer creates a virtual machine using Amazon EC2 in the AWS cloud. The customer is responsible for patching the OS and maintaining any software that is installed on the OS. Amazon is responsible for securing and maintaining the servers where the virtual machine is installed.

▶ A customer creates an application and hosts it on Azure App Service. The customer is now responsible for making sure the application security is sound and that updates are made to the application in a timely manner. Azure is responsible for patching the OS, ensuring the storage is secure and reliable, and making sure the network is secure and responsive.

▶ A customer uses Google Docs to create a document. Google is responsible for just about everything related to the application, although the customer is responsible for the data placed in the document and, in some cases, the security of this data. For example, Google Docs allows the user to share the document, making that function the responsibility of the user, not Google's responsibility.

ExamAlert

For the Cloud+ exam, you should know Table 1.1 by heart. You will be asked scenario-based questions and expected to know which entity is responsible for each component of the application.

CramQuiz

Answer these questions. The answers follow the last question. If you cannot answer these questions correctly, consider reading this chapter again until you can.

1. Your organization deploys virtual machines on AWS. This is an example of which deployment model?
   - ○ **A.** Public
   - ○ **B.** Private
   - ○ **C.** Hybrid
   - ○ **D.** Community

2. A VPC is an example of using _____.
   - ○ **A.** Multitenancy
   - ○ **B.** Multicloud
   - ○ **C.** Cloud within a cloud
   - ○ **D.** Community

3. Which of the following is an example of IaaS?
   - ○ **A.** Google App Engine
   - ○ **B.** Google Compute Engine
   - ○ **C.** Google Apps
   - ○ **D.** AWS Elastic Beanstalk

4. Which of the following is an example of SaaS?
   - ○ **A.** AWS Elastic Beanstalk
   - ○ **B.** AWS EC2
   - ○ **C.** Azure Compute
   - ○ **D.** Dropbox

5. A serverless application runs in which of the following environments?
   - ○ **A.** IaaS
   - ○ **B.** PaaS
   - ○ **C.** SaaS
   - ○ **D.** None of these answers are correct

CramQuiz Answers

1. Public
2. Cloud within a cloud
3. Google Compute Engine
4. Dropbox
5. None of these answers are correct

What Next?

If you want more practice on this chapter's exam objectives before you move on, remember that you can access all of the CramQuiz questions on the companion website. You can also create a custom exam by objectives with the practice exam software. Note any objectives you struggle with and go to that objective's material in this chapter.

CHAPTER 2

Capacity Planning

This chapter covers the following official CompTIA Cloud+ exam objective:

▶ 1.2 Explain the factors that contribute to capacity planning.

(For more information on the official CompTIA Cloud+ exam topics, see the Introduction.)

In this chapter you will learn about *capacity planning*, which is the ongoing process of ensuring that your resources meet the needs of your consumers (employees, customers, clients, and so on). You will first be introduced to requirements; you can use them to define what levels of components, such as hardware and software, are needed to meet consumer needs.

This chapter will also cover licensing models, which are necessary to determine the best cloud-based solution for your organization's business needs. You will also learn the basics of performance capacity planning, which is used to determine how many resources are needed during the lifecycle of your project or program.

CramSaver

If you can correctly answer these questions before going through this section, save time by skimming the ExamAlerts in this section and then completing the CramQuiz at the end of the section.

1. What are some of the hardware requirements that you should consider when implementing a cloud-based resource?

2. Name two common cloud template data formats.

3. Which licenses are based on the CPU?

Answers

1. vCPUs, GPUs, RAM, Storage, Network performance

2. JSON and YAML

3. Socket-based and core-based

Requirements

One of the first steps to capacity planning is to determine your business and technical requirements. Cloud-based projects tend to be very flexible and have different requirements. To best ensure you meet both current and future business and/or technical needs, you should explore the following requirements before performing any of the other steps of capacity planning.

Hardware Requirements

Some of the services that you deploy in the cloud provide you with the option of choosing different hardware. For example, if you create a virtual machine or a database, you are normally provided with the option of choosing how much RAM, hard disk space, and other hardware components you need.

The choice of hardware profile is important in regard to capacity planning. The more RAM, hard disk space, vCPUs, and so on that you choose, the more your service will end up costing. However, if you opt for less hardware resources, you risk having the service fail to perform.

The hardware that you need to consider when performing capacity planning includes:

> ▶ **vCPUs:** Virtual CPUs provide the processing power. If your instance needs to perform a lot of processing, you need to take that into consideration when determining how many vCPUs to allocate to your instance.

> ▶ **GPUs:** The graphics processing unit has a large impact on how images are processed on the system.

> ▶ **RAM:** Random-access memory is used to store data for applications that are running. You should consider reviewing the software requirements for all the applications that you intend to install on the instance(s). This also has an impact on your machine learning models as well as the capability to execute other functions.

> ▶ **Storage:** You not only need to consider how much storage your instance(s) would need but also the different storage types that the cloud vendor provides. They may differ based on storage requirements for databases, application data, or archival needs. See Chapter 12, "Storage in Cloud Environments," for more details on storage types.

▶ **Network performance:** Most of the data transiting into or out of your cloud instance will be across either a public network, such as the Internet, or one of the private channels offered by cloud platform providers, such as Direct Connect (AWS), Inter Connect (GCP), or Express Route (Azure). As a result, the speed of the network for your instance will be an important decision when it comes to capacity planning.

Software Requirements

The software that you need to deploy in your cloud environment is another key requirement to determine during the capacity planning phase. In fact, what software you decide to use may determine which cloud provider you will end up using.

For instance, consider a situation in which you have decided to migrate an existing on-premises database solution to the cloud. The constraints of the existing database solution will have an impact on which cloud database solution you migrate to. And, because different cloud providers have different database solutions, the cloud solution you decide to migrate to may be available only from some cloud providers.

When determining a software solution, consider your needs and evaluate solutions to ensure they can meet your needs. Determine a schedule of deployment and clearly define constraints during the capacity planning phase to limit any scope creep (when additional features are required after a solution is in the implementation phase).

Budgetary Requirements

If money were not a consideration, then capacity planning would be a much simpler process. However, any viable solution must take the bottom line into consideration. The budget of any cloud project should be determined in the capacity planning phase, and any solution that is selected should include some flexibility/buffer.

Business Need Analysis

There must be a strong reason to implement any new feature or software project in an organization. This reason is typically defined by a *business need analysis*. When you are conducting a business need analysis, the requirements of the business (the need) are clearly defined. Additionally, potential solutions are proposed that could meet the needs of the business. This analysis gives the decision makers in the organization the data needed to make the best choices of solutions.

Standard Templates

In cloud computing, a *template* is a reusable model that enables you to quickly implement a resource within the cloud. For example, if you want to implement a virtual machine in the cloud, you would normally need to provide information such as the amount of RAM, the type of operating system, the storage space, and so on. A template can provide some or even all of this information automatically, making the process of implementing multiple virtual machines much quicker compared to manually providing this information.

Templates can be used to automate the creation of many different types of cloud resources. They typically use a well-defined data format, such as JavaScript Object Notation (JSON) or YAML Ain't Markup Language (YAML). For example, the following is a simple template in JSON format to create an AWS S3 bucket (a storage container):

```
{
  "Resources" : {
    "SampleBucket" : {
      "Type" : "AWS::S3::Bucket"
    }
  }
}
```

The next example creates the same S3 bucket using YAML:

```
Resources:
  SampleBucket:
    Type: AWS::S3::Bucket
```

Licensing

When using the services of a cloud provider, you are utilizing resources (hardware, software, expertise, and so on) of the cloud provider. The cloud provider's business model is to make money by exchanging these resources for money. How this exchange is determined is based on the license.

A *license* is a component of the agreement or contract between the cloud provider and the client that determines how the client will be charged for the resources provided by the cloud provider. Most cloud providers offer a wide variety of license models to meet the various needs of their clients.

Per-user

With a *per-user license*, the client is charged a fee for each user who uses the resource. This model is very common in SaaS cloud resources, such as an email service or a service that manages customer contact data.

Socket-based

For licensing purposes, a *socket* refers to a CPU socket. The socket provides the connection between the CPU and the motherboard. Socket-based licenses are common on virtual machines and resources based on virtual machines, such as database servers.

This sort of license is not typically applicable to public cloud providers, but if your organization is deploying its own private cloud, this license may apply. Virtual machine software, like VMware, may include a socket-based license structure.

Compare socket-based licenses to core-based licenses, which are covered later.

Volume-based

If a cloud client has the need for a large amount of resources, the cloud provider will often provide a *volume-based license*. With this license, a discounted price is provided to the client for agreeing to use a larger amount of resources.

Volume-based licenses either require the client to pay in advance for the resources or agree to a long-term contract (typically one to three years in length).

Core-based

Older CPUs had just a single processing core. Modern CPUs typically offer multiple cores. A core is a part of the CPU that can perform the calculations required by the operating system or applications.

Core-based licenses are common on virtual machines and resources based on virtual machines, such as database servers. Often novice users tend to prefer core-based licenses to socket-based licenses because understanding the concept and purpose of a CPU core is generally easier than understanding the concept and purposes of CPU sockets.

Subscription

A *subscription* is a license model that is typically reserved for SaaS resources, such as M365 or Google Workscape. With a subscription the resource is made available to the client for a specific period of time, typically one year. Subscription models normally include either a per-user cost or a volume-based cost.

User Density

Consider a situation in which you need to deploy virtual machines for your employees to perform their work. You find yourself asking, "How many virtual machines do I need to deploy?" This is an important question to ask when planning your cloud implementation.

A major consideration in determining the answer to this question is user density. Think of the *user density* as a calculation of how many users can utilize a single system or resource without that resource being overutilized or underutilized. This is a critical calculation because

▶ If you miscalculate with a lower-than-optimal user density, you will end up paying more for resources. For example, if you have 100 users and calculate that 5 users should be assigned to each resource, but really 20 users could use each resource, you end up paying for 20 resources when 5 resources would be optimal.

▶ If you miscalculate with higher-than-optimal user density, you will end with resources that don't provide timely services to the user base. For example, if you calculate that a web server can handle 100 simultaneous user requests when it really can handle only 75 user requests, the server will likely respond slowly or become entirely unresponsive.

Calculating the right user density requires testing and a bit of guesswork. Anticipating exactly how users will utilize a resource can typically only be done by making educated guesses because users may be unpredictable. There are tools that help with these calculations, including tools that provide system load information and trend analysis tools.

System Load

System load is a term that refers to how busy a resource or its components are. For example, if the resource is a database, system load can refer to the average read and write operations to the database.

The statistics of the system load vary based on the resource itself and should be measured over time. The performance of your resources will be critical for capacity planning, and the system load provides a good insight into this performance. A sudden spike in system load typically is considered an anomaly, but a continuous or routine spike over a period of time, such as a day or week, could indicate that more resources are needed.

Trend analysis is used in conjunction with system load statistics to determine if additional (or even fewer) resources are required for optimal performances of a resource.

Trend Analysis

Consider this scenario: Your organization currently has three web servers to handle web traffic from customers and clients. Lately, some customers have been complaining that your web servers seem slow and sometimes unresponsive. You need to determine if this is an issue with your web servers or another problem (network, customer-side problems, and so on).

Using trend analysis can help you with this process. Using data accumulated over time, you will be able to determine if you need to add more resources or, in some cases, scale back and reduce the number of resources. To perform trend analysis, you will need to understand baselines, patterns, and anomalies.

Baselines

A *baseline* is statistical information that demonstrates the system load of a resource when under "normal" usage. A baseline is typically created when the resource is first deployed, and additional baselines are created as your environment evolves (such as when you add additional resources or increase the capabilities of a resource).

Baseline values are compared with future system loads to determine if a resource is being overtaxed or underutilized.

Patterns

A *pattern* can help you make smart and flexible capacity planning decisions. For example, consider a situation in which your company offers a new release of your software product every six months. By looking at previous baselines, you have determined that when a new version is released, there is a spike in traffic to your web servers. As a result of this, you can plan for this spike by increasing the number of web services prior to the release of the new version of the software. You can also plan on reducing the number of web servers a week after the software release, which patterns indicate is when web server traffic typically returns to normal.

Anomalies

An *anomaly* occurs when statistical information deviates from the standard or norm. These anomalies can be useful in some situations but can also cause problems when not properly understood.

For example, consider a sudden spike in traffic to your web server. This anomaly could be the result of hacking attempts against your company or the results of new interest in your company's products and services. Determining the cause for the anomaly is important because the reaction to the anomaly (if there is a reaction) should be carefully considered.

For example, if the cause for the spike in network traffic is a press release made by your company about a new software feature, you may decide to take the following actions:

- ▶ Temporarily include the number of web servers to respond in a timely manner to the new volume of requests.

- ▶ Contact the person who is responsible for press releases in your organization to coordinate future press releases with an increase in available web servers.

However, if the spike is due to massive hacking attacks, you likely don't want to increase the number of web servers because doing so just provides more availability to the hackers.

Performance Capacity Planning

The purpose of performance capacity planning is that you determine the number of available resources based on performance. In other words, your resources must meet the needs of the internal or external consumers in order for the performance to be acceptable to the consumer.

Performance capacity planning makes use of the system load statistics and trend analysis described in previous sections of this chapter. Keep in mind that this is an ongoing process, not something that you do once and then forget about it.

CramQuiz

Answer these questions. The answers follow the last question. If you cannot answer these questions correctly, consider reading this section again until you can.

1. When conducting a _____ analysis, the requirements of the business (the need) is clearly defined.

   ○ **A.** Business need

   ○ **B.** Trend

   ○ **C.** Hardware

   ○ **D.** Software

2. In what format is the following template?

```
{   "Resources" : {

    "SampleBucket" : {

       "Type" : "AWS::S3::Bucket"

     }

   }
}
```

   ○ **A.** XML

   ○ **B.** HTML

   ○ **C.** JSON

   ○ **D.** YAML

3. In what format is the following template?

```
Resources:

SampleBucket:

Type: AWS::S3::Bucket
```

   ○ **A.** XML

   ○ **B.** HTML

   ○ **C.** JSON

   ○ **D.** YAML

4. _____is a term that refers to how busy a resource or its components are.

- ○ **A.** Trend analysis
- ○ **B.** System load
- ○ **C.** User density
- ○ **D.** Anomaly

CramQuiz Answers

1. Business need analysis
2. JSON
3. YAML
4. System load

What Next?

If you want more practice on this chapter's exam objectives before you move on, remember that you can access all of the CramQuiz questions on the companion website. You can also create a custom exam by objectives with the practice exam software. Note any objectives you struggle with and go to that objective's material in this chapter.

CHAPTER 3

High Availability and Scaling in Cloud Environments

This chapter covers the following official CompTIA Cloud+ exam objective:

▶ 1.3 Explain the importance of high availability and scaling in cloud environments.

(For more information on the official CompTIA Cloud+ exam topics, see the Introduction.)

In this chapter you will learn about the components found with a cloud environment that are related to high availability and scalability. *High availability* is ensuring your cloud resources are highly available, accessible, and functioning properly at all times (or as close to all times as possible). *Scalability* is the capability to meet the increasing demand by scaling out (horizontal scaling) or scaling up (vertical scaling).

This chapter will include information on how hypervisors can affect high availability as well as how cloud providers use a technique called *oversubscription* that can impact high availability. You will also learn about regions and zones, which can be used to provide high availability.

You will also discover how networking components (switches, routers, load balancers, and firewalls) can impact high availability. Finally, you will learn about scalability, including auto-scaling, vertical scaling, horizontal scaling, and cloud bursting.

CramSaver

If you can correctly answer these questions before going through this section, save time by skimming the ExamAlerts in this section and then completing the CramQuiz at the end of the section.

1. Which type of hypervisor runs directly on the system hardware?

2. What type of hardware resources are oversubscribed by cloud providers?

3. What is the name for a collection of zones in a geographic location?

4. Which network component can affect high availability by blocking access to a resource?

Answers

1. A Type 1 hypervisor

2. Compute (vCPUs), network, and storage

3. A region

4. A firewall

Hypervisors

Some of the most common cloud-based resources will make use of virtual machines (VMs). A virtual machine is an operating system that shares hardware with other operating systems. Typically, this sharing would pose a problem because operating systems are designed to manage hardware devices directly and exclusively, which would lead to problems if two operating systems were to try to manage hardware devices concurrently.

This problem is solved with the introduction of the hypervisor. The hypervisor presents virtual hardware devices to the operating systems that are running as virtual machines. Each virtual machine is presented with a virtual CPU (vCPU), a virtual hard drive, a virtual network interface, and other virtual devices, depending on how the hypervisor is configured. So, what is managing the real (physical) hardware?

The answer depends on the type of the hypervisor. A Type 1 hypervisor runs directly on the system hardware, essentially acting as an operating system itself. This type of hypervisor directly manages the hardware and provides better performance than a Type 2 hypervisor.

A Type 2 hypervisor runs on a system that already has a host operating system. The Type 2 hypervisor works with the host operating system to manage the physical hardware, but it is ultimately the host operating system that has full control of the hardware. Because of the overhead that is created by the host operating system, Type 2 hypervisors are not commonly used in cloud computing solutions.

Affinity

While often associated with virtual machine technology, the term *affinity* can be applied to other cloud technologies. For virtual machines, think of affinity as a way of keeping virtual machines together, often on the same network or even the same hypervisor.

Most cloud environments are massive and include thousands of compute nodes (a fancy way of saying a computing device or a server). Many of these compute nodes will be physically close to one another, such as in the same data center or even the same rack. Others will be spread further apart in additional data centers or even in different buildings. This setup can present problems when two virtual machines need to communicate effectively.

For example, consider a virtual machine that hosts a web server that needs to read and write data to a database that is hosted on a separate virtual machine. While you could place the web server on a virtual machine that is hosted in the United Kingdom and place the database server on a virtual machine that is hosted in Japan, this arrangement really isn't effective because the distance between the two (both physically and the number of routers between the two) will certainly result in latency issues when transporting the data. It would be better in this case to use an affinity rule that will result in keeping these two virtual machines close.

Depending on the cloud provider, there may be rules that keep the virtual machines in the same geographic area or even on the same compute node.

Anti-affinity

As you might expect, *anti-affinity* is the opposite of affinity. This term means "keep these things separate." In terms of virtual machines, anti-affinity can mean "keep these virtual machines in different server rooms" or even "keep these virtual machines in different geographic regions."

To understand the purpose of anti-affinity, consider a situation in which you have a virtual machine that hosts a database. This server is located on the East Coast of the United States and you want to have a backup server to ensure that you don't lose any data in case of some sort of disaster in the data center where the database is located. In this case, it wouldn't be a good decision to also place this backup database in the East Coast geographic region, so you would use an anti-affinity rule to have the backup database stored in a different location.

Oversubscription

If you have been a frequent airline traveler, you probably have gotten used to announcements like the following: "We are looking for passengers who are willing to take a later flight in exchange for a voucher for future travel." This is the result of a practice in air travel called *overbooking*, in which the airline will book more passengers than there are seats because historically some of the passengers will cancel their flight at the last minute. This booking method tends to allow an airline to maximize the utilization of available seats, even if it does occasionally lead to some passengers having to be placed on other flights.

Cloud providers will use a similar technique. When a compute node is used to host multiple resources (virtual machines, databases, and so on), the cloud providers will allocate more hardware resources than would be physically possible to provide to maximize the revenue for that compute node. Cloud providers are essentially betting that clients won't use all of the physical or virtual hardware resources that are provisioned for a cloud instance, so the provider will "overbook" the compute node's resources. This process is called *oversubscribing*.

Just about any physical or virtual resource can be oversubscribed, but the most common three are the compute power (AKA, CPUs), the network, and the storage.

Compute

There are several components to the compute element of a cloud resource, including

▶ Physical CPUs

▶ Number of processors

▶ The number of cores

► Threads (also known as hyperthreading)

► vCPUs (virtual CPUs)

You may choose these values when you create a virtual machine. For example, on AWS there is an option when creating a virtual machine where you can specify the number of CPUs, the number of threads, and the number of vCPUs, as demonstrated in Figure 3.1.

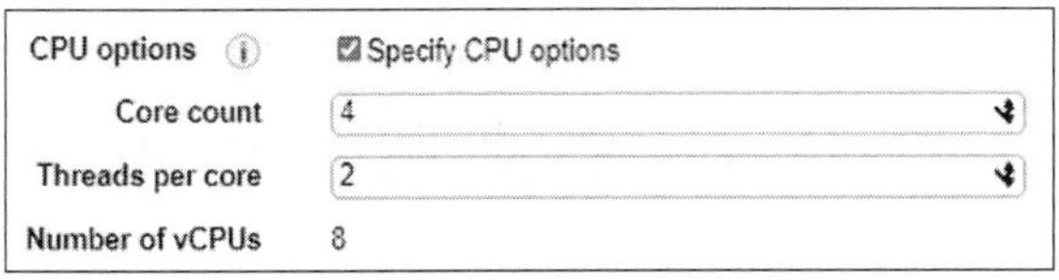

CPU options	Specify CPU options
Core count	4
Threads per core	2
Number of vCPUs	8

FIGURE 3.1 **CPU Compute Options**

Network

Cloud providers are aware that not all resources for their customers will be active at the same time. As a result, they will often oversubscribe network bandwidth.

For example, when you create a Relational Database Service (RDS) on AWS, you are required to choose the instance class, which includes the bandwidth for the database instance, as shown in Figure 3.2.

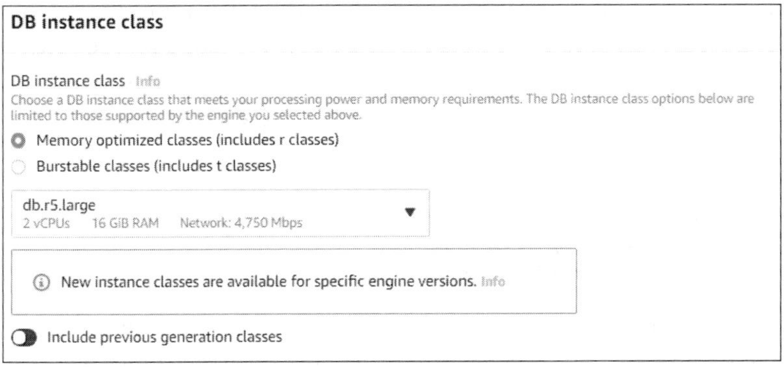

DB instance class

DB instance class Info
Choose a DB instance class that meets your processing power and memory requirements. The DB instance class options below are limited to those supported by the engine you selected above.

○ Memory optimized classes (includes r classes)
○ Burstable classes (includes t classes)

db.r5.large
2 vCPUs   16 GiB RAM   Network: 4,750 Mbps

ⓘ New instance classes are available for specific engine versions. Info

◐ Include previous generation classes

FIGURE 3.2 **Database Class**

Figure 3.2 indicates that the database instance will be allocated a maximum of 4,750 Mbps. If you added up all of the allocated bandwidth of all of the instances that are hosted on the physical system, you would likely discover that the total allocated bandwidth exceeds the actual bandwidth that is available for this system.

Storage

Storage is also often oversubscribed by cloud providers, but this one is a bit trickier. Often, two components of storage are allocated to a resource:

▶ **The size of the storage:** This is how much space the resource could use.

▶ **IOPS (the input/output operations per second):** This is how much data can be read from or written to the storage device.

As with CPU and network bandwidth, the cloud providers know that it is rare for all of the cloud customers to use 100 percent of the available shared storage space. Additionally, the odds are that not all of the customers who are sharing storage space will attempt to use the maximum IOPS. This means that the cloud provider can safely oversubscribe the storage allocation.

You may be wondering how cloud providers deal with situations in which oversubscription backfires. For example, it is almost inevitable that a vendor's customers will at some point exceed the actual capacity of CPU processing, network bandwidth, or storage. How do cloud providers prevent that from happening?

The solution is monitoring. Cloud providers have applications that routinely monitor the utilization of these hardware components. When a specific threshold is reached, resources are moved to another system. This solution prevents unhappy customers and ensures that the cloud provider complies with the service-level agreement (SLA), a legal contract that stipulates that the cloud provider will provide a minimum level of service.

Regions and Zones

Keep in mind that the focus of this chapter is on high availability and scaling. There are multiple purposes of regions and zones, but the focus in this section will be on how regions and zones provide high availability features.

Cloud providers have data centers across different continents and geographic areas of the world. These are called *regions*. For example, Figure 3.3 shows a map that demonstrates the regions for Microsoft Azure.

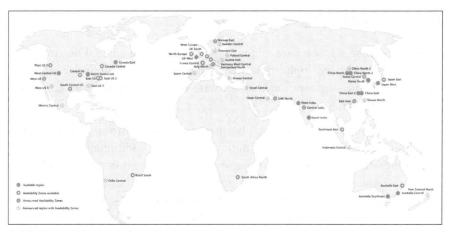

FIGURE 3.3   Microsoft Azure Regions

Within each region, the cloud provider will create multiple sets of data centers. These sets are called *zones* (sometimes also called *availability zones*). Each zone is connected via a private high-speed network to the other zones in that region.

The purpose of regions is to ensure that all of the cloud customers can place their resources close to the customer's user base. For example, if your organization's user base is primarily in Japan and you wanted to create a virtual machine for these users to access, you would not want to place the virtual machine in the United Kingdom. If you did, access to this resource would be slow, and it is possible that network issues may make the resource unavailable at times. As a result, regions support the goal of making resources highly available.

Zones also support high availability. Each zone has its separate physical resources, such as power supplies, to ensure that problems in one zone won't affect another. Additionally, because the zones are physically separated, some natural disasters that may affect one zone, like flooding or a fire, should not affect another zone. As a result, the cloud customer can better ensure high availability of its resources by providing a redundant instance in a different zone.

For example, suppose you had a virtual machine that hosts a critical web server. You can create a second virtual machine with a copy of that web server and host it in a different zone within a region. If the first virtual machine becomes unresponsive, web traffic could be redirected to the second virtual machine. You could also have the two web servers both handle the requests by implementing a load balancer (see the "Load Balancers" section later in this chapter).

Applications

A cloud application is software that is implemented in the cloud. For example, you may have a custom application that handles issuing payroll payments to all employees in your organization. The software that performs this task could be hosted in the cloud.

As you can imagine, some cloud applications are mission critical, making high availability of these applications an important feature. Additionally, the workload of these applications can increase over time, making it important to be able to use scaling to increase the performance of the applications. For example, the resources that were allocated to the payroll application may have been working as desired when your organization had 500 employees, but now that your company has grown to 6,000 employees, the application is no longer able to keep up. When you scale the application, it will have the capability to handle the increased workload.

Containers

A *container* is similar in some ways to a virtual machine; however, containers are not complete operating systems, but rather purpose-built compute components. They are much more "lightweight" in that they don't use as many resources (vCPU, RAM, storage, and so on) as virtual machines. In terms of high availability and scaling, they may be better suited than virtual machines in some cases because of the following reasons:

▶ Because high availability often means having duplicate instances, there is an added cost to highly available systems. Full virtual machines require more physical resources, making them more expensive than containers.

▶ Scaling often requires creating another instance of a resource. This process can take time, especially when creating a large resource, like a virtual machine. Containers can be created much more quickly, making them more ideal for scaling.

Containers are not always the ideal solution, however. For example, you may want to deploy an application that really needs a large amount of dedicated hardware resources. This may require the use of a virtual machine.

Clusters

A *cluster* is a collection of instances that provide the same function. For example, you could implement multiple virtual machines, each of which hosts the same web server.

Clusters provide two primary features. They ensure that the resource is highly available because if one server is not responding, another server in the cluster can respond to requests. Additionally, as demand grows, additional instances can be added to the cluster, making the cluster more scalable.

High Availability of Network Functions

The components of the network play a major role in high availability. Consider the role of each of following components described next.

Switches

Switches are used to direct network traffic between devices that are attached on the same physical network. Typically, switches will associate an IP address with a MAC address (hardware address) to ensure that the network traffic is sent to the correct device. Switches operate at Open Systems Interconnection (OSI) layer 2. The switch will send network traffic only to the port that the destination device is connected to.

Modern switches can be configured to provide high availability. This is done by having the switch monitor the activity of the device that is attached to the network port. If the device stops responding, the switch can start sending the network traffic to an alternate port where another device is configured to handle the request.

Note that in a cloud environment, the cloud vendor is responsible for setting up this feature. The customer does not have access to any layer 2 functions in the cloud.

Routers

Routers are used to connect similar and dissimilar networks together. This is typically done by having a switch send network traffic that is destined for a device outside of the local network to a router. Routers operate at OSI layer 3.

The flaw to this system is when a router becomes unresponsive. This lack of response can halt all network traffic between networks. One way to prevent this problem is by implementing one or more backup routers, so if one router is no longer responsive, switches can send network traffic to another router. This solution results in high availability of network traffic. High availability can be achieved by various mechanisms, such as Virtual Router Redundancy Protocol (VRRP), Gateway Load Balancing Protocol (GLBP), and Hot Standby Router Protocol (HSRP).

Note that in a cloud environment, the cloud vendor is responsible for setting up this feature. Customers have access to layer 3 functions and can set up their own routing outside of the default routing set up by the cloud provider.

Load Balancers

Consider the situation previously mentioned in which you have multiple servers configured with web servers that serve up your company's web pages. You might have this question: "How do the client web applications know which web server to contact?" The answer is a load balancer.

To understand how the load balancer performs its task, first look at Figure 3.4, which shows the steps that a web client would go through to access a web server. The web client first needs to know the IP address of the web server (private IPs are used in this example), which is determined by a DNS lookup. Then the web client sends the request to the web server using the appropriate IP address.

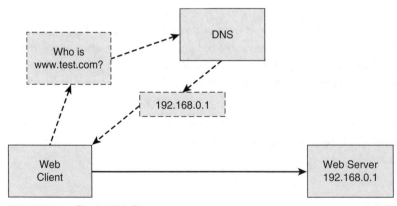

FIGURE 3.4 **Single Web Server**

When a load balancer is used, the DNS server is configured to report the IP address of the load balancer. The load balancer then redirects the incoming client request to one of the web servers that the load balancer has been configured to utilize. This method is demonstrated in Figure 3.5.

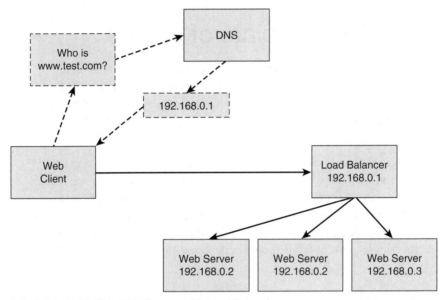

FIGURE 3.5 **Multiple Web Servers with Load Balancing**

In cloud computing, there are many different types of load balancing. Which methods are available really depend on the cloud provider. The most common methods are:

▶ **Round robin:** The load balancer sends the requests in a preset order equally between the servers.

▶ **Weighted:** Each server is given a weight, typically based on how capable the server is to respond. For example, a server that has more vCPUs, RAM, and bandwidth would be granted a higher weight. The load balancer sends more requests to the servers that have higher weight values.

▶ **Geographic-based:** The load balancer sends the client request to a server that is located closest to the client geographically.

Firewalls

A firewall can have an impact on high availability because the purpose of a firewall is to just allow or block traffic to a network. If a resource in a network is not available, the reason may be that a firewall rule has blocked access to that resource or the firewall is unavailable due to a failure (fail close configuration).

Avoid Single Points of Failure

To ensure high availability, you need to avoid any single points of failure. Avoiding them can be tricky because many components can impact the availability of a resource. For instance, while having just a single resource is an obvious single point of failure, having only a single network path to access the resource is another single point of failure.

To avoid single points of failure, you should map out how the resource is accessed and map the components required for the resource to work. Here's another example: you may have multiple web servers and multiple network paths to access the servers, but the servers rely on a database, and currently you have only a single instance of that database. If that database becomes unresponsive, this single point of failure could make the web server resource fail as well.

Scalability

In cloud computing, scalability is the capability of a resource to adapt to growing demands. This is a critical feature and often one of the compelling reasons to migrate on-premises systems to the cloud.

There are different methods used for scaling, including auto-scaling, horizontal scaling, vertical scaling, and cloud bursting.

Auto-scaling

Auto-scaling occurs when the scaling process happens automatically. For example, you could have a system in place in which, if the current resource reaches a specific threshold such as a specific number of client connections, a second resource is automatically started to handle additional requests.

> **Note**
>
> The terms *scalability* and *elasticity* are often used interchangeably, but although they are related, they do not really mean the same thing. Scaling is all about providing additional capability to handle additional demands, but it does not address when the demand diminishes.

For example, consider a scenario in which you spin up a new web server whenever existing web servers handle more than 50 client connections. Suppose in this scenario you now have five web servers, then at some point later, the client connections die down. This means you do not need five web servers any longer.

Elasticity can handle this situation. A cloud solution that provides elasticity means that those extra web servers would be deactivated when no longer needed. Think of elasticity as meaning not only the capability to scale up to meet demand but also the capability to scale down when the demand is no longer present.

Horizontal Scaling

When additional web servers are spun up to handle increased demand, this scenario is called *horizontal scaling*. With horizontal scaling, more resources are provided on the fly to meet demand. This approach is less intrusive.

Vertical Scaling

In *vertical scaling*, additional resources are not allocated, but rather the existing resource is beefed up to handle the demand. In cloud computing, this typically means that the resource is provided additional hardware, such as more vCPUs, RAM, or storage capacity. This can be an intrusive process because the instance may need to be shut down for changing the resource configuration.

Cloud Bursting

Consider the following scenario: your organization has already heavily invested in your own private cloud structure. This means you are using on-premises resources to provide cloud-based features. However, there is some concern in your organization that during peak times the resource available in your private cloud will not be able to handle the demand.

For example, each year your organization hosts an online conference, and the utilization of your web servers and video hosting software skyrockets. You want to be able to meet this demand without having to spend a lot of money on hardware resources that won't be used during the rest of the year. The solution: leverage cloud bursting.

With *cloud bursting* you configure your scaling (typically using auto-scaling) to make use of the resources of a cloud provider. You are essentially augmenting the capability of your private cloud to scale by using the resources of a public cloud. You can redirect the additional demand to cloud-based resources instead of on-premises by leveraging routing of traffic and load balancers.

CramQuiz

Answer these questions. The answers follow the last question. If you cannot answer these questions correctly, consider reading this section again until you can.

1. What is another term for threads?
   - ○ **A.** Hypervising
   - ○ **B.** Hyperthreading
   - ○ **C.** Hyperprocessor
   - ○ **D.** HyperCPU

2. _____ is a term that means "keep separate."
   - ○ **A.** Anti-affinity
   - ○ **B.** Multi-affinity
   - ○ **C.** Affinity
   - ○ **D.** None of these answers are correct

3. Which of the following is a component of storage that might be oversubscribed? (Choose two.)
   - ○ **A.** Type of storage
   - ○ **B.** Size of storage
   - ○ **C.** Location of storage
   - ○ **D.** IOPS

4. A region is made up of one or more _____.
   - ○ **A.** Access points
   - ○ **B.** Hypervisors
   - ○ **C.** Zones
   - ○ **D.** Containers

5. A _____ is a collection of instances that provide the same function.
   - ○ **A.** Zone
   - ○ **B.** Cluster
   - ○ **C.** Region
   - ○ **D.** Container

CramQuiz Answers

1. Hyperthreading
2. Anti-affinity
3. Size of storage and IOPS
4. Zones
5. Cluster

What Next?

If you want more practice on this chapter's exam objectives before you move on, remember that you can access all of the CramQuiz questions on the companion website. You can also create a custom exam by objectives with the practice exam software. Note any objectives you struggle with and go to that objective's material in this chapter.

CHAPTER 4

Solution Design in Support of the Business Requirements

This chapter covers the following official CompTIA Cloud+ exam objective:

▶ 1.4 Given a scenario, analyze the solution design in support of the business requirements.

(For more information on the official CompTIA Cloud+ exam topics, see the Introduction.)

In this chapter you will learn about designing cloud-based solutions. This will include a discussion on requirement analysis to determine what resources are required to build a solution that will fit the needs of the organization. You will also learn about different types of deployment environments as well as different forms of testing to determine the suitability of the solution.

CramSaver

If you can correctly answer these questions before going through this section, save time by skimming the ExamAlerts in this section and then completing the CramQuiz at the end of the section.

1. What is the first activity that is performed during requirement analysis?

2. In _____ as a Service, the entire application is hosted and maintained by the cloud vendor.

3. In a _____ environment testing is performed before changes are migrated to a production environment.

4. _____ testing is the process of probing a system or network to determine if there are any security vulnerabilities.

> **Answer**
>
> 1. Requirements gathering
> 2. Software
> 3. Quality Assurance (or QA)
> 4. Penetration

Requirement Analysis

Any organization that is planning on deploying a new system, software, or tool is likely going to first perform some sort of requirement analysis. This key process is designed to ensure that the deployment meets all of the needs of the user base and the organization.

Different processes can be used for requirements analysis, but typically they break down into four different types of activities:

- ▶ **Requirements gathering:** During this activity, internal users are queried to determine the requirements for the organization.

- ▶ **Requirements analyzing:** Responses from the requirements gathering activity may not always be clear or concise. During the requirement analysis phase, the data collected during the requirements gathering activity is reviewed and any inconsistencies are resolved.

- ▶ **Requirements modeling:** In this activity the information gathered from the previous two activities are converted into solutions that can be deployed.

- ▶ **Review and retrospective:** After the systems have been deployed, many teams will review the processes and issues and then share any findings. These findings may be used to adjust the process in the future. These are also known as learnings.

In relation to the Cloud+ certification exam, you will be expected to be able to answer questions related to how specific topics will affect the requirement analysis process. The rest of this section will focus on these topics.

Software

One of the components that you will need to take into consideration when performing a requirement analysis is which software you will utilize in the cloud.

This determination will be based on, in part, which type of cloud environment you will end up using. Several that you should consider include the following:

▶ **Software as a Service (SaaS):** In an SaaS software solution, the entire application is hosted and maintained by the cloud vendor. Examples of SaaS include Salesforce, Dropbox, Gmail, Webex, and DocuSign. One advantage of SaaS solutions is that the vendor handles all upgrades and maintenance of the software. Disadvantages include less control over your data (although the security of the data is primarily the customer's responsibility), the inability to customize the software to your organizational needs, and potential vendor lock-in (when your organization is so entrenched in a solution that switching to another solution is almost impossible).

▶ **Platform as a Service (PaaS):** In a PaaS solution, the cloud vendor provides a platform that you can use to install or develop a software solution. Examples of PaaS include OpenShift, AWS Elastic Beanstalk, and the Google App Engine. With a PaaS solution, the primary advantage is that you can deploy a customized software solution without having to be concerned about maintaining the underlying platform that the software runs on. With the PaaS solution, like the SaaS solution, there still may be concerns regarding control over your data and potential vendor lock-in. However, PaaS does offer more control over these issues, so the concern isn't as strong as with the SaaS solution.

▶ **Infrastructure as a Service (IaaS):** In an IaaS solution, the cloud vendor provides the infrastructure for you to install your operating system or software solution. With this solution the cloud vendor essentially provides the hardware structure (compute, networking, and storage) and you manage the rest, including the operating system and the software. Examples of IaaS include using Azure virtual machines and AWS EC2 instances. A major advantage of an IaaS software solution is control. You choose the platform (operating system), the amount of hardware resources used, and how the system is configured. This control may also be considered a disadvantage because you are also tasked with maintaining the operating system and the software.

Hardware

If you are using an SaaS or a PaaS solution, you likely don't have any choice regarding the hardware. However, if you are using an IaaS solution, hardware becomes an important component of requirement analysis.

Most cloud vendors provide different tiers or levels of hardware when you choose an IaaS solution. The more hardware resources, the higher the cost of the solution. The available options may be overwhelming because cloud vendors attempt to provide as many options as possible to their customers. For example, Figure 4.1 provides a brief glimpse of the different EC2 instance types.

Amazon EC2 Instance Types

Amazon EC2 provides a wide selection of instance types optimized to fit different use cases. Instance types comprise varying combinations of CPU, memory, storage, and networking capacity and give you the flexibility to choose the appropriate mix of resources for your applications. Each instance type includes one or more instance sizes, allowing you to scale your resources to the requirements of your target workload.

General Purpose

Compute Optimized

Memory Optimized

Accelerated Computing

Storage Optimized

Instance Features

Measuring Instance Performance

General Purpose

General purpose instances provide a balance of compute, memory and networking resources, and can be used for a variety of diverse workloads. These instances are ideal for applications that use these resources in equal proportions such as web servers and code repositories.

| Mac | T4g | T3 | T3a | T2 | M6g | M5 | M5a |
| M5n | M5zn | M4 | A1 | | | | |

Mac instances are powered by Apple Mac mini computers and built on the AWS Nitro System. This EC2 family gives developers access to macOS so they can develop, build, test, and sign applications that require the Xcode IDE.

- Intel core i7 processors with 3.2 GHz (4.6 GHz turbo)
- 6 physical / 12 logical cores
- 32 GiB of memory
- Instance storage is available via Amazon Elastic Block Store (EBS)
- Mac instances are dedicated, bare-metal instances which are accessible in the EC2 console as dedicated hosts

Instance Size	vCPU	Memory (GiB)	Instance Storage	Network Bandwidth (Gbps)	EBS Bandwidth (Mbps)
mac1.metal	12	32	EBS-Only	10	8,000

FIGURE 4.1 AWS EC2 Instance Types

Note that AWS has several categories (General Purpose, Compute Optimized, Memory Optimized, and so on), each of which has several different types of instances. For example, General Purpose has 11 instance types, including Mac, T4g, T3, and T2.

If there is documentation for the software solution that you are installing, you can use it to develop a general idea of what hardware requirements will fit the needs of the software. However, the ideal method to determine which instance type is right for you is to perform benchmarking tests. This would include testing the software on different instance types using a variety of usage loads to determine the best instance type.

Note that there are several factors to consider when choosing a hardware instance type, including the following:

▶ Type of physical CPU

▶ Number of vCPUs

▶ Amount of RAM

▶ Type, speed, location, and size of the storage

▶ Network bandwidth

Integration

When you are performing a requirement analysis for implementing a cloud-based solution, there is a good chance you want this solution to work with other components that you already have in place in your IT infrastructure. The concept of integration is how to best ensure that different solutions work well together.

Budgetary

Perhaps one day you will work for an organization that takes the approach of "price is not a consideration," but this day is likely to never come for most of us. When you're performing requirement analysis, it is important to explore multiple solutions and to find a solution that meets the budget that has been provided for the solution.

Obviously, exploring many solutions is not always possible, and you should be prepared to justify higher costs or offer alternative solutions that might not meet all of the requirements of the situation. Even if you do propose a solution that meets the needs of the situation and the budget, you may be asked to justify the costs and offer suggestions for a more cost-effective solution or, in other words, discuss the total cost of operations (TCO) and return on investment (ROI).

Compliance

If your organization must follow regulations of third-party organizations, such as the government or other regulatory organizations, compliance must also factor into the solution. When performing requirement analysis, be certain that you are aware of all compliance rules and ensure they are addressed properly when developing the solution. You will likely need to generate a report that verifies that the regulations are met by the solution, either by your organization's compliance officer or by the regulatory organization.

Service-Level Agreement (SLA)

An SLA is designed to protect both the cloud vendor and the customer by clearly defining the levels of service that the cloud vendor will provide within the outlined constraints. The SLA typically describes the minimum levels that the customer should expect for topics like the following:

▶ Availability

▶ Speed

▶ Responsiveness

The SLA also normally makes it clear what the cloud vendor is responsible for and what the customer is responsible for. Other topics that you might find in an SLA include data ownership, disaster recovery, and details on the hardware that the cloud vendor uses.

User and Business Needs

Recall that during requirements gathering, users are queried to determine the requirements for the organization. These needs are the driving force behind requirement analysis.

Security

If you have been paying attention to news coverage regarding security breaches in major organizations over the past decade or so, you probably realize any cloud solution must include a strong security environment. Before implementing a solution (and even after implementing one), you need to perform some testing to ensure the solution is not vulnerable to security breaches.

See the "Vulnerability Testing" and "Penetration Testing" sections later in this chapter for further details.

Network Requirements

Network requirements can turn into a big topic when it comes to requirement analysis. For example, you may need to consider where your users reside geographically to determine where and how to configure the network environment for your solution.

For the Cloud+ exam, you should focus on three network elements when performing a requirement analysis: sizing, subnetting, and routing.

Sizing

The sizing of the network is related to the bandwidth available in the network, but bandwidth alone is not the only consideration. If you have multiple instances within a network, they will compete for that bandwidth, so you need to consider collectively how much bandwidth is required for your network.

Subnetting

At times you will want to ensure that several related instances are able to communicate without having to leave the network where the instances are placed. This comes down to *subnetting*, which is the process of defining the number of possible hosts on the network.

For example, if you have a web server that uses a database server, it might be best to ensure they are both on the same subnet. This results in faster access for the web server to the database server. This also allows for a more secure connection because the traffic doesn't need to leave the local network.

However, there is also a security advantage of having the web server and database server on different subnets. If an attacker were to compromise a system in one subnet, that could make it easier to compromise other systems in the same subnet. So, having the web server and database server in different subnets can mitigate the chance that they are both compromised.

Routing

Routing is the process of transferring network packets from one network to another. This is a security consideration when performing requirement analysis because firewalls can be configured via the routing points to either allow or block the transferring of these network packets.

Environments

Another major consideration when performing a requirement analysis is to determine which environments you want to create. Each environment will play a specific role in your solution. Not all environments will be deployed in every situation, and each environment provides a benefit that must be weighed against the cost (typically budgetary cost, but there are other costs, such as manpower and maintenance costs).

For the Cloud+ certification exam, you should be aware of specific environments when asked questions regarding requirement analysis. Those environments are covered in the rest of this section.

Development

In a development environment you develop new software or modify existing software that your organization has been developing. While the development environment may be used to prepare for changes to a production environment, its primary purpose is to allow software developers to work in an environment that won't affect any live work.

Quality Assurance (QA)

Testing is performed in a QA environment before migrating changes to a production environment. Initially, the QA environment should mirror the current production environment. In the QA environment new features and configurations are tested to ensure they meet the needs of the users and organization.

Testing may include having regular users work in the environment to ensure that the environment works as it should. Eventually, after testing is complete, the changes made to the development environment are implemented in the production environment.

Staging

Some organizations utilize a staging environment to replicate the production environment. This staging environment can be used for several different purposes, including determining potential problems ahead of time in the production environment and as a replacement if the production environment fails or is compromised. It is also used when implementing a blue-green deployment (see the next section for more details).

Blue-Green

When using a blue-green deployment, you have two identical environments (production and staging). The production environment is live and used actively within your organization. The staging area is used in the final phase of deploying a new version of the solution. This means that changes made within your QA environment are applied to the staging environment, and some final tests are performed.

Once tests have passed successfully, the staging environment is converted into the production environment, and the production environment is now treated as the staging environment. If the solution still runs smoothly, changes are made to the original staging environment and then applied to the new staging environment. The result is that the two are identical again.

This is called a *blue-green deployment* because one environment is traditionally labeled *blue*, and the other is traditionally labeled *green*. Note that either blue or green can be the production or staging environment at any given time.

The advantages of using this method are smoother upgrades, less downtime, and the ability to quickly roll back a deployment to a previously working environment. The disadvantages of this system are the additional costs and time to maintain both environments.

Production

The production environment is the live environment that your organization uses.

Disaster Recovery (DR)

A DR environment is used specifically if the production environment is compromised. While a staging area can sometimes be used for DR, it is not an ideal

DR solution because at times during a new deployment it will not be identical to a production environment.

A DR is an identical copy to the production environment that has one specific purpose: a quick way to restore a compromised environment. Typically, the DR environment should be located in a different geographic location from the production environment so a physical disaster cannot disable both environments.

Testing Techniques

Another major component of requirement analysis is ensuring that the solution that has been developed will meet the needs of the organization. This requires several different types of tests to be performed.

For the Cloud+ exam, you should be aware of specific types of tests when performing requirement analysis. The rest of this section will cover these types of tests. Note that the actual tests that you will perform depend on the actual solution that you have developed. This book will cover these tests in general because the Cloud+ exam should not include specific tests for specific solutions.

Vulnerability Testing

Any solution has the potential to have security holes. With vulnerability testing the goal is to discover these security issues/holes and address them well before the software/solution goes live. This test can be performed manually or by using industry standard tools such as those provided by the Open Web Application Security Project (OWASP) and the Web Application Security Consortium (WASC).

Penetration Testing

Also called *pen testing* or *ethical hacking*, *penetration testing* is the process of probing a system or network to determine if there are any security vulnerabilities. The concept is to find the holes that an attacker would exploit before the environment is in production. Pen testing tools can aid in this process, including the following:

- ▶ **nmap:** A port scanning tool

- ▶ **Wireshark:** A network sniffer that can capture and display network traffic

- ▶ **Metasploit:** A security testing automation framework

> **Important Note**
>
> Most cloud vendors have limits on the pen testing that you can perform on systems within their cloud. Before performing any pen testing on any cloud resource, verify that this is allowed by the cloud vendor.

Performance Testing

Performance testing is a way to evaluate how responsive a solution is when a certain amount of work (called a *workload*) is placed on the solution. This testing should be able to determine weak points or bottlenecks in a solution and should test all major components (hardware, software, network, and so on) of the solution.

Regression Testing

When changes are made to software, it is important to ensure that the software works by performing regression testing. These tests are most often performed on development environments and QA environments.

Functional Testing

Consider a software program that allows you to edit documents. This software should have many different functions, including loading a document, saving a document, formatting a document, and others. Before deploying this software (or a new version of it), you can perform functional testing to ensure all of its functions work correctly.

Functional testing is performed on a QA environment. During a single function test, only one feature of the software, independent of any other feature, is tested. This is also considered a form of black-box testing because the tester isn't aware of how the program works, just how to perform the test and determine whether it is successful.

Usability Testing

Many software programs are operated directly by users. This means that a software vendor must ensure that users are able to use the software as it is intended. One way of verifying this is through usability testing in which users are asked to perform tasks using the software. The users then provide feedback about their experiences. This feedback is used to determine if the software needs adjustments or if it works as intended.

> **Note**
>
> The usability testing method is not intended to find errors in code. That would be the purpose of functional testing. Consider usability testing to answer the question, "Will average users be able to use this software when provided the proper directions, or will they run into problems?"

CramQuiz

Answer these questions. The answers follow the last question. If you cannot answer these questions correctly, consider reading this section again until you can.

1. What is the final activity in requirement analysis?

    ○ **A.** Requirements gathering

    ○ **B.** Requirements analyzing

    ○ **C.** Requirements modeling

    ○ **D.** Review and retrospective

2. A cloud provider provides you with a server in its environment so you can install a virtual machine. This is an example of what?

    ○ **A.** SaaS

    ○ **B.** PaaS

    ○ **C.** IaaS

    ○ **D.** DaaS

3. Which of the following would you not need to consider when reviewing the hardware for an IaaS solution?

    ○ **A.** Amount of RAM

    ○ **B.** Size of storage

    ○ **C.** Location of storage

    ○ **D.** Type of motherboard

4. On what type of environment would your software programmers work on code that they create for the organization?

   ○ **A.** Development

   ○ **B.** Quality assurance

   ○ **C.** Staging

   ○ **D.** Disaster recovery

5. What type of testing would a tool like nmap be used for?

   ○ **A.** Penetration testing

   ○ **B.** Performance testing

   ○ **C.** Regression testing

   ○ **D.** Functional testing

CramQuiz Answers

1. Review and retrospective
2. IaaS
3. Type of motherboard
4. Development
5. Penetration testing

What Next?

If you want more practice on this chapter's exam objectives before you move on, remember that you can access all of the CramQuiz questions on the companion website. You can also create a custom exam by objectives with the practice exam software. Note any objectives you struggle with and go to that objective's material in this chapter.

CHAPTER 5

Identity and Access Management

This chapter covers the following official CompTIA Cloud+ exam objective:

▶ 2.1 Given a scenario, configure identity and access management.

(For more information on the official CompTIA Cloud+ exam topics, see the Introduction.)

Security personnel spend a great deal of time ensuring that only authorized users are able to gain access to an organization's cloud environment. This means that a high priority is placed on identity and access management, the process of verifying a user and ensuring that the user is provided with the correct level of access to the cloud services.

In this chapter you will learn the essentials of identity and access management. This will include the concepts of privileged access management, account lifecycle management, and access control. You will also learn about directory services, federation, and multifactor authentication (MFA), key components to allowing users access to your cloud environment.

This chapter will also discuss certificates, including providing an understanding of public key infrastructure (PKI) and key management.

CramSaver

If you can correctly answer these questions before going through this section, save time by skimming the ExamAlerts in this section and then completing the CramQuiz at the end of the section.

1. What types of identities can be assigned to a role?

2. True or false: A CA is a form of directory services.

3. Name a protocol that is associated with federation.

4. True or false: A valid factor for MFA is something that a person is.

Answers

1. User accounts and cloud resources (or instances)

2. False

3. SAML1.1, SAML2, OAuth2, OpenID Connect, WS-Trust, or WS-Federation

4. True

Identification and Authorization

Identification occurs when a user provides some sort of value, such as a username, to indicate who he or she is. By itself, identification isn't enough to grant access to the system; the process of authentication must also be used. *Authentication* occurs when the user proves the identity by using another piece of information, such as a password or an access token.

After a user has been identified and authenticated, that user is granted access to resources within the system. When an authenticated user is either allowed or denied access to resources based on some sort of rule, this is the process of *authorization*.

In this section you will learn more about the process of identification and authorization. The chapter includes the various methods and techniques that are employed in a cloud environment to identify and authorize user accounts.

Before diving into different components of identification and authorization, you should be aware of a few terms that will be used:

▶ **User account:** Users in your organization (and, in many cases, customers) will need to log in to your cloud infrastructure or specific resources in your cloud infrastructure. This access typically requires each user to be assigned a unique user account.

▶ **Roles:** A role is a way to grant user accounts access to cloud resources. Most cloud environments also allow you to assign a cloud resource to a role. For example, you could add a virtual machine to a role that would allow the virtual machine to access a database resource. Roles relate to role-based access control (or RBAC).

▶ **Groups:** A group is a collection of user accounts. You can assign permissions to a group and manage which user accounts have these permissions by adding and removing user accounts to the group. A group may sound like a role, but there are some important differences. Only user accounts can be a member of a group (not cloud resources) and group assignment is normally directly tied with the user account, whereas a user (or resource) can temporarily take on a role to gain more access to another resource.

Privileged Access Management (PAM)

Through privileged access a user is granted rights that allow for escalated access to a resource. This access is not something granted to a regular user account in most cases but is reserved for individuals who need to have more administrative control over a resource.

Privileged access management (also referred to as PAM) is the process of administering the privileged access. The goal is to enforce a security principle called least privilege. This means providing only the access that an individual needs to perform the tasks that the user is responsible for.

A cloud-based example of PAM is the access provided to use and manage virtual machines. For instance, access to AWS EC2 instances are managed by AWS policies, like AmazonEC2FullAccess and AmazonEC2ReadOnlyAccess.

Note that for the Cloud+ exam you won't be asked specific questions about how PAM is implemented on specific cloud environments, so this example is designed solely to enhance your understanding of this topic.

Logical Access Management

To understand the concept of logical access management (also called logical access control), first consider a related topic: traditional physical access management. An example of physical access management is requiring a person to have a key to enter a building, a room, or a storage container. To be able to access the storage container, which is placed in a room, a person would need a key for both the storage container and a key for the room. Of course, to enter the room, the person must also have a key to enter the building. As the manager of the building, you manage access to the objects by either providing or removing the keys.

Logical access management provides a similar methodology to providing access to cloud-based resources. You may have one method to authenticate when accessing the entire cloud infrastructure and additional authentication methods to access individual resources within the cloud infrastructure. As with physical keys, an administrator can manage this access by adding or removing the logical access method.

Account Lifecycle Management

The concept of account lifecycle management is that there should be systems in place to handle each of the primary stages of a user account. These stages are:

▶ **Creation:** This stage must include specific procedures for an account to be created. User data must be gathered, the account creation must be authorized using a system that prevents compromise, and the account privileges must be clearly defined.

▶ **Updates:** In some cases, a user account may need to be updated. If the user takes a new role in the organization, processes must be put in place to either grant more privileges or remove unnecessary privileges.

▶ **Deactivation or deletion:** When a person no longer needs an account— for example, the person leaves the organization—there must be a procedure in place to either deactivate or delete the account. For security reasons, many organizations choose to deactivate accounts because there may be the need to review the account at a later date. Additionally, a new user account may need the same type of account as the one being deactivated, so deleting the account is not advisable because the old account can then be used as a template to create the new account.

Provision and Deprovision Accounts

Provisioning an account means creating or activating the account. Deprovisioning an account is deactivating or deleting the account. Also see the preceding "Account Lifecycle Management" section.

Access Controls

Access controls allow user accounts to gain access to a resource in your cloud infrastructure. There are several different types of access controls that you should be aware of, including role-based, discretionary, nondiscretionary, mandatory, and rule-based. The rest of this section covers these different types of access controls.

Role-Based

With role-based access control (normally referred to as RBAC), users are assigned a role, which defines what a user is able to do. A role normally mirrors an organizational role. For example, you could have a role named "database administrator" that would provide an account with the privileges to perform administrative tasks on the databases within the organization.

There are several advantages of RBAC, including the following:

▶ An administrator can easily add a user to a role or remove a user from a role.

▶ Roles can normally be temporarily deactivated. Deactivating may be necessary when a security breach has made the system vulnerable.

▶ Roles can be modified. When this happens, all user accounts associated with the role are also immediately modified.

Discretionary

Discretionary access control (normally referred to as DAC) leaves the job of securing a resource to the user rather than the administrator. It is also related to the user account identity and the groups that the user account belongs to. With DAC, a resource (normally called an *object* when discussing DAC) is owned by a user account, and the user account decides who can access the object.

A common example of DAC is how file permissions work on Linux systems. Each file is owned by a user account and has three sets of permissions: the user owner of the file, the group owner of the file, and all other user accounts. The owner of the file can change any of these three sets of permissions to allow or deny access to the file.

The primary advantage of DAC is that regular users are granted more control and don't need elevated privileges to change the access to resources that the user owns. The primary disadvantage of DAC is that regular users may not understand how the access control works and may unintentionally provide more access to an object than they intended.

Nondiscretionary

The method of nondiscretionary access control involves creating rules that govern which user accounts are provided access to resources. These rules can be associated with not only the user account but also other features like when the access is attempted and from where the user attempts the access. In other words, a nondiscretionary rule might state that a user can access a database only from 9 a.m. to 5 p.m., Monday through Friday, and only while logged in to a specific network.

Note that role-based access control (RBAC) and mandatory access control (MAC) are both considered nondiscretionary access control methods.

Mandatory

Mandatory access control is one of the highest forms of nondiscretionary access control. In systems that employ MAC, a policy is used to determine which accounts can access which resources. This policy defines identities, resources, and rules that determine which identities can access which resources.

Directory Services

In their simplest form, directory services are designed to store information about an organization or system. A simple but very powerful example of a directory service is Domain Name System (DNS), which stores IP addresses to host name mappings. When a user needs to access a system using an IP address but knows only the host name, a DNS server can be queried to look up the required information in its directory of information.

DNS doesn't have anything to do with identity and access management, but it does serve to provide a simple example of a directory service as well as highlight some of the features of a directory service. Other features of a directory service normally include the following:

▶ Hierarchical naming model to provide the ability to segment different collections of data

▶ Robust search capability to enable for searching of items within the directory using different types of searches

▶ Distributed data model so not all the data needs to be stored on a single server

▶ The capability to replicate data to multiple servers to avoid a single point of failure

▶ Data stored in a way that optimizes reading the data, not writing the data, because data is read much more often in a directory service than it is written

▶ An extensible schema, which is a component of a directory service that defines what data can be stored in the directory service

Note that for identity and access management the directory service doesn't, by itself, perform any identification or authorization functions. It can provide information that can be used to aid in these processes, but the directory service itself just provides information.

Lightweight Directory Access Protocol (LDAP)

LDAP is a protocol that is used by directory services that are typically used on Linux-based systems to store enterprisewide information, such as user account data. In relation to identity and access management, LDAP is one of the most commonly used directory service protocols. On Linux systems, OpenLDAP and Red Hat Directory Service are common directory services that utilize LDAP.

LDAP is also a key component of Microsoft's Active Directory (AD) product. AD makes use of the protocol to provide controlled access to the data stored within AD.

Federation

You may have accessed an organization's website and then been provided different methods of logging in to the system. For example, Figure 5.1 shows the login screen for developer.cisco.com.

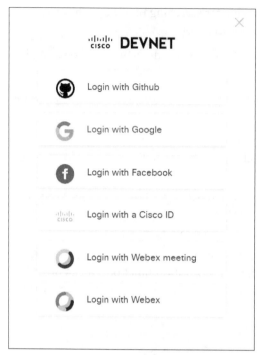

FIGURE 5.1   Federation Login Example

As you can see from Figure 5.1, you can log in to developer.cisco.com using several different types of accounts, including GitHub, Google, and Facebook. None of these login methods are organizations that Cisco owns or has any control over. However, these organizations have provided a certain level of trust as well as a method to allow other organizations to have the capability to authenticate a user.

In a sense, GitHub, Google, and Facebook have become identity providers. They provide a service that organizations like Cisco can use to identify and authenticate users. This service provides Cisco's customers with more options and prevents users from having to create yet another user account and password.

Several commonly used protocols are associated with federation identity management, including

- SAML1.1
- SAML2
- OAuth2

▶ OpenID Connect

▶ WS-Trust

▶ WS-Federation

Certificate Management

Consider a situation in which you want to log in to your bank's website and transfer some money. You open a web browser, type in the URL of your bank (or use a browser bookmark), and then log in to the bank. But how do you know that it is really your bank?

It is possible that your browser has been directed to a website that isn't your bank. This redirection may have been done by an individual or group that is trying to steal your login information to gain access to your bank account. You may have even seen this attempt in action. Figure 5.2 shows a message that your web browser will display if it appears that the server you are trying to connect to really isn't the correct server.

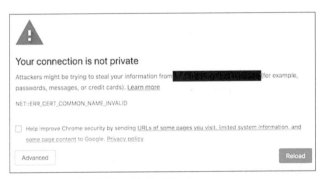

FIGURE 5.2 **Invalid Certificate Warning**

This discussion brings up another question: how does your web browser know that you are potentially communicating with a rogue server? The answer is by its certificate.

When you communicate using the HTTPS protocol (note that this does not apply to HTTP; the *S* must be in the URL), your browser knows that it must verify the validity of the web server's certificate. It does this by querying a certificate authority (CA), which is a trusted third-party organization that can look at a web server's certificate and verify that it is really the correct web server. You can look at your browser's settings and see a list of the CAs that your browser uses, as shown in Figure 5.3.

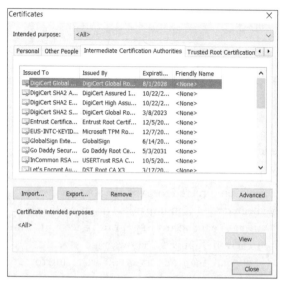

FIGURE 5.3 **List of CAs on a Google Chrome Browser**

> **Note**
>
> You can find more details about the certificates and how they are managed in the "Public Key Infrastructure (PKI)," "Secret Management," and "Key Management" sections later in this chapter.

Multifactor Authentication (MFA)

MFA is a method of authenticating a user that requires more than one way of verifying the identity of that user. For example, a regular authentication method would be to have the user provide a username and a password. With MFA, the user would also be required to provide another item that proved the identity of that user.

The *factor* in MFA is the other item that is required to authenticate the user. This factor can be something from one of three categories:

▶ **Something that the user has:** This could be a physical object, such as a bank card, a physical key, or a USB stick that contains a unique token.

▶ **Something that the user knows:** This can be another password, a PIN, or some other bit of information that only the user should know.

▶ **Something that the user is:** This can include a biometric-based scan for a fingerprint, voice print, iris (eye), palm, and so on.

> **Note**
>
> A newer category, somewhere the user is, has somewhat recently become a valid factor in MFA. This could be a factor that is verified by GPS, for example.

Another similar term that you may encounter is two-factor authentication. This is the simplest form of MFA because it requires only two factors to properly authenticate a user account. However, MFA in general can require more than two factors—for example, three factor with password, PIN from token, and fingerprint scan.

Single Sign-On (SSO)

SSO is a technique in which once a user has logged in to an environment, the user won't be asked to provide the account credentials to access other components in the environment until a timeout period has been reached. For example, you may log in to your company's cloud infrastructure and then access different elements of the cloud (database services, virtual machines, and so on) without being asked for your account information. After a period of time—for example, 12 hours—further access to this environment would require going through the authentication method again.

The primary advantage of SSO is that it makes it easier for the user to work in an environment without having to provide authentication information repeatedly across multiple internal sites or services. Disadvantages of SSO include the complexity of administrating the environment and the trust placed in users that they will physically secure the device that they used to access the environment. For example, if a user logs in to an environment that supports SSO and then loses control of the device (for example, someone steals the user's mobile device), the attacker may gain unauthorized access to the environment for a period of time.

Security Assertion Markup Language (SAML)

SAML is the technology that allows for SSO. It is a standard that allows for exchanging data related to authentication and authorization between systems. Complete details of SAML are beyond the scope of the Cloud+ certification exam, but you should realize its purpose in enabling SSO within an infrastructure.

Public Key Infrastructure (PKI)

As mentioned in the "Certificate Management" section earlier in this chapter, digital certificates are used to verify the identity of servers (primarily web servers, but other things can use certificates, such as VPN connections). Note that these certificates are also commonly called SSL/TLS certificates in context to HTTP services and functions, and they are based on the public key infrastructure (PKI).

PKI is a standard that defines how digital certificates are created, revoked, managed, stored, used, and distributed. It utilizes a pair of cryptographic keys (public and private), which not only allows the creation and verification of certificates but also provides a way to encrypt the data that is transported between the client and the server.

For the Cloud+ certification exam, you won't need to know all of the details of PKI, but you will need to know some key terms:

▶ **Digital certificate:** A unique value that contains a collection of data that is used to identify an entity (that is, a server). For example, think of certificates in your browser store.

▶ **CA:** Certificate authority; an entity that validates, signs, and issues the digital certificates. For example, Verisign CA or GeoTrust CA are public CAs; also, an organization may have an internal Microsoft Root CA for certificate signing.

▶ **Public key:** A unique cryptographic key that is publicly shared. Data encrypted by the public key can be decrypted only by the corresponding private key.

▶ **Private key:** A unique cryptographic key that is never shared. It is used to decrypt data that was encrypted by the corresponding public key.

▶ **CRL:** Certificate revocation list; a list that defines the certificates that the CA no longer considers valid. For example, a certificate that was deemed to be no longer secure but is valid can be declared as void in the CRL.

▶ **CSR:** Certificate signing request; a request to a CA to generate a digital certificate. The CSR must contain specific information, including the public key for the organization, and must be "signed," a process verifying that the organization making the CSR possessed the private key.

Secret Management

"Three may keep a secret, if two of them are dead."

—Benjamin Franklin, *Poor Richard's Almanack*

While a bit dramatic, this quote from hundreds of years ago illustrates that the importance of keeping a secret can't be understated. It also holds true for the private key in PKI (although no one must die to key this secret!).

Secret management just means that you should have some secure means to protect your private keys. Doing so may include ensuring that your private keys are stored in folders or directories that are secured by passwords, but in a high security cloud environment, it will likely mean using a tool that stores this information.

Most cloud vendors provide the means to store private keys securely. For example, AWS offers a product called AWS Secrets Manager, Google offers Cloud Key Management, and Azure has Key Vault. Some third-party organizations also will allow you to store and manage your private keys, such as HashiCorp's Vault and PKI Secrets Engine.

It is important to note that most of these tools not only store the private keys but also manage the process of creating and revoking the keys, which means they also manage the public keys for your organization. In other words, these tools help manage the certificate lifecycle.

Key Management

See the preceding "Secret Management" section.

CramQuiz

Answer these questions. The answers follow the last question. If you cannot answer these questions correctly, consider reading this section again until you can.

1. Which of the following is not considered a part of the account lifecycle management?

   ○ **A.** Creation

   ○ **B.** Updates

   ○ **C.** Verification

   ○ **D.** Deactivation

2. _____ access control leaves the job of securing a resource to the user rather than the administrator.

   ○ **A.** Role-based

   ○ **B.** Discretionary

   ○ **C.** Nondiscretionary

   ○ **D.** Mandatory

3. Which of the following is not considered a feature of directory services?

   ○ **A.** Hierarchical naming model

   ○ **B.** Distributed data model

   ○ **C.** Security enhanced model

   ○ **D.** An extensible schema

4. Which of the following is considered a directory service? (Choose two.)

   ○ **A.** DNS

   ○ **B.** Federation

   ○ **C.** Multifactor authentication

   ○ **D.** LDAP

5. _____ is the protocol that allows for SSO.

   ○ **A.** MFA

   ○ **B.** LDAP

   ○ **C.** SAML

   ○ **D.** PKI

CramQuiz Answers

1. Verification
2. Discretionary access control
3. Security enhanced model
4. DNS and LDAP
5. SAML

What Next?

If you want more practice on this chapter's exam objectives before you move on, remember that you can access all of the CramQuiz questions on the companion website. You can also create a custom exam by objectives with the practice exam software. Note any objectives you struggle with and go to that objective's material in this chapter.

CHAPTER 6

Secure a Network in a Cloud Environment

This chapter covers the following official CompTIA Cloud+ exam objective:

▶ 2.2 Given a scenario, secure a network in a cloud environment.

(For more information on the official CompTIA Cloud+ exam topics, see the Introduction.)

This chapter tackles the challenge of security in a cloud network environment. You will first learn about network segmentation, including the differences between VLAN, VxLAN, and GENEVE. Microsegmentation and tiering will also be covered in this chapter.

Securing the protocols that are commonly used in a cloud network will also be discussed in this chapter. This will include the basics of securing DNS using DoH, DoT, and DNSSEC; securing NTP with NTS; and using encryption protocols, including TLS and HTTPS.

Security-based network services, such as firewalls, ADCs, IPS, IDS, DLP, and NAC, are included in this chapter. You will also learn about some network hardening techniques, including disabling unnecessary ports, services, protocols, and ciphers.

CramSaver

If you can correctly answer these questions before going through this section, save time by skimming the ExamAlerts in this section and then completing the CramQuiz at the end of the section.

1. You are limited to _____ VLANs per network.

2. Which solutions will encrypt DNS traffic?

3. A _____ firewall is one that keeps track of the network packets that are allowed to pass through the firewall and allows responses to pass back through the firewall.

4. _____ is creating a list of servers, sites, or resources that you want to permit access to.

Answers

1. 4000

2. DNS over HTTPS (DoH) and DNS over TLS (DoT)

3. Stateful

4. Whitelisting

Network Segmentation

The purpose of network segmentation is to divide a network into smaller networks. The primary goals of network segmentation are to improve performance and increase security. In a public cloud environment, they are critical because your organization will often be sharing the underlying network with other organizations. The cloud vendor wants to ensure that your network traffic is not viewable by other organizations.

This section focuses on different methods of performing network segmentation.

Virtual LAN (VLAN)/Virtual Extensible LAN (VxLAN)/Generic Network Virtualization Encapsulation (GENEVE)

VLAN, VxLAN, and GENEVE are three commonly used network segmentation techniques. Each of these topics can be quite large and complex. For the

CompTIA Cloud+ exam, the most important point is to understand that they are used for network segmentation and to understand some of the differences.

VLAN is a well-established technology and has been around since the 1990s. The technique used to segment traffic on a network is to apply tags to the network frames. Networking devices use the tags to determine which endpoints to send broadcast messages to. VLANs apply the tag on the layer 2 frame. There is a limit of 4000 VLANs per network.

VxLAN was designed to handle scaling issues in large-scale deployments (particularly cloud environments and ISPs). VxLANs are similar to VLANs, but there are some differences, including where the tag is applied (it uses a larger field in the frame), which results in more possible network segments (up to 16 million).

Although VxLAN technology offers more flexibility and scalability than VLAN technology, one challenge is that it isn't the only alternative technology to VLANs. Different network technology vendors have provided other solutions, such as Network Virtualization using Generic Routing Encapsulation (NVGRE) and Stateless Transport Tunneling (STT). These other technologies provide similar features to VxLAN, but these technologies are not compatible with each other.

GENEVE is a newer network segmentation technology that is designed to support the features provided by VxLAN, NVGRE, and STT.

Microsegmentation

Microsegmentation is a security feature that enables administrators to logically divide virtual and physical resources into groups and apply a different set of security rules to each group. In terms of firewalls, microsegmentation is the process of creating zones within the same VLAN, for example.

With a firewall zone, you can create firewall rule sets that apply to a specific logical area of the network. Zones provide more flexibility for the firewall administrator, but they can also make it more difficult to troubleshoot problems if you are not aware of how the zones are configured and which resources belong to which zones.

Tiering

Tiering is a network segmentation technique that considers the function of the resources on the network. For example, one popular tiering segmentation method is to place resources in one of three categories: Web, Application, or Database.

Protocols

There are several protocols that either provide you with the capability to secure your network or that you should consider when using a more secure practice or technique. For example, you can use encryption techniques like IPsec, TLS, or HTTPS to provide a more secure network. However, technologies like DNS and NTP are not typically secure, so you should consider either using alternatives or implementing additional security features. This section focuses on these protocols.

Domain Name Service (DNS)

To learn the basics of DNS, see "DNS" in Chapter 13, "Cloud Networking Solutions." The following sections describe security features that you should consider implementing when managing a DNS service.

DNS over HTTPS (DoH)/DNS over TLS (DoT)

DNS data is normally sent across the network in plaintext format. This implementation poses a security risk because the privacy of the user could be compromised. It is also more vulnerable to a man-in-the-middle attack, an attack in which a rogue DNS server replaces the DNS results from the DNS server.

More secure solutions include DNS over HTTPS (DoH) and DNS over TLS (DoT). Both methods end up encrypting the network traffic.

DNS Security (DNSSEC)

Another potential security risk can exist in the DNS system. It is possible for a fake DNS server to provide incorrect data when a query is performed. This is known as *DNS cache poisoning* or *DNS spoofing*. The concern here is that the domain name to IP address translation of a sensitive system (like a bank's website) could point to a rogue server designed to capture usernames and passwords.

There is a way to limit the likelihood of DNS cache poisoning: use transaction signatures (TSIGs). With TSIGs, private and public digital signatures are used to ensure that DNS data is coming from the correct source. This technology can be used to verify zone transfers as well as DNS queries. The most common way to implement TSIGs for DNS is to use Domain Name System Security Extensions (DNSSEC).

Network Time Protocol (NTP)

To learn the basics of Network Time Protocol, see "NTP" in Chapter 13. The following section describes security features that you should consider implementing when managing an NTP service.

Network Time Security (NTS)

When you consider how important accurate time is, you can begin to understand the importance of having accurate clocks on resources. NTP provides a great method of providing an accurate clock, but it wasn't built to be highly secure, and there are concerns that a rogue NTP server can serve up inaccurate times to your NTP client resources.

NTS provides another layer on top of NTP, a layer that makes NTP more secure. One of the biggest additions that NTS offers is a key exchange function that is designed to ensure that NTP clients are connecting to the correct NTP server.

Encryption

To learn the basics of encryption, see "Encryption" in Chapter 7, "OS and Application Security Controls." The following sections describe security features that you should consider implementing when managing a NTP service.

IP Security (IPsec)

IP Security is a protocol that is designed to allow the transport of data between network nodes in a secure manner. IPsec is often used to create a secure VPN connection between two nodes in different physical networks. To securely transport the data, it establishes a connection between the two nodes and sends all data in an encrypted format.

IPsec can also be used to create VPNs from a single node to a remote network as well as a network-to-network VPN. Note that IPsec functions at Layer 3 (the network layer) of the OSI model.

Transport Layer Security (TLS)

Transport Layer Security is a cryptographic protocol used to secure data transfer and authenticate systems. Designed to replace SSL (Secure Sockets Layer), TLS is often generically called SSL.

TLS is used in conjunction with several protocols, including Voice over IP (VoIP), email, and instant messaging. It is also commonly used to make communications between a web client and web server by providing a protocol that is more secure than HTTP (the HTTPS protocol).

TLS provides two primary functions: preventing eavesdropping and tampering. Data sent via TLS is encrypted with a symmetric cipher after establishing a connection via an asymmetric cipher.

Hypertext Transfer Protocol Secure (HTTPS)

See the preceding "Transport Layer Security (TLS)" section.

Tunneling

Tunneling is the process of transporting data securely over a network via an encrypted connection. It is often used to implement VPN connections across multiple networks, like the Internet. This section provides some essential information about the protocols often used for tunneling: Secure Shell (SSH), Layer 2 Tunneling Protocol (L2TP), Point-to-Point Tunneling Protocol (PPTP), and generic routing encapsulation (GRE).

Secure Shell (SSH)

The Secure Shell is a network protocol that is used to securely transport data across a network. SSH has several functions, including

▶ The capability to log in to a remote system via a command-line interface

▶ The capability to remotely execute a command-line program on a remote system

▶ The capability to transfer files between systems, either using a command-line utility or an FTP-like utility

An SSH connection can also be established to create a secure tunnel between two systems through a method called *port forwarding*. After the tunnel is established, the client system doesn't send the network packet directly to the remote system but rather to the local SSH service. Then the local SSH service sends the network packet via the encrypted connection to the SSH service on the remote system. The remote SSH service then sends the data to the service on the remote system that the packet was designed to be sent to.

This method allows for several advantages. One advantage is that a protocol that is not normally secure can still send data across the network using an encrypted connection. A second advantage is that an SSH tunnel can be established for a brief period of time to perform the necessary operations. It doesn't have to be running all of the time, and it is easy to set up and tear down. Additionally, an SSH tunnel communicates on port 22, which is often not blocked by firewalls, so an SSH tunnel can be used to bypass the restrictions of a very secure firewall implementation.

Layer 2 Tunneling Protocol (L2TP)/ Point-to-Point Tunneling Protocol (PPTP)

Layer 2 Tunneling Protocol performs the tunneling at Layer 2 of the OSI model. OSI Layer 2 is also referred to as the data link layer. L2TP uses 256-bit encryption keys, making it a strong encryption protocol.

Point-to-Point Tunneling Protocol is a lower-level protocol, which is faster and easier to use than L2TP. However, PPTP encrypts using 128-bit encryption keys, so it is considered less secure than L2TP.

Generic Routing Encapsulation (GRE)

Cisco developed another protocol, called generic routing encapsulation, that is often designed to create encrypted VPN connections across the network. The method used by GRE is to encapsulate a data packet that doesn't use encryption with a GRE packet (which does use encryption). Once the GRE packet gets to the destination, the encapsulated packet is decrypted and processed by the destination system.

Network Services

This section focuses on network services that are used to secure a cloud environment.

Firewalls

See "Software Firewall" in Chapter 7.

Stateful

A stateful firewall is one that keeps track of the network packets that are allowed to pass through the firewall and allows responses to pass back through the firewall. For example, suppose your organization has a firewall that blocks most traffic into your network, but you have an application that queries a web server on the Internet. Normally, if the web server were to attempt to send network packets directly into your organization's network, the packets would be blocked by the firewall. But if the firewall is stateful, it will allow packets from the web server that are in response to the internal application queries. In other words, it opens a pinhole connection.

Stateless

A stateless firewall does not consider any connections or communications that have been established from within the organization. A stateless firewall must have all ports manually configured to be "unblocked" for communication to enter the network.

Web Application Firewall (WAF)

Most standard firewall software programs are designed to protect either a network or an entire operating system. Although there are certainly situations where you will want to implement that type of firewall in your cloud environment, there is a more specialized case where you will want to implement a more specific type of firewall: the web application firewall (WAF).

A WAF is designed to protect OSI layer 7 applications based on HTTP/HTTPS. This is important for cloud environments because applications can run separately from the operating system in a cloud infrastructure. A WAF is designed to filter and monitor inbound connections to applications by analyzing HTTP traffic. It helps protect your applications from attacks like SQL injections and cross-site scripting (known as *XSS*).

Note that dozens of different WAF programs are available, including several provided by major cloud vendors. For example, Amazon has AWS WAF, and Microsoft offers Azure Application Gateway with WAF.

Application Delivery Controller (ADC)

An application delivery controller is a program that provides several functions, including

- ▶ Acting as a web accelerator, which improves HTTP response time and reduces the load on the web servers

- ▶ Acting as a simple load balancer for web servers

- ▶ Providing controlled access to web servers because it is normally placed in the DMZ (between the inner and outer firewall)

Intrusion Protection System (IPS)/ Intrusion Detection System (IDS)

See "Host-Based IDS (HIDS)/Host-Based IPS (HIPS)" in Chapter 7.

Data Loss Prevention (DLP)

Consider how some stores attempt to limit loss through theft of inventory by using security control tags. A tag is placed on an item and is deactivated only if the item is sold. If that item isn't sold and someone tries to remove it from the store, an alarm goes off. In simpler words, data loss prevention offers protection against data exfiltration.

A similar concept is the basis of DLP software. This software actively monitors network traffic and tries to recognize the transmission of sensitive data. If discovered, the DLP should block the data from leaving the network.

Network Access Control (NAC)

Consider a situation in which your organization has implemented several software programs to secure your network and resources. This includes an antivirus program, a threat detection program, a device management program, data loss prevention, and others. Each program is designed to perform its function, but they all work independently, even though they are all part of the goal of endpoint security.

Think about network access control as a way of unifying these disjointed programs under a single administrative umbrella. NAC makes use of policies to control multiple aspects of a network to improve the security of the network while also making the protection of the network more visible and transparent to the NAC administrator.

Packet Brokers

You may have used a broker in real life to facilitate a complex process. For example, if you were trying to get a loan to buy a house, you could go to an individual lender, fill out a loan application, provide all of your financial information, and so on. Then to make sure you get the best deal, you would go through this process again and again with multiple lenders.

In real life a broker is an agent who provides a single point of contact instead of your having to work with multiple entities individually. Another example is a stock market broker who will handle the process of buying and selling stock for you (and hopefully provide you with sound advice on buying and selling stock).

A packet broker fulfills a similar function. It will receive network traffic, analyze the traffic, and manage the flow of the traffic. It can act as a filter and also monitor the network and provide administrators a single pane-of-glass view of network traffic. It isn't used in place of other security devices, like firewalls, DLP, or IPS/IDS devices, but rather in conjunction with these devices to provide a higher level of security.

Log and Event Monitoring

See "Logging" and "Monitoring" in Chapter 16, "Logging, Monitoring, and Alerting."

Network Flows

As you can probably tell by now, your organization's network can become very complex very quickly. With multiple security devices, VPNs, and other security features, understanding the flow of your network traffic becomes critical to ensuring your security policies are implemented correctly.

A *network flow* is a description of how packets are routed through your network. You can utilize network diagram software to generate a network map to better visualize the flow of network traffic in your cloud environment. This should also include the flow of network packets from your on-premises environment to your cloud environment (and vice versa).

Hardening and Configuration Changes

Improving security is often referred to as *hardening*. This section focuses on procedures and processes you can implement to improve the security of your cloud network.

Disabling Unnecessary Ports and Services

When you deploy a resource in a cloud environment, you should make sure that only necessary services are running on the resource. For example, suppose you deployed a Linux server in your cloud infrastructure and you performed an "out of the box" installation. This will likely result in many services running on the server that are not necessary, including the print service.

Unnecessary services are a potential security threat to your resource. Perform an analysis of which services are running on the resource and disable all that are not needed to perform the function of the resource.

Disabling Weak Protocols and Ciphers

You should have a list of protocols and ciphers that your company supports and allows in your cloud environment. Anything not on this list should not be allowed in your cloud infrastructure. Note that there are many protocols and ciphers, and providing a list here that would suit your organization's needs isn't feasible. The following brief list provides you with an idea of commonly used weak protocols and ciphers:

▶ FTP

▶ Telnet

▶ POP3

▶ IMAP

▶ SNMP v1 and v2

▶ RC2

▶ RC4

▶ MD5

▶ 3DES

▶ DES

Firmware Upgrades

Firmware software is the software that manages specific physical hardware devices on a system. This software is not typically installed on the file system for the resource but rather in special nonvolatile memory devices, like ROM.

This software is often overlooked in a security policy because it tends to just "work" as it is, and updating the software rarely provides any new critical features. However, firmware updates often do address security concerns, such as patching security holes. As a result, a security plan should include the regular patching of firmware.

Control Ingress and Egress Traffic

You have already learned about tools that control traffic flow, including firewalls, packet brokers, and DLP. These tools are designed to control traffic into your network (ingress traffic) and traffic leaving your network (egress traffic).

Whitelisting or Blacklisting

Whitelisting is creating a list of servers, sites, or resources that you want to permit access to. *Blacklisting* is creating a list of servers, sites, or resources that you want to block access to. These lists are often used in conjunction with software like firewalls or DLP software to control the ingress and egress flow of network traffic.

Proxy Servers

A *proxy server* is a system that serves to facilitate the communications between a client and a server. There are different advantages depending on the design of the proxy server. There are several different types of proxy servers, including the following:

▶ **Tunneling proxy:** This type of proxy is designed to act as a gateway between two networks. An example would be when an IPv4-based network needs to communicate with an IPv6-based network. See Figure 6.1 for a visual example of a tunneling proxy.

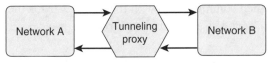

FIGURE 6.1 **Reverse Proxy**

▶ **Forward proxy:** This type of proxy is designed to work on the client side of the communication. For example, a web browser can point to a proxy server instead of communicating directly with the web server. Typically, when someone calls a system the proxy server, that person is referring to a system functioning as a forward proxy. See Figure 6.2 for a visual example of a forward proxy.

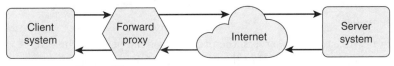

FIGURE 6.2 **Forward Proxy**

A forward proxy server can provide the following key functions:

▶ It can act as a filter by blocking access to external resources.

▶ It can act as a buffer between the client and the server because the server "sees" the request coming from the proxy, not the original client. This can hide the original client data, such as its IP address or location. Some users prefer this because it allows for anonymous browsing. This is also useful to get around restrictions—for example, a website that only allows access from a geographic region. In this case a proxy server located in the correct geographic region could permit the required access.

▶ Proxy servers can cache static data—for example, websites that have static web pages. When multiple proxy clients attempt to retrieve the same data, the proxy server can serve to speed up the process by returning the data directly rather than querying the web server repeatedly.

▶ The proxy server can be used to log client activity.

▶ **Reverse proxy:** A reverse proxy server is one that is configured on the server side. For example, instead of having web clients directly connect to your company web server, you have them connect to the proxy server initially. The proxy server then communicates with the web server for the required data. See Figure 6.3 for a visual example of a reverse proxy.

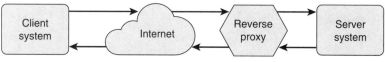

FIGURE 6.3   **Reverse Proxy**

There are several advantages for a reverse proxy server, including:

▶ Load balancing can be provided by the proxy server because it can send queries to multiple web servers.

▶ The proxy server can limit the load from the server by caching static data.

▶ For SSL-based web servers, the proxy server can perform the SSL-based operations instead of the web server. If the proxy server is equipped with SSL-accelerated hardware, this can be a tremendous advantage.

▶ The proxy server can effectively hide the web server from the client, making the web server more secure. Without direct access to the web server, it is more difficult to exploit it.

▶ The proxy server can optimize communication by compressing the data, increasing the speed of data transport.

Distributed Denial-of-Service (DDoS) Protection

A DDoS is an attack on your network or a resource within your network. Using multiple systems, a large number of network packets are sent with the goal of overwhelming systems within your network. There are many different forms of DDoS attacks, including

▶ HTTP floods

▶ DNS query floods

▶ SSL abuse

▶ SYN floods

▶ UDP reflection floods

Because there are many different DDoS attacks, there are different approaches to protecting your resources from these attacks, including

▶ Using DDoS mitigation software

▶ Reducing attack areas

▶ Preparing to scale up in the event of a successful attack

▶ Using analytic tools to discover abnormal traffic

▶ Utilizing WAF devices

CramQuiz

Answer these questions. The answers follow the last question. If you cannot answer these questions correctly, consider reading this section again until you can.

1. _____ is a security feature that enables administrators to logically divide resources into groups and apply a different set of security rules to each group.

   ○ **A.** VxLAN

   ○ **B.** Microsegmentation

   ○ **C.** GENEVE

   ○ **D.** VLAN

2. Transport Layer Security (TLS) is a cryptographic protocol used to secure data transfer and authenticate systems. It was designed to replace SSL.

   ○ **A.** TLS

   ○ **B.** IPsec

   ○ **C.** L2TP

   ○ **D.** PPTP

3. Which of the following is not a feature of an application delivery controller?

   ○ **A.** Can act as a web accelerator

   ○ **B.** Can act as a simple load balancer for web servers

   ○ **C.** Can provide controlled access to web servers

   ○ **D.** Can authenticate users

4. Which of the following would be considered an insecure protocol? (Choose two.)

- ○ **A.** IMAP
- ○ **B.** SSH
- ○ **C.** SNMP v2
- ○ **D.** TLS

CramQuiz Answers

1. Microsegmentation
2. TLS
3. Can authenticate users
4. IMAP and SNMP v2

What Next?

If you want more practice on this chapter's exam objectives before you move on, remember that you can access all of the CramQuiz questions on the companion website. You can also create a custom exam by objectives with the practice exam software. Note any objectives you struggle with and go to that objective's material in this chapter.

CHAPTER 7

OS and Application Security Controls

This chapter covers the following official CompTIA Cloud+ exam objective:

▶ 2.3 Given a scenario, apply the appropriate OS and application security controls.

(For more information on the official CompTIA Cloud+ exam topics, see the Introduction.)

The focus of this chapter is how you should apply security controls to operating systems and applications within a cloud infrastructure. You will first learn about the importance of developing policies and user permissions. Next, you will learn about improving the security of a system by using hardened baselines, an endpoint detection and response (EDR), a host-based intrusion detection system (HIDS), and a host-based instruction protection system (HIPS).

CramSaver

If you can correctly answer these questions before going through this section, save time by skimming the ExamAlerts in this section and then completing the CramQuiz at the end of the section.

1. When you create an application_____, you are specifying which applications can be installed and executed on that virtual machine or container.

2. Which command is used to display permissions in Linux?

3. A hardened _____ is a set of requirements for each system you deploy.

4. A(n) _____ build is a stable build that should be supported for a longer-than-average period of time.

Answers

1. Whitelist
2. ls
3. Baseline
4. LTS

Policies

A *policy* is a collection of rules that are designed to provide a higher level of security. Without policies, components of the cloud infrastructure, like user accounts and software, are more vulnerable. This section covers some of policies that you should consider implementing in your cloud environment.

Password Complexity

Clearly "cat1234" is not a very good password on any modern system, and you want to avoid having users create passwords that are this simple. Because password complexity is such a key component of any good security policy, most cloud vendors provide an easy way to implement a policy for the cloud accounts. For example, Figure 7.1 demonstrates the AWS password policy for IAM users.

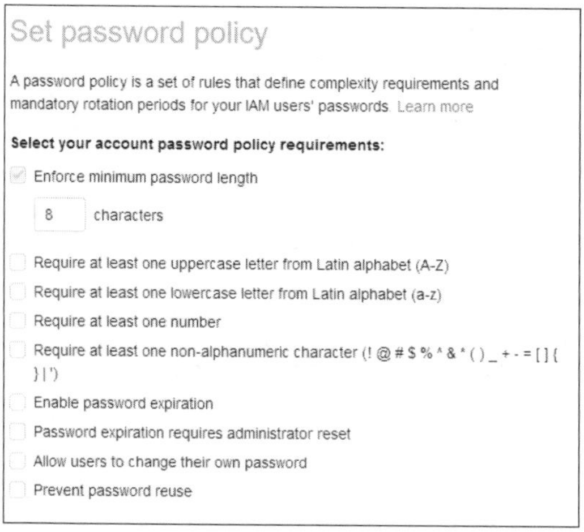

Set password policy

A password policy is a set of rules that define complexity requirements and mandatory rotation periods for your IAM users' passwords. Learn more

Select your account password policy requirements:

☑ Enforce minimum password length

    8   characters

☐ Require at least one uppercase letter from Latin alphabet (A-Z)
☐ Require at least one lowercase letter from Latin alphabet (a-z)
☐ Require at least one number
☐ Require at least one non-alphanumeric character (! @ # $ % ^ & * ( ) _ + - = [ ] {
   } | ')
☐ Enable password expiration
☐ Password expiration requires administrator reset
☐ Allow users to change their own password
☐ Prevent password reuse

FIGURE 7.1 **AWS Password Policy**

Note that the following are common complexity features that you can apply to most password policies:

▶ Enforce minimum number of characters in the password.

▶ Require at least one numeric character.

▶ Require at least one lowercase character.

▶ Require at least one uppercase character.

▶ Require at least one character that is not a number or an alpha character (sometimes called special characters).

Note that it is not just cloud accounts that you should apply a password complexity policy to. Other cloud resources, such as database engines and operating systems, also utilize user accounts, and these account passwords should also comply with the company password complexity policy.

Account Lockout

An account lockout policy defines in which situations an account is locked. This can include any of the following:

▶ An expiration date

▶ Too many attempts to log in to the account

▶ The number of days that the account is inactive

▶ Login attempts from unauthorized locations

Typically, an account lockout policy requires an administrator to remove the lockout. However, in some cases the account lockout could be removed after a predetermined period of time.

Application Whitelisting

When you deploy compute resources in the cloud (and on-premises as well), you should consider developing a policy for application whitelisting. When you create an application whitelist, you are specifying which applications can be installed and executed on that virtual machine or container.

The goal of this policy is to prevent malware from being installed or executed. Malware can be installed either intentionally by a user or unintentionally when clicking a link to a site that downloads and installs the malware.

Software Feature

Most software applications have features that may be considered a security risk. For example, an email application that opens attachments may result in opening a file that contains a virus or worm. A software feature policy is used to determine which features should be disabled to provide a higher level of security.

User/Group

Both cloud and operating system user accounts can be merged together into a group. Typically, this is done to provide access to resources or to apply a policy to a collection of user accounts.

For example, suppose you want to provide access to read data from a database for three user accounts: ned, fred, and ted. You could apply the permissions to access the database to each individual user. This approach can be manageable for a small number of user accounts, but what happens when there are hundreds or thousands of user accounts? What happens when accounts are routinely deleted and added to the environment?

Using groups helps administer permissions and account policies, but there also need to be company policies regarding how the groups are administered. For example, suppose that database contains payroll information. There should be a policy in place that determines what criteria must be met before someone is able to access this database.

User Permissions

To access cloud resources, a user must have the right permissions for those resources. In many cases, these permissions can be applied to specific resources or specific types of cloud resources. For example, you could create a permission that allows a user to read data from any database but then have permissions that allows that user to modify only specific databases.

In terms of operating systems, both of the primary operating systems used in cloud computing (Linux and Microsoft Windows) utilize permissions to protect files. For example, in Microsoft Windows you can go to the properties of a file by right-clicking the file and then choosing **Properties**. Then you click the **Security** tab, as shown in Figure 7.2, and you can modify the permissions of the file.

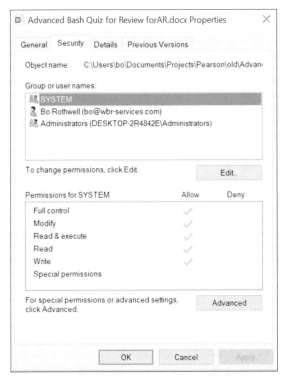

FIGURE 7.2   Changing the Permissions of a File in Windows

For Linux, every file and directory has standard permissions (also called *read, write, and execute* permissions) that either allow or disallow a user access. To view the permissions of a file or directory in Linux, use the **ls -l** command as follows:

```
[student@localhost ~]$ ls -l /etc/chrony.keys
-rw-r-----. 1 root chrony 62 May  9  2021 /etc/chrony.keys
```

The first 10 characters of the output denote the file type (if the character in the first position is a hyphen [–], it denotes a plain file, and **d** denotes a directory) and the permissions for the file. Permissions are broken into three sets: the user owner of the file (**root** in the preceding example), the group owner (**chrony**), and all other users (referred to as "others").

Each set has three possible permissions: read (symbolized by **r**), write (**w**), and execute (**x**). If a permission is set, the character that symbolizes the permission is displayed. Otherwise, a hyphen (–) character is displayed to indicate that permission is not set. Thus, **r-x** means "read and execute are set, but write is not set."

What read, write, and execute permissions really mean depends on whether the object is a file or directory. For files, these permissions mean the following:

▶ **Read:** Can view or copy file contents.

▶ **Write:** Can modify file contents.

▶ **Execute:** Can run the file like a program. After you create a program, you must make it executable before you can run it.

For directories, they mean the following:

▶ **Read:** Can list files in the directory.

▶ **Write:** Can add and delete files in the directory (requires execute permission).

▶ **Execute:** Can change into the directory (**cd**) or use it in a pathname.

The **chmod** command is used to change permissions on files. It can be used in two ways: the symbolic method and the octal method. With the octal method, the permissions are assigned numeric values:

▶ Read = 4

▶ Write = 2

▶ Execute = 1

With these numeric values, one number can be used to describe an entire permission set:

▶ 7 = **rwx**

▶ 6 = **rw-**

▶ 5 = **r-x**

▶ 4 = **r--**

▶ 3 = **-wx**

▶ 2 = **-w-**

▶ 1 = **--x**

▶ 0 = **---**

So, to change the permissions of a file to **rwxr-xr--,** you would execute the following command:

```
chmod 754 filename
```

With octal permissions, you should always provide three numbers, which will change all the permissions. But, what if you want to change only a single permission of the set? For that, you use the symbolic method by passing three values to the **chmod** command, as shown in Table 7.1.

TABLE 7.1 **Symbolic Permission Values**

Who	What	Permission
u = user owner	+	**r**
g = group owner	-	**w**
o = other	=	**x**
a= all sets		

The following example demonstrates how to add execute permission to all three sets (user owner, group owner, and others) using the symbolic method:

```
[student@localhost ~]$ ls -l display.sh
-rw-rw-r--. 1 student student 291 Apr 30 20:09 display.sh
[student@localhost ~]$ chmod a+x display.sh
[student@localhost ~]$ ls -l display.sh
-rwxrwxr-x. 1 student student 291 Apr 30 20:09 display.sh
```

Antivirus/Antimalware/Endpoint Detection and Response (EDR)

Just about any compute system has some sort of antivirus/antimalware software available, including traditional operating systems like Microsoft Windows and Linux, as well as mobile device operating systems like iOS (for the mobile OS by Apple) and Android. They have become commonplace and are especially important on cloud resources that are often easily accessible via the Internet.

In addition to installing these products on individual systems, many organizations make use of EDR software. This software monitors and records information on the endpoints (individual systems) into a central database. This information is used to determine what risks to the network are present.

By analyzing this information, organizations can develop a better understanding of the threats that are reaching the endpoints of the organization's network.

Host-Based IDS (HIDS)/Host-Based IPS (HIPS)

An intrusion detection system (IDS) is a software or hardware system that is designed to determine if an intrusion is occurring or has occurred on a network or a host. There are two major categories of IDS software: network-based and host-based.

A network-based IDS (NIDS) is software that monitors network packets to determine if an intrusion is taking or has taken place. A host-based IDS (HIDS) is installed on specific systems and monitors the state of the system itself to determine if an intrusion is in progress or has taken place.

There are many options available for these software programs, but the general concept is that an HIDS will utilize a database that describes what to monitor on the system. This can include monitoring actions that other software programs take, actions that users take, changes to the configuration of the operating system, and changes that are made to filesystems.

It is important to understand that an IDS is designed to monitor the system or the network for intrusions, but it is not designed to protect the system from intrusions. An IDS may take some actions, such as generating reports or sending alerts via email or SMS, but it doesn't take any direct action to protect the system or the network. It can generate alerts so an action can be taken manually.

An intrusion protection system (IPS) both monitors for intrusions and can take action if an intrusion is detected. For example, an HIPS may detect a suspicious login and, as a result, block access to the system from the source IP address.

The advantage of an IPS over an IDS is that potential threats may be neutralized quicker than if a human needed to get involved. The disadvantage of an IPS over an IDS is that false positives may result in disabling access for someone who should be allowed the access.

Hardened Baselines

Each resource should be designed to provide specific features and functions. For example, you might have a virtual machine that is designed to serve as a web host. Unfortunately, many operating systems have other features enabled when you perform an "out of the box" installation.

A *hardened baseline* is a set of requirements for each system you deploy. This baseline can include establishing rules on how different components of the system are configured, including the following:

▶ Operating system configurations

▶ Network configurations and services permitted on the network

▶ System monitoring configurations

▶ Data encryption methods

▶ Application configurations

▶ Security appliance configurations

▶ Backup policies and procedures

▶ Patching and update policies

The goal of hardened baselines is to establish specific rules and procedures to best ensure the security of any resource that your organization deploys. These baselines should be well established long before your organization deploys any resource in a production environment.

Single Function

As mentioned in the previous section, each resource should be designed to perform a single function. For example, a virtual machine that provides an organization's web server should not also function as the organization's mail server, NTP server, and file server.

The separating of functions is one of the primary advantages of cloud computing and a major reason to consider utilizing containers rather than full operating systems. In a cloud infrastructure you can customize the system resources (CPU, memory, and so on) to meet the need of the compute resource that you are deploying. You don't need to guess how much system resources your web server will need, and you don't have to feel compelled to "fill up" an expensive server with additional services.

By using a single function methodology, you provide a more secure environment. For example, maybe an attacker can hack into your web server (granted, this is bad), but if you use a single function methodology, the attacker doesn't automatically gain access to your mail server, NTP server, and file server.

File Integrity

See "Integrity" in Chapter 8, "Data Security and Compliance Controls in Cloud Environments."

Log and Event Monitoring

See "Monitoring" in Chapter 16, "Logging, Monitoring, and Alerting."

Configuration Management

See the following sections:

▶ "Hardening and Configuration Changes" in Chapter 6, "Secure a Network in a Cloud Environment."

▶ "Configuration Management Database (CMDB)" in Chapter 17, "Operation of a Cloud Environment."

Builds

When an organization develops software and the software is released, either internally or externally, the release is referred to as a *build*. This section explores different types of builds.

Stable

A *stable build* is designed to be a release that is ready for a production environment. Typically, if you are a customer who purchases software, that software is considered a stable build.

Prior to a software build being released, earlier releases are called *beta builds*. Some organizations like to have access to beta builds because this access provides them with early insight as to how the software will perform. However, beta builds come with little to no support or warranty. They are considered "use at your own risk" and should not be used in production environments.

Long-Term Support (LTS)

A *long-term support build* is a stable build that should be supported for a longer than average period of time. This can be an important issue for some organizations because moving to a new version of software can pose several challenges, including:

▶ Time, effort, and money to ensure that the new version performs within standards.

▶ Potential new licensing costs.

▶ The need to deal with potential inconsistencies or incompatibilities. For example, a newer version of software might not integrate with other software that the organization is already using.

▶ Additional training costs to teach existing employees and customers how the new version of the software behaves.

▶ Reduced production as employees attempt to use the new version of the software.

One disadvantage of utilizing an LTS build is that new features that are released with the regular stable build are not normally implemented in the LTS build.

Beta

See the earlier "Stable" section.

Canary

You may have heard how miners would take a canary bird into the mines with them to determine if the air held dangerous levels of toxic gases. The idea was that the canary had a faster breathing rate than humans and would show signs of the presence of toxic gases quicker than humans would.

A *canary build* works on a similar concept. New features are released to a specific set of beta testers (pilot users) to determine if the new features have any negative impact on the software. The features are provided in the new beta builds in a very specific manner and typically spread out over several beta releases. This type of build allows the developers some insight as to which new features may have caused an issue and allows the developers the time to fix the issues before releasing the software in a stable build.

Operating System (OS) Upgrades

See "Scheduled Updates" in Chapter 9, "Security Requirements."

Encryption

See "Encryption" in Chapter 8.

Application Programming Interface (API) Endpoint

An API is a technique that is used to provide a well-known communication method between a client and a server. A client will issue an API request to a server, typically using representational state transfer (REST; see "Authorization" in Chapter 23, "Troubleshoot Security Issues").

API calls across the Internet are common. Even if the API call is made within an enclosed network, it is important that the transmission itself be encrypted. For this reason, the endpoint of API connections is normally established with the HTTPS protocol.

Application

Applications often store and transmit data. To ensure the security of this data, all data in transit and all data at rest should be in an encrypted format. This is especially important in cloud environments because data is often more accessible as it is stored in a network-accessible location.

OS

Typically, in regard to OS encryption, what is really being encrypted is the storage disk or the filesystem where the OS resides. See the "Filesystem" section later in this chapter.

Storage

Most cloud-based storage devices provide some level of encryption although it might not be enabled by default. Cloud storage that is used to hold sensitive data should have the encryption option turned on.

Filesystem

The term *filesystem encryption* refers to any filesystem in which the file data (and, sometimes, metadata) is encrypted when the data is "at rest." The data is decrypted when needed by a user or program.

In some cases, the encryption is provided as a feature of a filesystem that can be turned on or off. In other cases, a separate application handles the encryption process.

In environments like the cloud, where the data on the filesystem can be accessed by multiple people, using an encrypted filesystem is an important part of security strategy.

> **Note**
>
> Encrypted filesystems are not the same as full disk encryption. With full disk encryption, the entire disk is encrypted when the operating system is inactive (shut down). When the system is booted, the data on the disk is encrypted.

Mandatory Access Control

Consider a situation in which a user logs in to an operating system and then wants to share a file with another user so that the other user can view the contents of the file. This change is typically accomplished by file permissions and, if the user owns the file, that user normally has the ability to make changes to the file permissions. This is referred to as discretionary access control (DAC).

The problem with DAC is that users don't always make the best choice when it comes to security. For example, suppose the user couldn't figure out how to change the permissions on the file so that the other user had access. Instead, the first user, either because of frustration or lack the time to research how to accomplish this task, decides to allow everyone the ability to view the file contents. Depending on the contents of the file, this can be a very poor security decision.

A mandatory access control (MAC) system is a set of rules that either allow or deny entities (users, software programs, and so on) access to a resource. However, unlike DAC, with MAC individual users don't have the ability to change the access rules. A MAC policy is used to manage the access rules, and the administrator should be the only one who can modify the policy.

MAC systems are popular on operating systems. Microsoft utilizes Mandatory Integrity Control to provide MAC on Windows. On Linux systems, SELinux and AppArmor are popular MAC systems.

Your cloud vendor likely also employs MAC. For example, as the cloud administrator for your organization, you can permit users the ability to access resources using either cloud permissions or policies.

Firewall Software

Firewall software is used to protect either a network or an individual resource. When firewall rules are put in place, the firewall can filter which network packets can enter a network or the operating system.

A large number of firewall programs are available. You shouldn't expect to be asked questions on the CompTIA Cloud+ exam on any specific firewall software. However, you should realize that firewalls provide many features and benefits, including the following:

▶ A firewall can block or allow packets based on any header information, like source IP address or destination port.

▶ In some cases a firewall can block or allow packets based on the content of the message.

▶ Firewall software can often provide advanced features, like Network Address Translation (NAT), malware filtering, intrusion prevention, and VPNs.

▶ Firewalls can be configured to log network packet information.

▶ Firewalls are not one directional. You can use a firewall to block access from resources within your network attempting to access an external resource.

CramQuiz

Answer these questions. The answers follow the last question. If you cannot answer these questions correctly, consider reading this section again until you can.

1. Which of the following is not normally a rule used to enforce more complex passwords?

    ○ **A.** Minimum number of characters in the password

    ○ **B.** Maximum number of characters in the password

    ○ **C.** Require at least one lowercase character

    ○ **D.** Require at least one uppercase character

2. Based on the following permissions, what can members of the chrony group do with the /etc/chrony.keys file?

```
[student@localhost ~]$ ls -l /etc/chrony.keys
-rw-r-----. 1 root chrony 62 May  9  2021 /etc/chrony.keys
```

- ○ **A.** Can only view the file
- ○ **B.** Can view and change the file
- ○ **C.** Can view and delete the file
- ○ **D.** Cannot do anything with the file

3. Which of the following is not normally a requirement for a hardened baseline?

- ○ **A.** Operating system configurations
- ○ **B.** System monitoring configurations
- ○ **C.** Application configurations
- ○ **D.** Cloud access configuration

4. Which build includes small beta releases over time?

- ○ **A.** Oriole
- ○ **B.** Canary
- ○ **C.** Goldfinch
- ○ **D.** Big bird

CramQuiz Answers

1. Maximum number of characters in the password
2. Can only view the file
3. Cloud access configuration
4. Canary

What Next?

If you want more practice on this chapter's exam objectives before you move on, remember that you can access all of the CramQuiz questions on the companion website. You can also create a custom exam by objectives with the practice exam software. Note any objectives you struggle with and go to that objective's material in this chapter.

CHAPTER 8

Data Security and Compliance Controls in Cloud Environments

This chapter covers the following official CompTIA Cloud+ exam objective:

▶ 2.4 Given a scenario, apply data security and compliance controls in cloud environments.

(For more information on the official CompTIA Cloud+ exam topics, see the Introduction.)

In this chapter you will learn about different data security and compliance controls that are available in cloud environments. You will learn about how encryption and integrity affect an organization's data. You will also learn how to secure data by classifying and segmenting the data, as well as controlling access to the data.

Also discussed in this chapter is how laws and regulations impact data security, including the concept of a legal host. Lastly, you will learn about records management, a process in which rules are put in place to determine how long data is maintained and how to properly destroy the data when it is no longer needed.

CramSaver

If you can correctly answer these questions before going through this section, save time by skimming the ExamAlerts in this section and then completing the CramQuiz at the end of the section.

1. Data at rest and data in transit are two forms of data encryption. What is the third?

2. A _____ algorithm is a mathematical function that is applied to data that should return a unique result.

3. True or false: Data classification may be dependent on who can view the data.

4. In relation to data security, data _____ is the process of placing data into different locations based on who should be able to access the data.

Answers

1. Data in use
2. Hashing
3. True
4. Segmentation

Encryption

Encryption is the process of transforming data from its original form to a form that, when viewed, does not reveal the original data. There are three different forms of encryption:

▶ **Data at rest:** Data is encrypted when it is stored. This method can either be performed by you prior to uploading the data to storage, or in some cases, it can be performed by a function that is provided by the cloud provider. When you perform the data encryption, it is your responsibility to decrypt the data when the original data is needed. When the cloud provider encrypts the data, the decryption process must be performed by the cloud provider.

▶ **Data in transit:** Data is encrypted before it is sent and decrypted when received. This form of encryption could involve several different techniques, but in most cases for cloud computing environments it means that the data is encrypted by a network device that then sends the data across the network.

▶ **Data in use:** Data is encrypted when being actively used, which typically means while it is stored in random-access memory (RAM). Because some exploits may make data in RAM vulnerable, this form of encryption may be very important to ensuring data integrity.

Many different technologies can be used to encrypt data, and which technology you use will depend on several factors, including which cloud provider you utilize. These technologies fall into one of two methods of encryption:

▶ **Symmetric encryption:** With this method you use the same key (a unique value of some sort) to both encrypt and decrypt the data.

▶ **Asymmetric encryption:** With this method you use a different key to encrypt and decrypt the data. One key is referred to as the *public key*, and the other is called the *private key*. An example of using this encryption method would be if you wanted someone to send data to you across the network. You provide the public key to this person, and this person then encrypts the data. The only way to decrypt the data is to use the private key, which you would never share with anyone else.

Integrity

While data encryption is focused on keeping prying eyes from seeing the original data, data *integrity* is focused on assuring the data is accurate and consistent. Doing so requires ensuring data integrity through all stages of the data life-cycle, which includes transporting, storing, retrieving, and processing data.

Several tools can be used to ensure data integrity, including hashing algorithms, digital signatures, and file integrity monitoring (FIM).

Hashing Algorithms

A *hashing algorithm* is a mathematical function that is applied to data that should return a unique result. Unlike encryption, in which the result of the encryption process is data that could be decrypted back to the original format, hash data is one-way, making it impossible to return the original data. The purpose of a hash isn't to hide or encrypt the data, but rather to ensure that the data you have received matches up with the original.

Consider a situation in which you receive a database with sensitive information. Your organization is going to use this information to help make some critical decisions on future products. You received this data from a trusted third-party source, but how can you be certain that a "bad actor" didn't intercept the data and inject false information?

Your third-party source could use a hashing algorithm and send the resulting hash separately. Then you could take the data that you have received, perform the same hashing algorithm, and then compare the results with the hash from the third-party. If they match, you know you have unaltered data.

There are many different types of hashing algorithms. Each has specific advantages and disadvantages, but for the CompTIA Cloud+ certification exam, you should be familiar with the names of these algorithms:

▶ MD5

▶ SHA-1

▶ SHA-2

▶ SHA-3

▶ RIPEMD-160

Digital Signatures

Suppose a friend sends you a letter. How would you know that it really came from that person? One method is to have your friend add a signature to the bottom of the letter. If you recognize the signature, you can be more certain that it came from your friend.

Digital signatures are used in the same way but are a bit more complicated in how they are implemented. Digital signatures make use of asymmetric cryptography in which the signature is encrypted using the private key of an individual or organization. The public key is made well known through another means. The signature that has been encrypted with the private key can only be decrypted by the public key. Successful decryption verifies the data came from the correct source.

File Integrity Monitoring (FIM)

In some cases, it is important to determine if data within a file has changed. The process that handles this determination is called *file integrity monitoring*. With FIM a checksum is created when the file is in a known state called a *baseline*. This checksum is a value that is based on the current contents and, in some cases, additional file attributes, such as the file owner and permissions.

To determine if a file or a file attribute has been changed, you can take another checksum sometime in the future. When you're comparing the original checksum to the new checksum, if they match, the current file is the same as the original. This technique can be used to determine if someone has tampered with a key operating system file or a file that has been downloaded from a remote server.

Classification

Consider how you would treat data that contains credit card information compared to how you would treat data that contains comments that have been made regarding your company website. The data that contains credit card information is much more sensitive than the data that contains customer comments, so you would want to treat the data differently.

In this situation data classification becomes important. With data classification, you place data into different categories depending on how you want to treat the data. These categories can be based on rules related to how sensitive the data is, who should be able to read the data, who should be able to modify the data, and how long the data should be available. Unless you are storing data that is related to compliance regulations (like SOC 2, GDPR, PCI-DSS, or HIPAA), the data classification criteria are up to you. See the "Impact of Laws and Regulations" section in this chapter for more details on compliance regulations.

For example, you may consider classifying data based on who is permitted to access the data. In this case you may use the following commonly used categories:

▶ **Public:** This data is available to anyone, including those who are not a part of your organization. This typically includes information found on your public website, announcements made on social media sites, and data found in your company press releases.

▶ **Internal:** This data should be available only to members of your organization. An example of this data would be upcoming enhancements to a software product that your organization creates.

▶ **Confidential:** This data should be available only to select individuals who have the need to access this information. This could include personally identifiable information (PII), such as an employee Social Security number. Often the rules for handling this data are also governed by compliance regulations.

▶ **Restricted:** This data may seem similar to confidential data, but it is normally more related to proprietary information, company secrets, and in some cases, data that is regarded by the government as secret.

In the cloud there are different techniques to handle different types of data. These techniques could include placing different types of data into different storage locations. Chapter 12, "Storage in Cloud Environments," will discuss different storage solutions that are typically found in a cloud environment.

You can also make use of metadata. *Metadata* is data that is associated with the "real data," and it is used to describe or classify the "real data." In cloud environments, metadata is normally created by using a feature called *tags*. Tags are flexible in that you can create a key-value pair that describes components of the data. Figure 8.1 demonstrates applying tags to data in AWS.

Key (128 characters maximum)	Value (256 characters maximum)
Category	Restricted
Department	Sales
Owner	Sarah Rothwell

FIGURE 8.1 **AWS Tags**

Segmentation

In relation to data security, data *segmentation* is the process of placing data into different locations based on who should be able to access the data. For example, it would be a good practice to place employee PII in a different location (like a different database) from the data contained in press releases.

Data segmentation may also be a requirement for compliance regulations. For example, a regulation may require that specific data never leave a country. The reason is typically that laws govern the use of this data, and once the data leaves the country, those laws no longer have effect. In this case, data segmentation may be related to the region in which you store the data. See the "Impact of Laws and Regulations" section in this chapter for further details.

Access Control

Access control is the technique that determines who can access a resource. In terms of data access control, accessing the resource can include viewing, modifying, and destroying the data.

In most cloud environments, the definition of "who" can include both people and other resources. For example, you may have a payroll application that needs to access secure data about employees that is stored in a database. There must be access control rules in place that permit or block access for both people and resources.

People are given user accounts to access cloud resources. These user accounts are granted access to resources by using permissions.

Applications are assigned to roles, which are similar to user accounts in that permissions can be applied to roles just as they are applied to user accounts. However, applications can never be assigned to user accounts (in some cases a user may be assigned to a role, depending on the cloud environment that you are working in).

To learn more about how user accounts and roles impact access to resources, see Chapter 5, "Identity and Access Management."

Impact of Laws and Regulations

As previously mentioned, many laws and regulations govern how data is treated in an organization. They will vary depending on where your data is located. For example, the laws that govern data in the United States are different from the laws that govern data in the European Union (EU).

The laws and rules are numerous and vary based on the industry of your organization. For example, if your company is a retailer and you accept credit card payments, you will likely need to follow PCI Security Standards when dealing with credit card data. If your organization is a hospital, you will need to follow HIPAA regulations when dealing with patient data.

For the certification exam, it likely is not worthwhile to memorize a bunch of laws and regulations. Many organizations have full-time staff devoted to ensuring these laws are followed. Being aware of the impact of these laws is most critical for the exam.

Legal Hold

Organizations cannot just delete information whenever they want. Some information, such as employee records, must be maintained for specific periods of time in the event of investigations or litigation. The term *legal hold* is used by an organization's legal department to indicate how long specific data must be stored and how it should be made available in the event it is needed.

Records Management

Organizations often end up creating, gathering, and accumulating a lot of data. The volumes of information stored by an organization can result in high costs because storing data is not free. While cloud vendors provide many ways of storing data, they will charge to store data, so organizations typically do not want to keep data for longer than necessary.

Records management is the process of determining how and for how long to store data. This large topic includes data classification and encryption, as well as versioning, retention policies, and destruction policies.

Versioning

Versioning is the process of keeping track of file content changes over time. Many cloud technologies provide versioning as a feature that can be enabled, so the versioning happens automatically whenever a data record is changed.

Retention

Retention refers to a policy that determines how long data should be stored. A retention schedule is created that will determine when data is destroyed and how older data is stored until it is to be destroyed.

Destruction

The destruction of data must be clearly defined when developing a records management plan. When the data is to be destroyed is one key element to define, but also how the data is to be destroyed should be clearly stated in the plan. Data can be destroyed by physical destruction of records, degaussing, or zeroizing.

Write Once Read Many

Write once read many, also referred to as WORM, is a form of write protection in which the data can be written only once and then it cannot be modified. This is a critical feature when you need to ensure that data has not been tampered with after it was created.

Data Loss Prevention (DLP)

Data loss prevention is the process of ensuring that sensitive data is not mis-used, accessed, or lost. It is designed to prevent a data breach that may include accessing, modifying, or destroying data. In some cases, the DLP process must be clearly defined because the data is regulated by laws and regulations. In other cases, the DLP may be the result of wanting to keep classified informa-tion secure.

Some cloud providers will include DLP as a software tool. For example, Google Cloud has a product called Cloud DLP, which enables you to view how data is stored and processed, configure data inspection and monitoring, and reduce the risk of data loss. In other cases, the features of DLP may be associ-ated with a specific data-based product. For example, there are techniques that you can use for DLP when storing data in AWS S3 buckets.

Cloud Access Security Broker (CASB)

CASB is a software tool that can be located either on-premises or in the cloud. It is designed to provide an interface between cloud resources (applications) and cloud users. It monitors access to cloud resources including data, issues warnings when a cloud resource may have been compromised, and enforces security policies.

CASBs also provide the means to perform audits, so access to data resources in the past can be analyzed. They are also often used for compliance reporting because they provide insights to data access over time.

CramQuiz

Answer these questions. The answers follow the last question. If you cannot answer these questions correctly, consider reading this section again until you can.

1. Which is not a form of data encryption?
   - ○ **A.** Data in use
   - ○ **B.** Data at rest
   - ○ **C.** Data in transit
   - ○ **D.** Data in the cloud

2. With this method you use a key (a unique value of some sort) to both encrypt and decrypt the data.

- ○ **A.** Antisymmetric encryption
- ○ **B.** Asymmetric encryption
- ○ **C.** Symmetric encryption
- ○ **D.** None of these answers are correct

3. Digital signatures make use of _____ cryptography in which the signature is encrypted using the private key of an individual or organization.

- ○ **A.** Asymmetric
- ○ **B.** Symmetric
- ○ **C.** Antisymmetric
- ○ **D.** Hashing

4. With _____ a checksum is created when the file is in a known state called a baseline.

- ○ **A.** Digital signatures
- ○ **B.** Hashing algorithms
- ○ **C.** File integrity monitoring
- ○ **D.** Data classification

5. The term _____ is used by an organization's legal department to indicate how long specific data must be stored and how it should be made available in the event it is needed.

- ○ **A.** Records management
- ○ **B.** Retention
- ○ **C.** WORM
- ○ **D.** Legal hold

CramQuiz Answers

1. Data in the cloud
2. Symmetric encryption
3. Asymmetric
4. File integrity monitoring
5. Legal hold

What Next?

If you want more practice on this chapter's exam objectives before you move on, remember that you can access all of the CramQuiz questions on the companion website. You can also create a custom exam by objectives with the practice exam software. Note any objectives you struggle with and go to that objective's material in this chapter.

CHAPTER 9

Security Requirements

This chapter covers the following official CompTIA Cloud+ exam objective:

▶ 2.5 Given a scenario, implement measures to meet security requirements.

(For more information on the official CompTIA Cloud+ exam topics, see the Introduction.)

The focus of this chapter is to ensure you are aware of tools and features to best ensure that you are implementing measures to meet security requirements. The first section focuses on vulnerabilities and the tools and techniques to find and resolve these vulnerabilities.

This chapter will also describe security patches, including hot fixes, virtual patches, signature updates, and rollups.

Lastly, you will learn about different topics such as handling default accounts to understanding the impact that security tools have on systems and services.

CramSaver

If you can correctly answer these questions before going through this section, save time by skimming the ExamAlerts in this section and then completing the CramQuiz at the end of the section.

1. The nmap utility is a _____ scanner.

2. A scan for default user accounts is called a _____ scan.

3. An _____-based scan is one that is run from an application that is installed locally on a resource.

4. A virtual patch is a type of _____ patch.

Answers

1. Port
2. Credential
3. Agent
4. Hot fix

Tools

This section focuses on different categories of scanning tools that you may use in your cloud infrastructure. Specifically, you will learn about vulnerability scanners and port scanners.

Vulnerability Scanners

Vulnerability scanners are tools that can automatically scan resources within your cloud infrastructure looking for possible vulnerabilities. These scanners use known exploits to test the cloud resources for these weaknesses and generate reports. The most well-known types of vulnerability scanners are related to the Open Web Application Security Project (OWASP), an organization that supports the development of tools and procedures that are designed to improve the security of software.

Additional vulnerability scanners are covered, including default and common credential scans, credentialed scans, network-based scans, and agent-based scans.

Port Scanners

A port scanner is a tool that probes network ports on a system to determine which logical ports are open. In this case, "open" means that the system will respond to a communication attempt on the port. Attackers use port scanners to find possible ways to infiltrate a system. Because you are responsible for the security of a cloud environment, you should use port scanners to ensure that the logical ports on virtual machines (VMs) and other services are not open unless they are meant to be open.

One of the most popular port scanning tools is called nmap. It can be configured to scan for a variety of ports via different protocols, such as TCP, IP, and ICMP.

Note that, legally, port scanning can be considered as an attack by itself. Be sure you have the rights to scan the ports of a system before using a port scanning tool.

Vulnerability Assessment

The goal of using vulnerability scanners is to generate a *vulnerability assessment*. This report is a review of the potential weaknesses of a system. The assessment consists of four phases:

▶ **Identification:** During this phase, you use vulnerability scanners.

▶ **Analysis:** Using the data gathered from the vulnerability scanners, in this phase you determine the root cause of the weaknesses.

▶ **Risk assessment:** Using a ranking score, in this phase you determine which vulnerabilities are the most severe and develop a plan to address these vulnerabilities.

▶ **Remediation:** In this phase, you implement the plan.

The rest of this section provides details about specific types of vulnerability scans.

Default and Common Credential Scans

The concept of a *credential scan* (not to be confused with a *credentialed scan*, discussed next) is to scan for common user accounts. For example, the most common user account on a Linux-based system is the root user account because it exists on Linux systems by default (it also provides the highest privileged access to the system).

Attackers will use brute-force scans to determine which user accounts exist. This technique works because many authentication tools provide a different error message to indicate when an account doesn't exist versus when an incorrect password is provided during an attempted login. After determining that a system has an account with a specific name, the attacker attempts a second attack to guess the account password.

Note that default accounts are the ones that exist by default on a system, like the root user account on Linux systems or the Administrator account on Microsoft Windows systems. Common accounts are not on the system by default but are commonly created accounts, like those with simple usernames like bob, sue, and ted.

Credentialed Scans

A *credentialed scan* is different from a *credential scan*, even though they look similar in name. In a credentialed scan, vulnerability scanning tools are used by an account that is actually logged in to the system (or sometimes network) being scanned. For example, if you were trying to find vulnerabilities on your own cloud resource, you could run a scan from a remote system, or you could log in to the resource using a credential (user account) that you have access to. The results of a credentialed scan indicate what would be vulnerable if an attacker were able to gain access to the system (successfully attack a user account).

Network-Based Scans

The purpose of a *network-based scan* is to scan the network itself looking for vulnerabilities in the network across devices or platforms.

Agent-Based Scans

An *agent-based scan* is executed from an application that is installed locally on a PC. It is often compared to a credentialed scan, but an agent-based scan doesn't use a credentialed account; instead, it runs as a system application. It also is typically run with administrative privileges, so it may have the capability to run deeper scans than a credentialed scan. Lastly, it is often scheduled to run periodically, whereas typically a credentialed scan is started manually by a user.

Service Availabilities Scans

A *service availabilities scan* is used to determine whether a specific service (web server, database server, mail server, and so on) is available. It may be run within the cloud infrastructure or from outside the cloud infrastructure, depending on whether the service being scanned should be available within the cloud or from outside the cloud.

Security Patches

A *security patch* is a specific type of software update that is designed to address a vulnerability. Software updates are normally scheduled in advance; for example, an update for a particular software program may come out every three months. When a vulnerability is made known to the software vendor, the announcement is often not near the date of a regular software update. Even if it were near a regularly scheduled update, the steps to implement the vulnerability fix in the new release might pose a logistical challenge because the update has new changes to the software.

A patch is used instead to create a temporary fix to the problem. Patches will be released as needed, often without advance warning. You can keep up with patches by either subscribing to the software vendor's notification system or viewing Common Vulnerabilities and Exposures (CVE) notices on https://cve.mitre.org/.

Hot Fixes

When you see the term *hot fix*, think *quick fix*. A hot fix isn't intended to be a long-term solution, but rather something to fix the problem while the software vendor works on a more robust and permanent fix. A virtual patch (see the "Virtual Patches" section) is an example of a hot fix.

Scheduled Updates

As mentioned previously, a scheduled update isn't a patch, but it may contain code that addresses vulnerabilities like a patch does. Most likely the vulnerabilities have been addressed via previous patches, but occasionally a new vulnerability is fixed with a scheduled update.

Virtual Patches

Virtual patches don't really address a vulnerability directly but make use of another tool like a web application firewall (WAF) to provide a short-term fix to the problem. With a virtual patch, a small application is attached to the software with the goal of blocking access that the vulnerability is currently allowing.

Signature Updates

Signature update is a term associated with antivirus software. A virus signature is much like a fingerprint of the virus. Antivirus programs use this signature to determine whether a virus has infected a system. Ensuring the antivirus signatures are up to date on a system is a very high priority.

Rollups

A *rollup* is a collection of hot fixes. In some cases, the rollup might contain more than just security updates, but the main focus is to address a collection of security or critical issues with a single update.

Risk Register

A *risk register* is a document that security professionals and project managers use as part of risk management. It should enable the viewer of the document to determine the impact of a risk versus the probability that the risk activity might take place.

Risk registers are often tied to some sort of regulatory compliance and are often requested during a compliance audit. A risk register is often stored in a spreadsheet, but it can also be displayed as a scatterplot graphic.

Prioritization of Patch Applications

The prioritization of patch applications is determining what patches should be installed first. This process is often strongly associated with the organization's risk register.

Deactivate Default Accounts

As mentioned in the "Default and Common Credential Scans" section, default accounts are often subject to attacking attempts. As a result, deactivating these default accounts is a good practice.

In some cases, deactivating might not be possible because the default account may be tightly entwined with the operating system or some software packages. In those cases, you should lock down the account as tightly as possible.

Here's an example of locking a default account: the root account on Linux systems is provided administrative rights because it has a user ID (UID) of 0. Any other account with a UID of 0 is also granted administrative rights. So, you can deactivate the root account (lock out the password and change the login shell to /dev/null) after you create another account with a UID of 0 (use an unusual name that isn't easy to guess, like zen0270). Note that this approach is only partially effective because anyone who is able to access the system with another user account is able to see that there is an alternative administrative account, but this technique makes external attacking attempts more difficult.

Impacts of Security Tools on Systems and Services

Installing and using security tools may seem like a no-brainer, but they do come with a potential cost. One of the biggest concerns is that an attacker may gain access to your system using a regular user account and then launch the security tools to find vulnerabilities in your environment.

Security tools might also have an impact on the performance of a resource. For example, an exhaustive port scan may lead to network connectivity issues on systems within the network, and some of these are production systems.

Security tools may also provide a false sense of...well, security. The idea is "we have these great tools that keep us safe, so we aren't at any risk." Security tools are only part of an effective security policy and should not be relied on as the complete security policy.

Lastly, some security tools are proactive, meaning that they have potential to automatically lock down a system or service if a vulnerability is detected— for example, Internet Protocol Security (IPS) or next-generation firewalls (NGFWs). On one hand, this is a good thing because it can limit the exposure of a system. On the other hand, this could end up making a system or service unavailable, which could have a bigger negative impact than if the vulnerability were just reported and handled manually (especially in cases of false positives).

CramQuiz

Answer these questions. The answers follow the last question. If you cannot answer these questions correctly, consider reading this section again until you can.

1. Which of the following is not considered a vulnerability scan type?

   ○ **A.** Credentialed

   ○ **B.** Network-based

   ○ **C.** Agent-based

   ○ **D.** Inactive

2. What is the third step of vulnerability assessment?

   ○ **A.** Risk assessment

   ○ **B.** Analysis

   ○ **C.** Identification

   ○ **D.** Remediation

3. In a(n) _____ scan, vulnerability scanning tools are used by an account that is actually logged in to the system (or sometimes network) being scanned.

   ○ **A.** Agent-based

   ○ **B.** Credential

   ○ **C.** Credentialed

   ○ **D.** Account

4. Which of the following is associated with updates to virus scanning programs?

   ○ **A.** Signature updates

   ○ **B.** Scan updates

   ○ **C.** Malware updates

   ○ **D.** Worm updates

5. A risk register is a document that security professionals and project managers use to address risk _____.

   ○ **A.** Management

   ○ **B.** Reports

   ○ **C.** Tools

   ○ **D.** Assessments

CramQuiz Answers

1. Inactive
2. Risk assessment
3. Credentialed
4. Signature updates
5. Management

What Next?

If you want more practice on this chapter's exam objectives before you move on, remember that you can access all of the CramQuiz questions on the companion website. You can also create a custom exam by objectives with the practice exam software. Note any objectives you struggle with and go to that objective's material in this chapter.

CHAPTER 10

Incident Response Procedures

This chapter covers the following official CompTIA Cloud+ exam objective:

▶ 2.6 Explain the importance of incident response procedures.

(For more information on the official CompTIA Cloud+ exam topics, see the Introduction.)

What is an incident? In many cases an *incident* refers to a security breach, often the result of a cyberattack. However, in a broader sense, an incident can include other events that are not really an attack but can affect the operations of your organization. You can consider natural disasters, accidental loss of company technology, and similar events as incidents.

In this chapter you will learn how to implement incident response procedures, including how to prepare for an incident and how to react when an incident occurs. Note that each incident is different and, as a result, needs to be handled differently.

The goal of this chapter reflects the Cloud+ 2.6 exam objective (see the beginning of this chapter) and is not intended to provide complete coverage of incident reporting.

CramSaver

If you can correctly answer these questions before going through this section, save time by skimming the ExamAlerts in this section and then completing the CramQuiz at the end of the section.

1. A(n) _____ is used to clearly define who to contact, when to make the contact, and how to contact each person when an incident occurs.

2. A(n) _____ is an exercise in which individuals of an incident response team are gathered and presented with a scenario. The goal is to walk through the steps that would be taken to handle the incident.

3. What should be the first phase of an incident response process?

4. The _____ of an incident describes how widespread the effect of the incident is.

Answers

1. Call tree
2. Tabletop
3. Preparation
4. Scope

Preparation

A quote often attributed to Woody Allen states that "80 percent of success is showing up." In terms of incident response, you might consider following a slightly different philosophy: "80 percent of incident response is preparation."

Putting together a practical, well-thought-out incident response plan is key to successfully dealing with any serious incident. However, the plan must include several important elements, such as good documentation, a process to train key personnel, and a clear definition of the roles and responsibilities of the incident response team.

Documentation

When you're dealing with an incident, it is critical to be able to rely on good documentation. Documentation provides the information that the incident response team needs to address the incident in a timely manner. Without documentation, it is often hard to determine what actions to take, by whom, and exactly what steps to take when performing these actions.

Good documentation should include all of the following:

▶ Be verified for accuracy.

▶ Be up to date.

▶ Be easily accessible.

▶ Be available from more than one source.

▶ Be clear and concise.

▶ Be reviewed by the incident response team in advance.

▶ Include roles and responsibilities.

▶ Include a communication plan.

Call Trees

When an incident takes place, people need to be notified. A *call tree* is used to clearly define who to contact, when to make the contact, and how to contact each person.

Often there are multiple call trees within an organization to handle different types of incidents, and different individuals may have different sets of call trees. Say a website administrator notices that the company website may have been hacked. The website administrator may have the following call tree that needs to be followed:

1. Call the direct manager immediately.

2. Call the other website administrators immediately.

After assessing the situation, the manager may discover that sensitive company information has been compromised. This discovery results in the manager using another call tree to do the following:

1. Call the CIO immediately.

2. Call the IT security manager immediately.

3. Call the HR manager after conducting a review of what data has been compromised.

A regular review of a company's call trees is necessary to ensure that the correct individuals are contacted. A review is also important because turnover in a company can impact the call tree. Changes in contact data (new phone numbers, changes in positions within the company, and so on) can also affect the call tree.

Training

Training for incident response is an ongoing process. During the training process, each individual needs to be made aware of responsibilities and procedures to follow.

Tabletops

A *tabletop* is an exercise in which individuals of an incident response team are gathered and presented with a scenario. The goal is to walk through the steps that would be taken to handle the incident. This exercise is called a tabletop because traditionally it was conducted with all participants in the same room, typically a conference room, and all the work was performed "on the tabletop." In other words, this exercise does not include any actual actions but is more of a verbal walkthrough of the actions that should take place.

You might wonder what sorts of scenarios could be used in a tabletop exercise. There are many good suggestions available, including the following suggestions found on the Washington State Office of Cybersecurity (https://cybersecurity.wa.gov/tabletop-exercises):

▶ An employee casually remarks about how generous state officials are to provide the handful of USB drives embossed with the state logo on the conference room table. After making some inquiries, you find there is no state program to provide USB drives to employees.

▶ Your agency has received various complaints about slow Internet access and that your website is inaccessible. After further investigation, it is determined that your agency is a victim of a DNS amplification attack that is currently overwhelming your DNS server and network bandwidth.

▶ Local news reports indicate that a major chemical plant, located two miles away, has had a significant toxic chemical leak. There is a chemical cloud, and your office building is in the path of the plume.

▶ A pandemic flu starts. Employees start calling in sick, but it's not clear if they are ill or afraid to go out in public. Enough people are absent that the organization struggles to maintain the IT infrastructure.

Documented Incident Types/Categories

The purpose of identifying *incident types* or *incident categories* is to generate a method of organizing incidents into groups. For example, you may decide to create an incident category called "natural disasters," which would include incidents such as fires, floods, and earthquakes, but this category would not include an incident like a hacking attempt.

Creating incident categories is important for several reasons, including the following:

▶ **Determining impact:** Different types of incidents will have different impacts on your organization. For example, a natural disaster could affect the entire organization, whereas a hacking attempt may impact only the IT department. Additionally, some types of incidents will have long-term impacts, whereas others will have short-term impacts.

▶ **Determining the response order:** You could also decide to place incidents into the severity of the incident. For example, suppose the following two incidents occur at roughly the same time: (1) An employee loses a company laptop that contains potentially sensitive information, and (2) the company's primary data center suffers major damage due to fire. Of the two incidents, you would probably categorize the damage to the data center as a higher priority than the lost laptop. Without categorizing based on severity, the priority might be placed on the less severe incident.

▶ **Helping to determine weak spots in your organization:** If you place incidents into categories, it can be easier to determine where your company's weak spots are. The reason is that an analysis of incidents sorted by category will highlight which types of incidents happen more often, as well as how long it takes to respond to and address each incident type.

▶ **Helping to determine the response level:** Categories are often based on the severity of the incident. Categorizing this way allows you to determine the appropriate response for an incident. For example, consider Figure 10.1, a table from the DevOps Zone (https://dzone.com/articles/how-to-classify-incidents) that demonstrates the response that should be taken based on the severity of the incident and the impact on the customer.

Severity Level	Situation	Customer Impact	Response
Severity One	Pages failing to load	Service unusable to customers, SLA violations	All hands on deck
Severity Two	Pages loading 200% slower	Service extremely tedious to use, customer retention threatened	Senior engineering teams and management alerted
Severity Three	Pages loading 50% slower	Service annoying to use, customers, complaining	Senior engineering teams alerted
Severity Four	Pages loading 10% slower	Service usage not impacted to the extent customers complain but could indicate further issues	Relevant engineering teams alerted
Severity Five	Pages loading 1% slower	Unnoticeable to customers	Incident logged into ticketing systems, but no immediate escalation or alerting necessary

FIGURE 10.1   **Response Based on Severity Category**

Roles and Responsibilities

Tasks that need to be performed when handling an incident are divided into roles. A *role* is typically associated with a position in an organization (for example, a customer support manager). Each role is given specific responsibilities to handle during the incident. Examples of roles include the following:

▶ Incident manager

▶ Incident coordinator

▶ Technical lead

▶ Communications manager

▶ Incident operator

▶ Service desk agent

▶ Service desk manager

▶ Customer support manager

▶ SME (subject matter expert)

▶ Documenter (also called the scribe)

▶ User

To make the responsibilities for each role clearer, an RACI matrix is often used. (RACI stands for Responsible, Accountable, Consulted, and Informed.) This matrix makes it easy to determine which role is responsible for handling specific actions or activities. See Figure 10.2 for an example of an RACI matrix provided by Micro Focus (https://docs.microfocus.com/SM/9.60/ Hybrid/Content/BestPracticesGuide_PD/IncidentManagmentBestPractice/ RACI_matrix_for_IM.htm).

Process ID	Activity	Incident Manager	Incident Coordinator	Incident Analyst	Incident Operator	Service Desk Agent	Service Desk Manager	User
SO 2.1	Incident Logging and Categorization	A	I			R	R	
SO 2.2	Incident Assignment	A	R	R				
SO 2.3	Incident Investigation and Diagnosis	A	C/I	R				C/I
SO 2.4	Incident Resolution and Recovery	A	C/I	R				C/I
SO 2.5	Incident Review and Closure	A	C/I	R	I	I		I
SO 2.6	Incident Escalation	R/A	R	I				
SO 2.7	SLA Monitoring	A/I	I	I		R		
SO 2.8	OLA and UC Monitoring	A/I	R	I				
SO 2.9	Complaint Handling	A/I					R	C/I

FIGURE 10.2 Sample RACI Matrix

Incident Response Procedures

Planning is a critical part of incident response, but if the right actions are not taken when the incident occurs, the planning is meaningless. The process for handling incidents is typically broken into phases. Different organizations have broken these phases down in different ways. For example, the SANS (SysAdmin, Audit, Network, and Security) Institute has described the following six phases of Incident Response:

1. Preparation

2. Identification

3. Containment

4. Eradication

5. Recovery

6. Lessons Learned

Because the Preparation phase was covered earlier in this chapter, the remainder of this chapter will focus on the other five phases.

Identification

To respond to an incident, you first need to identify the incident. Sometimes identification is easy; for example, a power outage is easy to identify. In other cases, the incident may be noticeable only when specific monitoring processes are put in place.

When you're identifying an incident, it is best to collect as much information as possible. An identification report sheet should include specific questions like the following:

▶ When did the incident take place?

▶ What led to the discovery of the incident?

▶ Who (or what) discovered the incident?

▶ What has the incident impacted?

▶ How does the incident affect users and services?

▶ If a breach occurred, what was the point of entry?

▶ What is the scope of the breach?

Scope

The *scope* of an incident describes how widespread the effect of the incident is. For example, consider a security breach in which a hacker gains access to your company's web server. Is only the web server affected, or was the hacker able to then launch further attacks on other systems (database servers, development servers, and the like) and breach more systems?

The scope of the incident will have a major impact on how to handle the incident. You also don't want to fix only some of the problems that the incident created and then have to go back and fix more problems at a later time.

Investigation

The identification phase also includes a component referred to as the *investigation*. The answers to the questions asked during the identification may not be plain or obvious. Investigation may be required to fully understand the incident and the scope of the problem.

The investigation steps will be different depending on the incident. For example, you would not look at login log file entries to determine the details about why a fire broke out, but you may look at monitoring equipment, such as temperature gauges.

Containment, Eradication, and Recovery

Containment is the process of ensuring that the systems that have been affected by the incident no longer pose a threat or an issue. For example, if a hacker has breached the security of your web server, keeping that web server isolated and separate from the rest of the network provides containment.

Containment typically includes at least three components: isolation, evidence acquisition, and chain of custody. These components will be covered in later sections.

After the affected systems have been contained, the process of eradication can begin. In this process you remove any changes that have caused the incident. In the recovery part of this step, you fix any of the problems that the incident caused.

It is important to note that incident response plans should treat containment, eradication, and recovery as distinct phases of the incident response plan. Attempting to do all of these steps at once will lead to incomplete solutions and will leave your organization open to more potential incidents.

Isolation

Isolation is the process of separating systems that have been affected by an incident from the rest of your operations.

Evidence Acquisition

Collecting evidence serves multiple purposes. This evidence can be used to prevent further incidents or make the recovery process of future incidents easier and quicker. The evidence may also be used to handle internal disciplinary actions or even to take legal action against an individual or another organization.

Chain of Custody

The chain of custody is a document that describes how evidence is handled during the lifecycle of evidence gathering. This document is critical when taking any legal action against an individual or when reporting possible crimes to the authorities.

Postincident and Lessons Learned

You work isn't done yet. After the incident has been resolved, the results need to be documented and reviewed. Many organizations conduct a postmortem in which the incident, its cause, and the effect it had on the organization are discussed.

Based on this information, the portmortem team creates a report of what was learned during the incident response process and what actions should be taken to avoid future incidents.

Root Cause Analysis

A critical component of the postincident process is determining the root cause. The incident is analyzed to determine the primary cause of the incident, which can then be used to help determine what lessons were learned by the incident and how to prevent similar incidents in the future.

CramQuiz

Answer these questions. The answers follow the last question. If you cannot answer these questions correctly, consider reading this section again until you can.

1. Which of the following is not likely to be a reason for creating incident categories?

   ○ **A.** Determining impact

   ○ **B.** Determining the response order

   ○ **C.** Determining who attacked your organization

   ○ **D.** Determining weak spots in your organization

2. What does the I in RACI stand for?

   ○ **A.** Informed

   ○ **B.** Illustrated

   ○ **C.** Ignored

   ○ **D.** Immobilized

3. What is the last phase of incident response?

   ○ **A.** Containment

   ○ **B.** Eradication

   ○ **C.** Recovery

   ○ **D.** Lessons Learned

4. _____ is the process of ensuring that the systems that have been affected by the incident no longer pose a threat or an issue.

   ○ **A.** Confinement

   ○ **B.** Eradication

   ○ **C.** Containment

   ○ **D.** None of these answers are correct

5. The _____ is a document that describes how evidence is handled during the lifecycle of evidence gathering.

   ○ **A.** Chain of information

   ○ **B.** Chain of authority

   ○ **C.** Chain of evidence

   ○ **D.** Chain of custody

CramQuiz Answers

1. Determining who attacked your organization
2. Informed
3. Lessons Learned
4. Containment
5. Chain of custody

What Next?

If you want more practice on this chapter's exam objectives before you move on, remember that you can access all of the CramQuiz questions on the companion website. You can also create a custom exam by objectives with the practice exam software. Note any objectives you struggle with and go to that objective's material in this chapter.

CHAPTER 11

Integrate Components into a Cloud Solution

This chapter covers the following official CompTIA Cloud+ exam objective:

▶ 3.1 Given a scenario, integrate components into a cloud solution.

(For more information on the official CompTIA Cloud+ exam topics, see the Introduction.)

This is the first chapter of a collection of chapters that focus on cloud deployment. Deployment is the process of creating resources within a cloud environment. The first part of this chapter will focus on subscription services, including what a subscription service is and the different types of subscription services.

Next, you will learn about deploying different types of resources, including compute, storage, network, and applications. Note that compute, storage, and network resources are covered in further detail in separate dedicated chapters.

This chapter will also cover templates, including OS templates, solution templates, and variables. Lastly, the chapter will discuss containers.

CramSaver

If you can correctly answer these questions before going through this section, save time by skimming the ExamAlerts in this section and then completing the CramQuiz at the end of the section.

1. Cloud vendors like RingCentral, Vonage, and Microsoft 365 Business Voice provide _____ service.

2. Cloud-based messaging is considered _____ as a Service.

3. In an IaaS solution a cloud vendor provides the _____ for you to develop or install your software solution.

4. What type of storage resource is typically used for compute resources (virtual machines specifically) to store data, including the operating system of the computer resource?

Answers

1. VoIP
2. Software
3. Infrastructure
4. Block storage

Subscription Services

With a subscription-based service, you typically pay up front (most subscriptions last for one year) to have access to a cloud-based service. Compare this with a pay-as-you-go model in which you pay for the service only for as long as you use it.

The cost of the subscription-based service depends on the length of the contract and the volume of use. For example, your organization opts in for a one-year contract for up to 5,000 accounts from a cloud vendor that provides email services. If you opted for a two-year contract, the cost per year would likely be less because the cloud vendor secures a longer period of revenue.

However, it is challenging for organizations to guess how many seats (that is, accounts) they will need each year, so while they may cost more overall, it is typically better to go with shorter-term versus longer-term contracts. With subscription-based services, it is not uncommon for the customer to end up overpaying for seats that are not used.

The following subscription-based services are typically offered by cloud vendors as well as software vendors as SaaS offerings:

▶ Communications

▶ Email

▶ Voice over IP (VoIP)

▶ Messaging

▶ Collaboration

Each service is described in greater detail later in this chapter.

An alternative to subscription-based services is consumption-based. However, the service types that are normally good for subscription-based services tend to be bad choices for consumption-based services. With consumption-based services you pay for what you consume (use). For example, an email service that is consumption-based would end up costing more if your employees send and receive more emails (or larger emails), but on a subscription-based plan, the costs would typically remain the same. Some subscription-based plans do impose limitations, which can result in a higher cost if your organization goes over the limits, so there can be a consumption-based pricing structure attached to a subscription-based plan.

File Subscriptions

File subscriptions are part of a service that enables your employees and customers to store files (data) in the cloud. This service is considered Software as a Service (SaaS) but also falls under the category of Storage as a Service (STaaS). See the "SaaS" section later in this chapter for more details.

File subscriptions are a popular cloud service, and as a result, many options are available. Google Drive, Microsoft OneDrive, and Dropbox are just a few of the popular options.

Communications

While many people use cell phones to make and receive phone calls, traditional phone calls were placed on land-line devices, and the communication took place over the public switched telephone network (PSTN). This technique, which dates back to the 1800s, uses copper wires and is still commonly used today. However, this medium for communication has limitations (analog voice only) and requires a vast infrastructure that doesn't exist throughout the world.

A more modern alternative is to use a communication option called *voice over IP (VoIP)* that is provided by organizations like cloud vendors. With VoIP, phone calls are placed over an Internet broadband connection. This connection requires converting the sound into a digital signal. Cloud vendors like Ring-Central, Vonage, and Microsoft 365 Business Voice provide VoIP service. This service is considered a SaaS, but also falls under the category of Communication as a Service (CaaS). See the "SaaS" section later in this chapter for more details.

Email

In all likelihood you have used a cloud-based email service. At the time this book was written, there are approximately 4 billion email users worldwide and over 1.8 billion of them use Gmail, just one of many cloud-based email services. That means that about 45 percent of all email users in the world use one of the many different cloud-based email services. Additional popular cloud-based email providers include Outlook, Zoho Mail, and Yahoo! Mail.

Cloud-based email services are considered a SaaS. See the "SaaS" section later in this chapter for more details.

Voice over IP (VoIP)

For more information on VoIP, see the "Communications" section earlier in this chapter.

Messaging

A messaging application enables you to send a message (text, video, images, and so on) to another individual, either directly to a mobile device or a computer. Almost all messaging services, including Facebook Messenger and WhatsApp, are cloud-based services. Cloud-based messaging is considered a SaaS. See the "SaaS" section later in this chapter for more details.

Collaboration

Collaboration services provide a variety of features all designed to allow organizations to work together to solve problems, create new products, or perform other business-related activities. Most of these tools provide some sort of messaging feature that includes the ability to send messages to an individual or a group. Other features may include video conferencing, forums, file transfer capability, and project management features.

Examples of collaboration tools include Slack, Microsoft Teams, and Trello. Cloud-based collaboration services are considered a SaaS. See the "SaaS" section later in this chapter for more details.

Virtual Desktop Infrastructure (VDI)

At this point you should understand what a virtual machine (VM) is. If not, please review the "Deploying Virtual Machines (VMs) and Custom Images" section later in this chapter. A virtual desktop infrastructure (VDI) leverages the power of a virtual machine to provide virtual desktops to users.

Imagine a scenario in which you are often traveling. You don't want to carry your system with you, but you want to be able to access the IT infrastructure in your organization. Using a mobile device, you can connect to a virtual machine via the Internet and bring up your desktop environment.

There are several advantages of VDI:

▶ Because the desktops reside on a virtual machine, the administration of these desktops is easier. With centralized management, updates and patches can be applied easily, by administrators, without the need for regular users to handle these operations.

▶ Because of the higher level of centralized control, VDI is typically more secure than individual user computers.

▶ Using a VDI solution can reduce the costs of buying hardware (laptops) for each user. Users can use more affordable devices (mobile phones, tablets, and so on) but can still use a laptop if they choose.

▶ Given that the virtual desktop is remotely available, it can be reached in most cases wherever an Internet connection is available. Some networking issues (firewalls, for example) may hinder this access.

Note that VDI itself would be considered a Platform as a Service (PaaS), but the virtual machines themselves would be considered an Infrastructure as a Service (IaaS). See the "PaaS" and "IaaS" sections later in this chapter for more details.

Directory and Identity Services

For more information on directory and identity services, see "Directory Services" in Chapter 5, "Identity and Access Management."

Cloud Resources

Cloud resource is a broad term that refers to some sort of system in the cloud. A resource can be a wide range of things: a virtual machine, an email service, a firewall, or a database. Think about it this way: if it is something in the cloud, it is considered a cloud resource.

IaaS

In an IaaS solution a cloud vendor provides the infrastructure for you to develop or install your software solution. With this solution the cloud vendor essentially provides the hardware structure (compute, networking, and storage), and you manage the rest, including the operating system and the software. Examples of IaaS include using Azure virtual machines and AWS EC2 instances. A major advantage of an IaaS software solution is control. You choose the platform (operating system), the amount of hardware resources used, and how the system is configured. This control may also be considered a disadvantage because you are also tasked with maintaining the operating system and the software.

PaaS

In a PaaS solution the cloud vendor provides a platform that you can use to install or develop a software solution. Examples of PaaS include OpenShift, AWS Elastic Beanstalk, and the Google App Engine. With a PaaS solution the primary advantage is that you can deploy a customized software solution without having to maintain the platform that the software runs on. With a PaaS solution, like the SaaS solution, you still may have concerns regarding control over your data and potential vendor lock-in. However, PaaS does offer more control over these issues, so the concern isn't as strong as with the SaaS solution.

SaaS

In a SaaS software solution the entire application is hosted and maintained by the cloud vendor. Examples of SaaS include Salesforce, Dropbox, Gmail, Webex, and DocuSign. One advantage of SaaS solutions is that the vendor handles all maintenance of the software. Disadvantages include a lack of control over your data, the inability to customize the software to your organizational needs, and potential vendor lock-in (when your organization is so entrenched in a solution that it is almost impossible to switch to another solution).

Provisioning Resources

When you, as a cloud customer/consumer, create a resource in a cloud provider's environment, this process is referred to as *provisioning a resource*. A wide variety of resource types is available in the cloud. They can include compute resources, storage resources, network resources, and applications.

Resources can be provisioned either manually or automatically as the need arises. The remainder of this chapter will focus on different types of resources that can be provisioned in the cloud as well as how they may be provisioned.

Compute

A *cloud compute resource* is any resource that has a primary goal of performing any sort of computation operation. This typically means virtual machines and containers, both of which are covered in more detail later in this chapter.

Note that *cloud computing* is a more generic term that means to use cloud resources to perform operations. In other words, the terms *cloud compute resource* and *cloud computing* are not synonymous.

Storage

A storage resource is anything that is used in the cloud to store data. There are three different types of cloud storage resources:

- ▶ **Block storage:** This type of storage resource is typically used for compute resources (virtual machines specifically) to store data, including the operating system of the computer resource. If you are used to non-cloud storage devices, think of a block storage resource like a hard disk or a partition. Examples include AWS Elastic Block Storage (EBS), Microsoft Azure Blob storage, and Google Cloud Persistent Disks. Block storage typically is raw storage space and normally requires a filesystem to be placed on the storage resource for it to be used. This typically happens during the installation process of a virtual machine.

- ▶ **File storage:** This type of storage resource acts much like a network filesystem (also referred to as a network-attached storage, or NAS). This type of storage is used when you need to be able to share the files with multiple resources. For example, two virtual machines may need to be able to access the same files (or share files between the two VMs). Examples of file storage include AWS Elastic File System (EFS), Azure Files, and Google Cloud Filestore.

- ▶ **Object storage:** Object storage is a feature in which objects (unstructured data like emails, videos, graphics, text, or any other time of data) can be stored in a cloud environment. Object storage doesn't use traditional filesystem storage features but rather organizes the data into "groups" (similar to a folder in a filesystem). Data is typically accessed using a URL, like you would use to access a web page. Object storage is durable and highly available, supports encryption, and can be used in a flexible manner that supports different backup and archiving features. Examples include AWS Simple Storage Service (S3), Google Cloud Storage, and IBM Cloud Object Storage.

Note that databases are not included in the list of storage devices. Databases do store data, but they provide more functionality than typical storage devices; therefore, they belong in a separate category of cloud resources.

> **Note**
>
> While there is some coverage of databases on the CompTIA Cloud+ exam, this isn't a major topic in any of the exam objectives.

Network

As with systems within your own IT infrastructure, cloud resources need network configuration to communicate between the resource and to systems on the Internet. However, network cloud provisioning is a bit different from what you might be used to in your own IT infrastructure on-premises.

The network in a typical IT infrastructure on-premises consists of the physical network connections and the individual network settings on each system within the network. In a cloud environment, the physical network is already in place, installed by the cloud provider. However, several different organizations may share that same physical network, so you need to create your own private network within that physical network (such as a VPC in AWS and GCP, and a VNet in Azure).

An entire chapter is devoted to provisioning the network in a cloud environment. Chapter 13, "Cloud Networking Solutions," covers a variety of cloud networking solutions that are listed in the CompTIA Cloud+ certification exam objectives.

Application

Other common cloud resources are applications. An application resource is a program that is running in a cloud environment. Because applications may need more hardware resources (RAM, storage, and so on) in different scenarios, the cloud is an excellent location to host applications because resources can be allocated on the fly.

Serverless

See "Serverless" in Chapter 1, "Different Types of Cloud Models."

Deploying Virtual Machines (VMs) and Custom Images

To make the process of deploying a virtual machine easy, most cloud vendors provide prebuilt images. An image is the operating system in its raw format. When you launch a virtual machine using an image, the resulting active operating system is referred to as an *instance*.

In some cases, the prebuilt instances provided by the cloud vendor might not suit your specific needs. In those cases, you can use tools provided by the cloud vendor to produce your own custom image. Doing so normally involves using an existing image, provisioning the virtual machine, customizing the operating system (including adding customized applications), and then converting the virtual machine into an image that you can use later.

Templates

When you deploy a virtual machine or other cloud resources, such as a database, there are typically a lot of questions that you need to answer. A *template* is a file that is used to answer these questions automatically.

Cloud templates are typically constructed in a data model/format that is easier to work with. In almost all cases the data format is an industry standard format. The most common formats used for templates are JSON, YAML, and XML.

OS Templates

An OS template is used to deploy a virtual machine. The questions that you are asked can vary. For example, in AWS you are asked the following:

▶ The image type for the operating system.

▶ The instance type, which is how AWS refers to the hardware specifications for the virtual machine (how much RAM, how many virtual CPUs,
and so on).

▶ Additional instance details, such as how many instances and which virtual
network to assign the instance(s) to. See Figure 11.1 for an example of
some of these details.

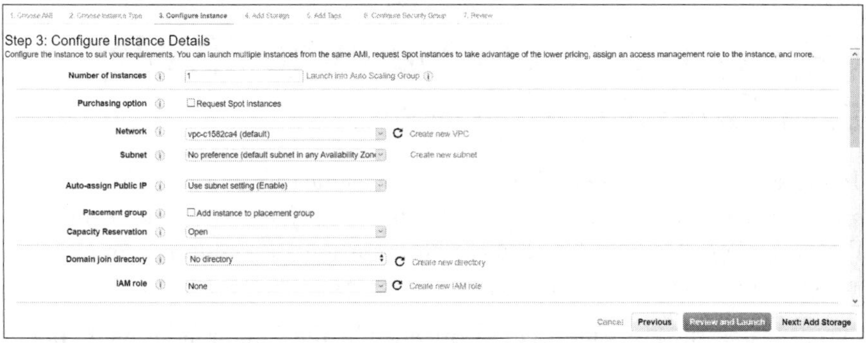

FIGURE 11.1   **AWS Instance Details**

▶ The storage type(s). See the "Persistent Storage" section later in this
chapter for more details.

▶ The tags associated with the instance. You use tags in AWS to group
instances together based on identifiers that you define.

▶ The security group that the instance is associated with. In AWS the security group acts as a virtual firewall.

By creating an OS template, you can automate your installations. This capability is important for situations in which you need to rapidly deploy a virtual
machine, such as when using an auto-scaling solution. See "Auto-scaling" in
Chapter 3, "High Availability and Scaling in Cloud Environments," for more
details.

Solution Templates

A solution template is designed to deploy a non-OS resource in the cloud. This
is a pretty wide field and can include resources like databases, web servers, and
virtual networks.

Identity Management

Identity management is covered in detail in Chapter 5.

Containers

Consider containers as alternatives to virtual machines. While virtual machines are a great solution for many cases, if you need to run just a single application, you might be better off with a serverless solution (see the "Serverless" section in Chapter 1) or a container.

A container acts, in many ways, like a virtual machine. It appears to have access to an operating system (unless it's a serverless solution, which uses less hardware resources than either virtual machines or containers), but it really has a very small footprint. A container will share much of the operating system with other containers, which means that container itself can be much smaller than a full virtual machine.

A container can host a web server, a mail server, or any number of other applications, including applications that your organization builds. The advantages of using a container versus a virtual machine are that a container should cost your organization less to deploy in the cloud, it can be deployed quicker than a virtual machine, and it scales very well.

Configure Variables

When you use a template (see the "Templates" section earlier in this chapter), you can use variables to customize the template. You use a variable when you want to have options when deploying the resource using a template.

For example, suppose you want to create a template that will deploy a virtual machine, but you don't want to answer the question of the type of instance within the template itself. You can tell the template to accept a value that is passed into the template when the template is used. That value is then assigned to a variable that is used to indicate the type of the instance.

Configure Secrets

See the "Secret Management" section in Chapter 5.

Persistent Storage

Recall from the "Storage" section earlier in this chapter that there are three types of storage in the cloud: block, file, and object. When you're deploying a virtual machine, the operating system is stored on a block storage resource. This storage device is persistent, meaning that even if you power off the virtual machine, the data is still retained on the storage device.

Most cloud vendors have a nonpersistent storage option for additional storage resources. For example, AWS offers a feature called an instance store. This block storage resource is available as long as the virtual machine is running. When the virtual machine is powered off, the instance store is deleted, making this a nonpersistent storage solution.

Auto-scaling

See "Auto-scaling" in Chapter 3.

Postdeployment Validation

If you are using an automated method of deploying a cloud resource, you should have some method of validating the success of the deployment after the deployment completed. Some cloud vendors have tools in place to validate some cloud resource deployments, but this task will likely require you to build a customized method to validate the deployment.

This is one of the reasons why automation tools are very popular. Tools like Jenkins, Ansible, and Chef (among many others) not only automate the deployment of resources but also validate the deployment. Cloud vendors often have their own automation tools. For more details, see Chapter 19, "Automation and Orchestration Techniques."

CramQuiz

Answer these questions. The answers follow the last question. If you cannot answer these questions correctly, consider reading this section again until you can.

1. Cloud-based email services are considered a(n) _____.

    ○ **A.** SaaS

    ○ **B.** PaaS

    ○ **C.** IaaS

    ○ **D.** DaaS

2. VDI is considered what type of service?

    ○ **A.** SaaS

    ○ **B.** PaaS

    ○ **C.** IaaS

    ○ **D.** DaaS

3. This type of storage resource acts much like a network filesystem.

    ○ **A.** Block storage

    ○ **B.** File storage

    ○ **C.** Object storage

    ○ **D.** Database storage

4. Which of the following is a common form of a cloud template? (Choose two.)

    ○ **A.** JSON

    ○ **B.** HTML

    ○ **C.** TXT

    ○ **D.** YAML

5. Which of the following uses the least amount of hardware resources?

    ○ **A.** A virtual machine

    ○ **B.** A container

    ○ **C.** A serverless application

    ○ **D.** None of these answers are correct

CramQuiz Answers

1. SaaS

2. PaaS

3. File storage

4. JSON and YAML

5. A serverless application

What Next?

If you want more practice on this chapter's exam objectives before you move on, remember that you can access all of the CramQuiz questions on the companion website. You can also create a custom exam by objectives with the practice exam software. Note any objectives you struggle with and go to that objective's material in this chapter.

CHAPTER 12

Storage in Cloud Environments

This chapter covers the following official CompTIA Cloud+ exam objective:

▶ 3.2 Given a scenario, provision storage in cloud environments.

(For more information on the official CompTIA Cloud+ exam topics, see the Introduction.)

One of the most often-used resources in the cloud is storage. In fact, many organizations that steadfastly stick with on-premises solutions for computing, networking, and applications will use a massive amount of cloud storage.

The focus of this chapter is the many features of cloud storage that you need to know for the CompTIA Cloud+ exam. You will learn more about the different types of cloud storage: block, file, and object. The chapter will also cover the different storage tiers and protocols.

You will be introduced to RAID storage as well as different cloud storage features related to reducing costs and limiting data loss. Lastly, you will learn about user quotas and software-defined storage.

CramSaver

If you can correctly answer these questions before going through this section, save time by skimming the ExamAlerts in this section and then completing the CramQuiz at the end of the section.

1. A(n) _____ is a network-accessible storage device designed for high-speed access to block storage.

2. Flash storage is any storage that is placed on a(n) _____.

3. Which version of NFS is the most recent?

4. Data _____ is the process of ensuring there is no redundant data within a storage resource (or between storage resources).

Answers

1. Storage-area network (SAN)
2. Solid-state drive (SSD)
3. NFSv4
4. Deduplication

Types

In a cloud environment there are three types of storage resources: block, file, and object. These storage types were introduced in Chapter 11, "Integrate Components into a Cloud Solution." However, the current exam objective adds some additional topics that you should be aware of. In this section, you'll learn about these additional topics.

Block

See the "Storage" section in Chapter 11 for a description of block storage.

Storage-Area Network (SAN)

A storage-area network is a network-accessible storage device designed for high-speed access to block storage. In a sense it isn't really a cloud topic because traditionally SAN devices are physical devices that you use in your local-area network (LAN). However, this topic is a CompTIA Cloud+ objective because a SAN is the on-premises solution that is most like cloud block storage.

Understanding what a SAN is used for is important because you may be asked a question like this: "You are an administrator who is migrating some on-premises systems to a cloud infrastructure. You have been asked which cloud solution would be used to perform the function of your SAN devices. What type of storage would be used in this case?" And, of course, the answer would be a block storage device.

Note that a subobjective of SAN for the CompTIA exam is SAN zoning. With SAN zoning, traffic between the storage device (called the *target*) and the client system (called the *initiator*) is segmented, resulting in better security and performance. See "Network Segmentation" in Chapter 6, "Secure a Network in a Cloud Environment," for more details regarding network segmentation.

File

See the "Storage" section of Chapter 11 for a description of file storage.

Network-Attached Storage (NAS)

Network-attached storage is, as its name states, storage that is accessible via a network. However, NAS is different from the SAN device discussed earlier in this chapter in that is it a file-based storage device, not a block-based storage device.

Object

See the "Storage" section of Chapter 11 for a description of object storage.

Tenants

There are two types of tenants in cloud computing:

▶ **Single-tenant:** This is a solution in which a resource or an infrastructure serves only a single customer. In small- to-mid-sized companies, this is the standard type of tenant. The organizations all share resources, but resources outside the organization are not shared.

▶ **Multitenant:** This is a solution in which a resource or an infrastructure serves multiple customers. These customers could be business units within a large organization or even separate organizations.

The biggest advantages of a single-tenant solution are that it is more secure and the organization typically has more control over the cloud environment. However, typically a multitenant solution will be more cost effective (due to volume discounts), and there will be more flexibility to integrate between the different business units or organizations.

Buckets

When you are dealing with a file-based storage solution, files are organized into folders (sometimes called *directories*). For object-based storage solutions, the term used to organize objects is *buckets*. In other words, a bucket is the container that is used to "hold" your object data.

Tiers

For this exam topic, the term *tiers* refers to different levels of storage that provide different features. Typically, these levels are based on the hardware that the storage resource uses to store the data.

For the CompTIA Cloud+ certification, you should be aware of four tiers of storage: flash, hybrid, spinning disks, and long-term.

Flash

Flash storage is any storage that is placed on a solid-state drive (SSD). These hardware devices are known for being faster than other storage devices, like spinning disks. This faster speed comes at a higher cost, however.

Hybrid

A hybrid tier is one in which you use your own on-premises storage devices, but if they start to become full, the available space is supplemented with cloud-based storage. This solution limits how much you have to spend on storage devices because you can buy just what you think you need. If you miscalculate or there is a sudden high demand for storage space, cloud-based storage is available at an "only pay for what you use" price.

Spinning Disks

Spinning disks, also called *magnetic drives*, are traditional hard drives in which data is stored on rapidly spinning platters that are coated with a magnetic material. Spinning disks are slower than SSD drives, but if used in a cloud solution, they are typically more cost effective because spinning disks are less expensive for the cloud vendor to purchase. Note that you will also see spinning disks referred to as *hard disk drives (HDDs)*.

Long-Term

Long-term storage typically refers to tape storage or cold storage. You may have some data that you don't need on a daily basis, but you still need it stored somewhere safely, perhaps in case your organization ever faces an audit or security analysis. Most cloud vendors provide a long-term storage solution that is much more affordable than using SSD or spinning disks. However, access to this data is likely going to be slow and may also require advanced notice before the data is directly available.

Input/Output Operations per Second (IOPS) and Read/Write

The primary speed calculation of a storage device is the input/output operations per second, or IOPS. This is a value that you must take into consideration when choosing which underlying storage type you want to use for your storage resource.

For example, consider Figure 12.1, which demonstrates some differences between two different HDD options that AWS provides for EBS resources.

	Throughput Optimized HDD	Cold HDD
Volume type	st1	sc1
Durability	99.8–99.9% durability (0.1–0.2% annual failure rate)	99.8–99.9% durability (0.1–0.2% annual failure rate)
Use cases	• Big data • Data warehouses • Log processing	• Throughput-oriented storage for data that is infrequently accessed • Scenarios where the lowest storage cost is important
Volume size	125 GiB–16 TiB	125 GiB–16 TiB
Max IOPS per volume (1 MiB I/O)	500	250
Max throughput per volume	500 MiB/s	250 MiB/s
Amazon EBS Multi-attach	Not supported	Not supported
Boot volume	Not supported	Not supported

FIGURE 12.1 **AWS HDD Storage Options**

Note that the durability and the volume size values are identical. The difference between these HDD types is the Max IOPS per Volume (which, in turn, affects the Max Throughput per Volume). The greater speed of the Throughput Optimized HDD makes it more suitable for cases in which large amounts of data need to be transferred (big data, data warehouses, log processing, and so on).

As you might expect, the IOPS for HDD devices is less than for SDD devices, as you can see from Figure 12.2, which demonstrates different SDD options that AWS provides for EBS resources.

	General Purpose SSD		Provisioned IOPS SSD		
Volume type	gp3	gp2	io2 Block Express ≠	io2	io1
Durability	99.8–99.9% durability (0.1–0.2% annual failure rate)	99.8–99.9% durability (0.1–0.2% annual failure rate)	99.999% durability (0.001% annual failure rate)		99.8–99.9% durability (0.1–0.2% annual failure rate)
Use cases	• Low-latency interactive apps • Development and test environments		Workloads that require submillisecond latency, and sustained IOPS performance or more than 64,000 IOPS or 1,000 MiB/s of through-put	• Workloads that require sustained IOPS performance or more than 16,000 IOPS • I/O-Intensive database workloads	
Volume size	1 GiB–16 TiB		4 GiB–64TiB		4 GiB–16 TiB
Max IOPS per volume (16 KiB I/O)	16,000		256,000		64,000 †
Max throughput per volume	1,000 MiB/s	250 MiB/s*	4,000 MiB/s		1,000 MiB/s †
Amazon EBS Multi-attach	Not supported		Not supported		Supported
Boot volume	Supported				

FIGURE 12.2   **AWS SDD Storage Options**

Note that the term *input* refers to writing data to the disk and *output* refers to reading data from the disk.

Protocols

Several protocols can be used with storage devices and resources. Some of these protocols, like NFS, CIFS, and iSCSI, are designed to allow you to access storage across the network. Others, like FC and NVMe-oF, are designed to provide high-speed access to drives. In this section you will learn the essentials of each of these protocols.

Network File System (NFS)

Network File System is a distributed file system protocol that has been used since 1984. It is a very popular way of sharing file systems across the network on UNIX and Linux systems.

NFS works by sharing a local file system (or part of a file system) using a collection of NFS server daemons (a *daemon* is a program that normally functions without needing to interact with or be controlled by a human). On the NFS client system, a system administrator uses a process called *mounting* to make the NFS shared file system available via a directory in the local file system.

As an older software protocol, NFS has gone through many revisions. The most current protocol, called NFSv4, was last revised in 2015. While it is still very popular and has had many modern features added recently, NFS does have some drawbacks when compared to CIFS. For example, operations to share an NFS resource and to access the NFS resource on the client side require administrative rights. With CIFS, regular users can typically share a file system resource.

Common Internet File System (CIFS)

Common Internet File System is a distributed file system protocol created by Microsoft. This protocol allows a user or administrator to share part of a file system. Regular users can also access the shares (after providing authentication credentials and assuming they have the correct permissions) by performing operations like mounting network drives.

This type of distributed file system is popular because software programs on Windows, Linux, Mac OS, and UNIX can share file systems and also access the file systems. This makes the protocol more flexible. On Linux and UNIX systems the Samba software is used to share and access shares.

Note that CIFS is often used interchangeably with another protocol: Server Message Block (SMB). SMB was created by IBM and, like NFS, has been around since the mid-1980s. CIFS is based on SMB, but it was more of an implementation of SMB and not the exact same protocol as the original SMB. With all that said, CIFS, while widely referred to in documentation, isn't really a protocol that is in use on modern systems. Microsoft has been using the native SMB protocol (either SMB 2.0 or SMB 3.0) since the introduction of Windows Vista in 2006. If you see mention of CIFS in modern documentation, it really refers to SMB.

Internet Small Computer System Interface (iSCSI)

Internet Small Computer System Interface is a protocol that allows communication to block devices across the network. With this protocol you can share a block device (SSD drive, HDD drive, SAN device, and so on) across the network for a client system to use. The block device can then be formatted with a local file system and then used like a local file system would be used (mounted on a Linux or UNIX system or assigned a drive letter on a Microsoft Windows system).

There are some key terms that you should be aware of for iSCSI. The device being shared is referred to as the *iSCSI target*, and the system that is accessing the share is referred to as an *iSCSI initiator*. You should also be aware that iSCSI can be implemented over Fibre Channel.

Fibre Channel (FC)

Fibre Channel is a protocol that is designed to provide high-speed data transfer of storage devices. It can be used to connect systems to SANs, iSCSI, and local data storage.

FC is a pretty robust and flexible protocol, so much so that you can find entire books devoted to this protocol. For the CompTIA Cloud+ exam, you should at least know the following basics of FC:

▶ Normally, optical fiber cables are used as the media to transfer data because these cables have very fast throughput. However, the protocol can be implemented on copper cabling as well.

▶ If iSCSI is implemented with FC, the actual protocol used is called Fibre Channel Protocol (FCP).

▶ FC can also be used with another protocol: Non-Volatile Memory Express (NVMe). This version is called NVMe-oF.

▶ You may be asked an exam question related to the data rates (speed) of FC. Currently, the following data rates are supported: 1, 2, 4, 8, 16, 32, 64, and 128 gigabits per second.

Non-Volatile Memory Express over Fabrics (NVMe-oF)

When SSD devices first appeared on the market, they were faster than the spinning disks, but they were connected to the motherboard, which used older protocols (SAS and SATA) to transfer data. Initially, this wasn't a problem, but the faster the SSD devices became, the more often these older protocols created bottlenecks. There was a need for a faster transfer protocol, and the solution was NVMe.

Why is NVMe faster than the older protocols? In a nutshell, it provides more "lanes" of input/output (I/O), which allows for a higher overall throughput.

This was a great protocol for local SSD devices, but there was also a need for a faster protocol for communicating with network devices. The result of this is NVMe-oF, or Non-Volatile Memory Express over Fabrics.

Redundant Array of Inexpensive Disks (RAID)

When a hard disk fails, typically all of the data on the disk is lost. Certain professionals may be able to recover some of the data, but that can be time-consuming and expensive, and ultimately the professionals may not be able to recover the data that you really need.

Redundant Array of Inexpensive Disks is a technology that was originally designed to provide a solution to the problem of hard disk failure. RAID is a technology that has been actively used for many decades. In fact, the technology for RAID actually predates the term *RAID*. The original concept, now referred to as RAID 1, was to mitigate the loss of a hard disk by having a second, completely redundant disk.

In addition to RAID 1, there are other types of RAID. The RAID types that are listed on the CompTIA Cloud+ exam are described next.

0

RAID 0 provides no redundancy but rather increases available storage by merging multiple hard disks (or partitions) into a single device. For example, three hard disks of 30 GB each can produce a RAID 0 device with 90 GB of storage space. Data is written to each physical device (hard disk/partition) in stripes, which results in the requirement of each physical device needing to be the same size to avoid wasting storage space. RAID 0 can improve the performance of reading data from the devices. See Figure 12.3 for a graphic that illustrates RAID 0.

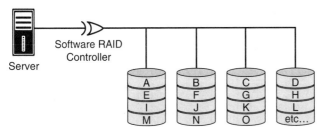

FIGURE 12.3   **RAID 0**

1

In RAID 1, also called *mirroring*, two or more disk drives appear to be one single storage device. Data that is written to one disk drive is also written to all of the others. If one drive fails, the data is still available on the other drives. See Figure 12.4 for a graphic that illustrates RAID 1.

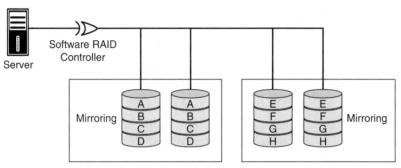

FIGURE 12.4 **RAID 1**

5

RAID 5 provides more efficient use of the physical storage devices. Unlike RAID 1, which completely mirrors all data to all physical storage devices, RAID 5 writes different data to each physical storage device with the exception of one device, which is used to store parity data. In the event that a physical storage device is lost or damaged, the data on that device can be restored by using the parity data and the real data on the other storage devices. RAID 5 requires at least three storage devices and can have a negative impact on system performance, so software RAID (RAID performed by the kernel) is not commonly used. However, hardware RAID (RAID performed by a separate processing chip) is fairly common on high-end servers. See Figure 12.5 for a graphic that illustrates RAID 5.

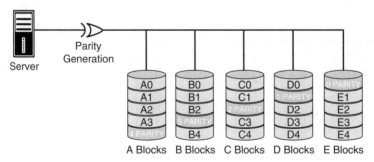

FIGURE 12.5 **RAID 5**

6

RAID 6 is much like RAID 5, except that instead of one parity device, two parity devices are used. This provides better redundancy but also increases the cost involved as an additional storage devices is needed.

10

Also called RAID 1+0, RAID 10 combines the advantages of both RAID 1 and RAID 0. First, two or more sets of two devices are placed into multiple RAID 1 devices. This provides redundancy. Then they are merged together into a RAID 0 device to create a much larger storage container. See Figure 12.6 for a graphic that illustrates RAID 10.

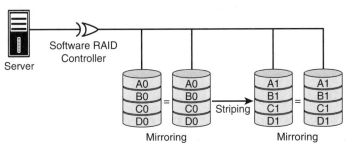

FIGURE 12.6 **RAID 10**

Storage System Features

There are several different storage system features that you should be aware of for the CompTIA certification exam. They includes compression, deduplication, thin provisioning, thick provisioning, and replication. These features typically fall into one of two primary categories:

- ▶ **Cost savings:** With cloud storage, you pay for the space that you use (in some cases, typically object storage, you also pay for the process of transferring the data, such as when you download data). The less storage space that you use, the less you pay.

- ▶ **Data loss prevention:** One of the great features of cloud storage is that there are methods to best prevent data loss.

Next, you'll learn the commonly used storage features and the benefit of using them.

Compression

Compression is the process of reducing the size of data using a mathematical algorithm. Data is run through the algorithm, resulting in compressed data that is stored in the cloud (or on-premises). When the data is needed, another algorithm will convert the data back into the original uncompressed format.

Compression reduces the space you use in the cloud storage environment, reducing your costs. In some cases, particularly object storage, the compression is handled by the cloud vendor. In other cases, like data stored in file storage, the encrypting is handled by the customer.

> **Note**
>
> Compression is often coupled with another feature called encryption. See "Storage" in Chapter 7, "OS and Application Security Controls," for additional details.

Deduplication

Data deduplication is the process of ensuring there is no redundant data within a storage resource (or between storage resources). In some situations, a cloud vendor may have tools to perform this process, but in many cases, you may need to create your own methods to perform deduplication tasks. By eliminating redundant data, you end up using less cloud storage, resulting in lower costs.

Thin Provisioning

Recall that you pay for the amount of storage that you use. In some cases, like object storage, this is very straightforward. A 10 MB object results in a charge for 10 MB of storage.

However, in other cases, such as block storage, what you pay for isn't exactly what you use, but rather what you reserve. For example, if you create a 10 GB block storage device, you are charged 10 GB, even if you don't use all of the space that you asked for. This makes sense because that space can't be used for any of the cloud vendor's other customers. But you don't want to pay for space that you aren't actually using.

The process of reserving the entire storage space of a block-based storage resource is called *thick provisioning*. An alternative, called *thin provisioning*, allows you to reserve part of the overall size of the block resource—essentially what you currently need, plus a bit more in case more data is written to the block storage.

For example, if you provision a 10 GB block store and then use only 2 GB of the space, a little over 2 GB is reserved for your use (say, 2.5 GB for this example). You pay only for 2.5 GB, unless you start adding more data to the block store. In that case, more space is reserved for your use.

Thin provisioning results in lower costs; however, it does come with a potential drawback. Reserving additional space can take some time, which means if large amounts of data are written to the block storage, the write process may fail because the required space wasn't reserved quickly enough.

Thick Provisioning

See the preceding "Thin Provisioning" section.

Replication

Data replication is the process of ensuring data is backed up to another storage resource. In the event that your data is lost or becomes unavailable on the original data resource, it will then be available in the backed-up resource. Data replication can be done in the cloud at a zonal or regional level.

As with many of the features discussed in this section, there are cases in which cloud vendors will offer replication as an automatic feature and some cases where it will be the responsibility of the cloud customer. In either case, replication will result in higher costs, but it will also serve to prevent data loss.

User Quotas

A *user quota* is a limitation placed on a user when using storage. This limit may include how much space the user can use or how many files or objects the user can store. The goal of user quotas is either to reduce costs (remember, space used equals higher costs) or prevent a user from using up all of the allocated space for a storage resource (typically a block storage resource).

Hyperconverged

See "Hyperconverged" in Chapter 14, "Compute Sizing for a Deployment."

Software-Defined Storage (SDS)

Software-defined storage is a technology that is designed to simplify using storage. Many cloud vendors have massive numbers of storage devices, and they are very difficult to manage individually. With SDS, these storage devices are "collected" into one massive storage collection (or more). When space is needed to provision a block storage resource, a file storage resource, or an object storage resource, the SDS program is asked for space. The SDS program manages where the actual data is stored.

CramQuiz

Answer these questions. The answers follow the last question. If you cannot answer these questions correctly, consider reading this section again until you can.

1. Which of the following is a solution in which a resource or an infrastructure serves only a single customer?
   - ○ **A.** Single-tenant
   - ○ **B.** Prime-tenant
   - ○ **C.** One-tenant
   - ○ **D.** Only-tenant

2. Which of the following types of storage is the slowest?
   - ○ **A.** Spinning disks
   - ○ **B.** Long-term
   - ○ **C.** Flash
   - ○ **D.** Hybrid

3. _____ is a protocol that allows communication to block devices across the network.
   - ○ **A.** CIFS
   - ○ **B.** SMB
   - ○ **C.** NFS
   - ○ **D.** iSCSI

4. Which RAID level provides no redundancy?
   - ○ **A.** 0
   - ○ **B.** 1
   - ○ **C.** 5
   - ○ **D.** 10

5. Which feature allocates only some of the provisioned space?

- ○ **A.** Small provisioning
- ○ **B.** Minimal provisioning
- ○ **C.** Thick provisioning
- ○ **D.** None of these answers are correct

CramQuiz Answers

1. Single-tenant

2. Long-term

3. iSCSI

4. 0

5. None of these answers are correct. (Thin provisioning is correct.)

What Next?

If you want more practice on this chapter's exam objectives before you move on, remember that you can access all of the CramQuiz questions on the companion website. You can also create a custom exam by objectives with the practice exam software. Note any objectives you struggle with and go to that objective's material in this chapter.

CHAPTER 13

Cloud Networking Solutions

This chapter covers the following official CompTIA Cloud+ exam objective:

▶ 3.3 Given a scenario, deploy cloud networking solutions.

(For more information on the official CompTIA Cloud+ exam topics, see the Introduction.)

This chapter focuses on the different resources and components that you will typically deploy in a cloud network environment. You will first learn about some commonly deployed services, including DHCP, NTP, DNS, CDN, and IPAM.

Next, you will learn about some of the concepts behind virtual private networks (VPNs), including the differences between site-to-site, point-to-point, and point-to-site. Included in this section is a discussion on IPsec and MPLS.

The last few sections of this chapter will cover virtual routing concepts, network appliances, and the concept of a virtual private cloud (VPC).

CramSaver

If you can correctly answer these questions before going through this section, save time by skimming the ExamAlerts in this section and then completing the CramQuiz at the end of the section.

1. _____ is designed to resolve issues regarding the system time synchronization of server and client systems.

2. The domains .com, .org, and .net are examples of _____-level domains.

3. A(n) _____ VPN is used to connect two networks via a VPN.

4. In _____ routing the routing table is updated based on near-real-time changes made in the network.

> **Answers**
>
> 1. Network Time Protocol (NTP)
> 2. Top
> 3. Site-to-site
> 4. Dynamic

Services

In cloud computing, you can configure different types of network services. For the purposes of the exam objectives described in this chapter, we will cover the DHCP, DNS, NTP, CDN, and IPAM network services.

Dynamic Host Configuration Protocol (DHCP)

Dynamic Host Configuration Protocol enables you to dynamically assign network-related information to client systems. This information can include providing a system with an IP address, subnet mask, and DNS server information.

A DHCP server provides DHCP client systems with this network information automatically. When a system is configured as a DHCP client, it sends a request for DHCP servers to provide this network information. When this data is received, the client automatically configures itself, enabling the system to communicate on the network.

Network Time Protocol (NTP)

Network Time Protocol is designed to resolve issues regarding the system time synchronization of server and client systems. Having an accurate system time is important for several reasons, including:

▶ **Log files:** These files have timestamps embedded within log entries. These timestamps are often critical to determine exactly when an error or security breach occurred. Inaccurate system times will result in inaccurate timestamps, which can lead to problems both in determining the cause of problems as well as potential legal issues (log files are sometimes used in legal cases but can be disregarded by the court system if the timestamps are not accurate).

▶ **Client/server interactions:** Some services require the client and server systems to be in sync regarding system time. If these systems are not in sync, the service may fail completely. For example, the server and client negotiating a secure connection using digital certificates should have the right system time.

▶ **Searches for file by timestamp:** Users and administrators will often search for lost or missing files using timestamps. If the system time isn't accurate, the file timestamps won't be accurate, making it difficult to find files.

▶ **Transaction log timestamps:** Many transaction operations include timestamps. For example, each email that is sent or received has a timestamp of these actions. Another example is banking and credit card transactions. It is critical to ensure these timestamps are as accurate as possible for both security and reliability of the transactions.

The purpose of NTP is to ensure accurate system times. A system is configured as an NTP client, which will set the system time based on data received from one or more NTP servers. Typically, three or more NTP servers are used to best ensure the most accurate time.

Organizations may deploy their own NTP servers, but there are also publicly available servers on pool.ntp.org. Servers are categorized by how accurate they are. This is done by assigning a "stratum" value to the server. This is a numeric value from 0 to 15, in which the lower the value, the more accurate the clock is considered to be.

A clock that advertises itself as a "stratum-0" is one that likely gets its timestamps from an atomic clock and has very little delay in responding to NTP requests. A clock that advertises itself as a "stratum-1" gets its timestamps from "stratum-0" servers.

Domain Name Service (DNS)

Domain Name Service is a protocol designed to provide name-to-IP address resolution. It is part of the standard TCP/IP protocol suite and one of several protocols that can provide this functionality; others include NIS and LDAP.

What distinguishes DNS from other similar protocols is that the sole focus of DNS is name resolution; NIS and LDAP provide other resolution operations, such as network user and group accounts. DNS is also the de facto standard name resolution solution for the majority of systems connected to the Internet.

The following important terms are associated with DNS:

▶ **Host:** Typically, a host is a computer that is attached to a network. Another way of looking at the term is that a host is a device that can communicate on a network.

▶ **Domain Name:** Hosts on the Internet address each other by using IP address numbers. These numbers are difficult for humans to remember, so a unique name is often assigned to a host. When this name is registered on an authorized DNS server, the name is considered a domain name.

▶ **Top-Level Domain:** Domain names are organized in a tree-like structure, much like files are organized in a virtual filesystem structure. The top level of the DNS structure is simply referred to as "dot" and symbolized by the . character. The domains directly beneath . are the top-level domains, or TLDs. The original top-level domains were .com, .org, .net, .int, .edu, .gov, and .mil. Many others have been added in recent years.

▶ **FQDN:** A fully qualified domain name is the domain name of a host starting from the top of the DNS structure. For example, the name www. onecoursesource.com. would be a FQDN. Notice the . character at the end of the FQDN. It is the domain above the top-level. This character is often omitted when regular users provide a domain name because the. is assumed to be the last character of the FQDN in most cases. However, you should get used to including the . character if you are going to administer DNS servers because it will be required in some of the DNS server configuration files.

▶ **Subdomain:** A subdomain is any domain that is a component of a larger domain. For example, suppose you wanted to have three domains in your organization to functionally organize the hosts. You might call these domains sales, eng, and support. If your company's domain is onecoursesource.com., these three subdomains would be called

sales.onecoursesource.com.

eng.onecoursesource.com.

support.onecoursesource.com.

▶ **Name server:** A name server is a system that responds to DNS client requests. Name servers provide the translation from IP address to domain names (and sometimes provide the opposite: domain name to IP address translation). Note: A name server either has a copy of this information stored locally (called a *zone file*) or stores information obtained by other name servers temporarily in memory or passes on the query to another server (or servers) that has the information.

▶ **Authoritative name server:** An authoritative name server is one that returns results based on information stored locally on the system (the original master records).

▶ **Zone file:** The zone file is the name of the file that is used to store IP address to domain name translation information (that is, the DNS records). This file also contains information that is used to define the domain itself.

▶ **Record:** Within the zone file, a record is an entry that defines a single chunk of information for the zone, such as the data that would translate an IP address to domain name.

▶ **Caching name server:** A caching name server is one that returns results based on information obtained from another name server, such as an authoritative name server. The primary advantage of a caching name server is that it can speed up the IP address to domain name resolution because it will cache results and be able to respond to future requests using the information in this cache.

▶ **TTL:** The data stored in a caching name server is typically not stored permanently. The name server that provides the data also provided the caching name server with a time to live (TTL). The caching name server will store the information in memory until this TTL period ends. Typically, this period of time is 24 hours, but it can vary depending on how often the records in the authoritative name server are updated.

▶ **DNS forwarder:** A DNS forwarder is a DNS server designed to take DNS queries from an internal network and send the queries to an external DNS server.

▶ **Forward lookup:** This is the process of translating an IP address into a domain name. Most DNS servers provide this functionality.

▶ **Reverse lookup:** This is the process of translating a domain name into an IP address. While many DNS servers provide this functionality, it is less common than a forward lookup.

Content Delivery Network (CDN)

Imagine a scenario in which your organization services customers that are primarily located in the United States. One of your most popular services is located on a server located in a cloud environment that is geographically located on the East Coast of the United States. Most of your customers are in the same geographic area, so having the service located close to the customers reduces latency and provides faster access to your service.

However, the board of directors has just approved a new initiative that is designed to expand your customer base internationally. There are now plans in place to service customers in Europe and Asia, with the possibility to expand to other geographic regions in the future. Having a service that is geographically based on the East Coast of the United States only means that these new customers will likely experience lower response times.

This is a scenario in which a Content Delivery Network (CDN) would provide a better solution. Content is distributed geographically, and proxy servers are used to "point" the client to the closest source (or edge) for the content. Examples of CDN solutions include Amazon CloudFront, Google App Engine, and Azure CDN.

IP Address Management (IPAM)

IP Address Management is a collection of tools, including DNS and DHCP, that enable you to deploy and manage an IP address infrastructure.

Virtual Private Networks (VPNs)

A virtual private network is a service that allows for a virtual network over a public network. This allows data to be shared across public networks in a secure manner.

Site-to-site

A site-to-site VPN is used to connect two sites via a VPN, where sites can be, for example, a headquarters (HQ) office and a remote office or two HQ offices. This type of network is typically used when an organization has remote offices (sites) that are a great distance apart (further apart than a LAN). The expense of a dedicated network connection between the remote offices is too great, but a secure means of communication is required. When a VPN is established between the different sites across the Internet, the communications are secured at a reasonable cost.

Point-to-Point

In a point-to-point VPN, a VPN connection is established between two specific hosts. An example of this would be when you use a VPN service (like Nord-VPN or ExpressVPN) to ensure your privacy when surfing the Internet. Some organizations may also set up a point-to-point VPN for a remote employee or customer to access a specific system, such as an internal web server or database.

Point-to-Site

In a point-to-site VPN, a VPN connection is established between a host and a network. Many organizations use this technique to allow employees to remotely connect to the organization's private network. This is also known as remote-access VPN, and these VPNs can leverage IPsec or SSL/TLS as protocols.

IPsec

Internet Protocol Security is a collection of protocols designed to allow for encrypted connections between different hosts. A common use of IPsec is to create a VPN between two hosts. IPsec is used both for site-to-site and point-to-site VPN connectivity.

Multiprotocol Label Switching (MPLS)

Multiprotocol Label Switching is a technique that routes network packets from one network to another. Because the technique isn't associated with any specific protocol, it can be used to route network traffic for many different protocols.

MPLS VPN allows for VPN connections across an MPLS environment. There are three different types of MPLS VPNs: point-to-point, Layer 2, and Layer 3.

Virtual Routing

One of the challenges of a cloud environment is that within a single physical network, there may be resources for many different customers. All customers will expect that their network data will be kept separate from other customers. Normally, in a physical network, data is broadcast and visible to all hosts on the network because all hosts are within the same IP network (see more about IP networks in the "Subnetting" section later in this chapter).

To avoid a scenario in which one customer can see another customer's data, each customer is placed with a different IP network. This works fine while data stays within the physical network but poses a problem when the data needs to leave the physical network. Normally, a router is used to handle this situation, but routers typically have a single routing table that applies to the entire network. The routing table informs the router of how to handle network traffic between two networks.

Virtual routing (also called Virtual Route Forwarding, or VRF) is a technology that allows for a router to have multiple instances of a routing table. This technology allows for multiple IP networks to use the router (that is, the gateway).

Dynamic and Static Routing

In dynamic routing the routing table is updated based on changes made in the network. A dynamic routing system can "self-heal" when routes become slow or unavailable.

With static routing, the routing table is managed manually. An administrator must manually edit the routing table.

Because of how often cloud environments change, virtual routing is often dynamic. As new IP networks are implemented by customers, virtual routing tables must be automatically updated to handle the changes in the network.

Virtual Network Interface Controller (vNIC)

A network interface controller (NIC) is a physical device that allows a host to communicate on the network. Most resources in the cloud are virtual in nature and need to share the NIC in order to communicate on the network. The resource is provided a vNIC that is associated with the physical NIC.

Subnetting

To understand subnetting, you first need to understand some basics of IPv4 addresses. An IPv4 address consists of four numbers separated by a dot character—for example, 192.168.100.25. Each number reprints an octet, a number that can be represented by a binary value:

        11000000.10101000.01100100.00011001

The number 192 can be represented by the binary number 11000000 because each binary value represents a numeric value, as shown in Figure 13.1.

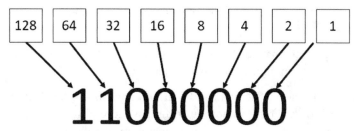

FIGURE 13.1 Binary Representation of Numeric Values

IPv4 addresses are divided into classes. There are five classes total. These classes are defined by the first octet (the first number of the IP address). For example, the IP address of 192.168.100.25 uses the 192 value to define which of the five primary classes the IP resides within. Table 13.1 describes these standard IPv4 address classes.

TABLE 13.1 **IPv4 Classes**

Class	Description
A	Ranges from 1.x.x.x to 126.x.x.x. Allows for 127 networks, each with up to 16 million hosts. The first octet defines the network address, and the remaining octets define the host addresses.
B	Ranges from 128.x.x.x to 191.x.x.x. Allows for approximately 16,000 networks, each with up to 65,000 hosts.
C	Ranges from 192.x.x.x to 223.x.x.x. Allows for approximately 2 million networks, each with up to 254 million hosts.
D	Ranges from 224.x.x.x to 239.x.x.x. Only used for multicast groups.
E	Ranges from 240.x.x.x to 254.x.x.x. Only used for research and development.

So, a class A network of 55.x.x.x can have up to 16 million host IP addresses that run from 55.0.0.1 (55.0.0.0 is reserved for the network itself) to 55.254.254.254 (technically, the highest value is 255, but those IP addresses are reserved for broadcasting messages to the entire network).

Organizations that have been assigned large networks (class A or B, although even class C networks apply here) do not want to have millions or even thousands of hosts on a single network. Subnetting provides a method of dividing a large network into smaller sections. This is accomplished by making smaller networks (subnetworks) by using IP addresses that are normally used by hosts to define the network and broadcast IP addresses.

There are two common network situations in which you should know how subnets work:

▶ When a system already has an IP address and a subnet address, you want to know how to determine the subnetwork that is created.

▶ When you have a larger IP network and want to know how to divide it into smaller networks. This is important if you have several smaller physical networks in your organization because each physical network must be on a separate subnetwork.

In both of these situations, there are many IP address calculators freely available on the Internet to aid you in the process. The purpose of showing you how to perform these tasks by hand is to aid you in understanding how subnetting works.

Suppose you were using a full Class C network of 192.168.100.0. This means that the first three octets (192.168.100.0) are used for the network address, the last possible IP address is the broadcast address (192.168.100.255), and all other IP addresses (192.168.100.1 to 192.168.1.254) can be assigned to hosts on the network.

Perhaps having 254 hosts in a single physical network does not work for your situation and you want to divide this class C network into smaller networks. Before doing this, consider how the network is defined in the first place by looking at Table 13.2.

TABLE 13.2 **Class C Network Definition**

Category	IP Address	Binary Format of IP Address
Address	192.168.100.25	11000000.10101000.01100100.00011001
Netmask	255.255.255.0 or 24	11111111.11111111.11111111.00000000
Network	192.168.100.0	11000000.10101000.01100100.00000000
Broadcast	192.168.100.255	11000000.10101000.01100100.00011111
First IP	192.168.100.1	11000000.10101000.01100100.00010001
Last IP	192.168.100.254	11000000.10101000.01100100.00011110
Maximum hosts in network	254	

In Table 13.2, the IP address is displayed in both dotted decimal notation (192.168.100.25) and binary format. The subnet mask is displayed in three formats:

▶ VLSM (Variable Length Subnet Mask), essentially the same format as dotted decimal notation.

▶ CIDR (Classless Inter-Domain Routing), the same value as the VLSM but described in a different format. This value is the number of "1" values in the binary format (add them up and you will get 24 "1" values for the Netmask in Table 13.2).

▶ Binary format.

To determine which part of the IP address represents the network, just look at all of the bits in the binary format that are a value of "1" for both the IP address and the subnet mask. To make this easier to see, this has been highlighted in gray in Table 13.2.

The first possible address in this network defines the network itself (192.168.100.0 in Table 13.2), and the last possible address in this network defines the broadcast address (192.168.100.255 in Table 13.2).

The example in Table 13.2 is straightforward because it is one of the standard classes. Look at the example in Table 13.3 to see how a different, nonstandard subnet (255.255.255.240) would affect the various IP addresses.

TABLE 13.3 **Nonstandard Subnet Mask Example**

Category	IP Address	Binary Format of IP Address
Address	192.168.100.25	11000000.10101000.01100100.00011001
Netmask	255.255.255.240 or 28	11111111.11111111.11111111.11110000
Network	192.168.100.0	11000000.10101000.01100100.00000000
Broadcast	192.168.100.31	11000000.10101000.01100100.00001111
First IP	192.168.100.17	11000000.10101000.01100100.00010001
Last IP	192.168.100.30	11000000.10101000.01100100.00011110
Maximum hosts in network	14	

> **Note**
>
> It may take some time to understand the process of subnetting. We highly encourage you to practice by using one of the many subnet calculators freely available on the Internet, such as the one found at the following address: https://www.adminsub.net/ipv4-subnet-calculator.

Network Appliances

A network appliance is any device that is designed to manage the flow of network traffic from and to a network segment. There are many different types of network appliances, but for the CompTIA Cloud+ exam objective, the two network appliances you should know about are load balancers and firewalls.

Load Balancers

Consider a scenario in which you need to access the website of a large organization. This website responds to millions of requests daily. If there really was just a single web server in this situation, it would cause several potential problems, including the following:

▶ **Single point of failure:** If the web server were to go down, experience an error, or have a network connectivity issue, the entire company's website would no longer be available.

▶ **Too many requests:** A single website can handle only so many requests before it becomes unable to respond to all client requests.

▶ **Latency issues:** The single web server can only be physically located in a single place. For example, suppose the web server is located in Germany. That would result in good response times for that country and others that are geographically close, but clients that are geographically further away, in New Zealand, for example, would experience latency issues.

A better solution would be to have multiple, identical web servers located in different geographic regions in the world. However, it would be difficult to tell the client system which specific web server to send requests to. This is where a load balancer comes in handy.

With a load balancer, the client request is sent to the load balancer resource. Then the load balancer will forward the request to a specific web server. Note: While a web server is given as an example here, the server can be other types. The load balancer can check for the health of server instances by sending periodic keep-alive packets, and if an instance is not available, it can redirect incoming requests from a client to another active instance.

There are different types of load balancers. Each cloud vendor offers its own specific types, but generally they fall into one of the following categories:

▶ **Round robin:** The load balancer sends client requests equally to the servers in a rotation system.

▶ **IP hash:** Client requests are sent to a specific server based on the client IP address.

▶ **Least connections:** The load balancer monitors client/server connections and sends the next client request to the server that has the least number of current connections. This is also known as *least busy* or *least used*.

▶ **Least response time:** The load balancer monitors client/server connections and sends the next client request to the server that has the least number of current connections and the lowest average response time.

▶ **Least bandwidth:** The load balancer monitors client/server connection bandwidth and sends the request to the server that has the least amount of traffic.

Firewalls

A cloud firewall (sometimes referred to as a Firewall as a Service, or FaaS) is a resource that performs the same function as a regular firewall. These firewalls are commonly deployed in a VPC (see the "Virtual Private Cloud (VPC)" section next).

The goal of a firewall is to inspect network traffic and determine if the traffic should be forwarded on to another network (or, in the case of host-based firewalls, a firewall determines if network traffic should be sent to the local operating system). Firewalls are typically used to protect a network from malicious traffic, but they can also be used to block network traffic from leaving an internal network.

Virtual Private Cloud (VPC)

A virtual private cloud is a feature provided by many cloud vendors (like Google Cloud and AWS) that enables you to create a virtual network within your cloud account. Note: Microsoft Azure's equivalent to VPC is called Azure VNet (Virtual Network).

Each cloud vendor will provide slightly different components in their VPC environment, but the following components are the most common:

▶ **Subnet:** This component defines the IP address range of the resources within the VPC.

▶ **Routing table:** Just as with a regular routing table, this table contains a set of rules that are used to determine how to route network traffic.

▶ **Gateway:** This router is used to communicate between the VPC resources and a network outside the VPC. It is often referred to as the *Internet gateway* because this router typically provides access to the Internet for your VPC resources.

▶ **Firewall:** See the preceding "Firewalls" section for more information.

▶ **Endpoint:** This optional feature is used to allow a direct or private connection between two VPCs or between the VPC and an on-premises network.

Hub and Spoke

In situations in which the VPCs of an organization need to communicate with each other internally (not via the Internet), there are two primary ways to configure this communication. One method, hub and spoke, uses a primary or central VPC (the hub VPC) that is configured to communicate with each of the other VPCs (the spoke VPCs). The spoke VPCs have no direct communication between each other, but the hub VPC can be configured to allow communication to pass through the hub, enabling spoke VPCs to communicate.

The advantage of this method is that the hub VPC can control all communication, making it easier to allow or block communication between the VPCs. The disadvantage is that it creates a single point of failure.

An alternative to hub-and-spoke VPC is peering VPC, which is covered next.

Peering

When using peering, VPCs are configured to directly communicate between each other, without requiring any access to the Internet. In an environment with many VPCs, peering can be very complex and difficult to manage, making hub and spoke a better solution.

VLAN/VxLAN/GENEVE

For more information about VLAN, VxLAN, and GENEVE, see "Network Segmentation" in Chapter 6, "Secure a Network in a Cloud Environment."

Single Root Input/Output Virtualization (SR-IOV)

On physical systems there is a connection called Peripheral Component Interconnect Express (PCIe). This connection allows you to connect devices like graphic cards, network cards, sound cards, and other similar devices.

In a virtual environment, SR-IOV can be used to represent a PCIe device as multiple virtual devices. This is done by providing virtual functions, allowing for separate configurations for each virtual machine. For example, an SR-IOV network card could be presented as four separate network cards, each with its own network port that can be configured differently for four different virtual machines.

Software-Defined Network (SDN)

See "Software-Defined Networks (SDN)" in Chapter 18.

CramQuiz

Answer these questions. The answers follow the last question. If you cannot answer these questions correctly, consider reading this section again until you can.

1. The caching name server will store the information in memory until the _____ period ends.

   ○ **A.** TTL

   ○ **B.** Zone record

   ○ **C.** FQDN

   ○ **D.** Domain

2. _____ is a technique that routes network packets from one network to another.

   ○ **A.** IPsec

   ○ **B.** MPLS

   ○ **C.** VPN

   ○ **D.** IPAM

3. Which IP class is the following IP address: 132.99.85.107?

   ○ **A.** A

   ○ **B.** B

   ○ **C.** C

   ○ **D.** D

4. What is the maximum number of hosts in the network 192.168.100.25/26?

   ○ **A.** 56

   ○ **B.** 60

   ○ **C.** 62

   ○ **D.** 66

5. Which type of load balancer would consider both the number of connections and the server response time?

   ○ **A.** IP hash

   ○ **B.** Least connections

   ○ **C.** Least bandwidth

   ○ **D.** None of these answers are correct

CramQuiz Answers

1. TTL

2. MPLS

3. B

4. 62

5. None of these answers are correct (Least response time is correct.)

What Next?

If you want more practice on this chapter's exam objectives before you move on, remember that you can access all of the CramQuiz questions on the companion website. You can also create a custom exam by objectives with the practice exam software. Note any objectives you struggle with and go to that objective's material in this chapter.

CHAPTER 14

Compute Sizing for a Deployment

This chapter covers the following official CompTIA Cloud+ exam objective:

▶ 3.4 Given a scenario, configure the appropriate compute sizing for a deployment.

(For more information on the official CompTIA Cloud+ exam topics, see the Introduction.)

Your organization is now ready to deploy virtual machines or instances in the cloud. However, before launching any instances, some questions will need to be answered: How much will it cost? How powerful will it be? What hardware resources will be available to the virtual machine?

You need to know how to determine the right compute size to fix the needs of what you will be using the virtual machine for. If money were no object, you could just deploy the virtual machine on the biggest instance type, getting the maximum CPU performance, highest amount of memory, and massive amounts of storage space. But, of course, money is an important factor. This chapter focuses on the considerations you need to make when determining the correct compute size for a virtual machine deployment.

CramSaver

If you can correctly answer these questions before going through this section, save time by skimming the ExamAlerts in this section and then completing the CramQuiz at the end of the section.

1. A(n) _____ is essentially a hardware emulator.

2. Which type of hypervisor utilizes a host operating system to communicate with hardware?

3. A(n) _____ is a processor designed to handle graphics rendering data.

4. _____ of memory means that RAM is provided to a virtual machine only as requested.

Answers

1. Hypervisor
2. Type 2
3. Graphics processing unit (GPU)
4. Dynamic allocation

Virtualization

One of the primary reasons to migrate on-premises solutions to the cloud is to replace operating systems that run on individual physical systems. Virtualization is the technology that enables multiple operating systems to share a single physical system. Although this technology is utilized in an on-premises environment, it is heavily used in cloud environments.

Virtualization enables you to place multiple operating systems on a single hardware platform or server. These operating systems share hardware components, such as the CPU, RAM (memory), storage, and the network interface.

Hypervisors

Normally, an operating system requires direct access to system hardware, and the operating system won't share this access with another operating system. Virtualization enables operating systems to share hardware. To allow this sort of abstracted access, a software program called a *hypervisor* is used.

A hypervisor presents to each operating system virtual devices that behave like real hardware devices. A hypervisor can emulate just about any hardware device, like CPUs, USB devices, and network interfaces. When the virtualized operating system communicates with a virtual hardware device, the hypervisor manages the process of communicating with the physical hardware.

There are two types of hypervisors: type 1 and type 2.

Type 1

A *type 1 hypervisor*, also called a *bare metal hypervisor*, runs directly on the physical hardware. It essentially takes on the role of the primary operating system. Type 1 hypervisors are faster than type 2 hypervisors because they have direct access to the system hardware. Figure 14.1 shows a type 1 hypervisor.

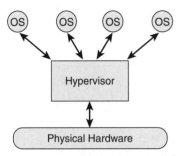

FIGURE 14.1   **Type 1 Hypervisor**

In most cases, the hypervisor in cloud computing is a type 1 hypervisor. There are some exceptions. For example, some cloud providers allow you to reserve an entire server. If you did that, you could opt to use a type 2 hypervisor to manage your own virtual machines.

Type 2

A *type 2 hypervisor* doesn't interact directly with the physical hardware but instead interacts with a host operating system. In this scenario, the virtualized OSs are referred to as *guest operating systems*.

While type 2 hypervisors are good for testing different operating systems on a system that already has a host operating system, they generally are not a good choice for production environments. Not only are the virtualized OSs hampered by the extra layer that the hypervisor must go through to access the hardware, but there are also security concerns. The host OS may be able to impact the guest OSs, including potentially installing malware on the guest virtual machines (this is known as *hyperjacking*). Figure 14.2 shows a type 2 hypervisor.

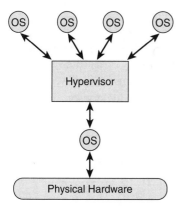

FIGURE 14.2   **Type 2 Hypervisor**

Simultaneous Multithreading (SMT)

Multithreading is a somewhat complicated and large topic. It essentially refers to the capability of a CPU core to execute multiple threads simultaneously.

SMT is one of two types of multithreading (the other is called *temporal multithreading* and is not an exam objective). If a cloud vendor provides the option to implement multithreading on a virtual machine, it is likely SMT, not temporal.

Cloud vendors will also often allow you to either use SMT or temporal multithreading to disable this feature. For example, Figure 14.3 shows the CPU options when creating an AWS virtual machine.

CPU options ⓘ	☑ Specify CPU options	
Core count	24	⬦
Threads per core	2	⬦
Number of vCPUs	48	

FIGURE 14.3   **CPU options**

The choice of whether to use SMT is not a simple one. Some applications don't take advantage of SMT, and as a result, performance may suffer. Additionally, high performance computing (HPC) isn't designed to utilize SMT, so it would be best to disable this feature. Benchmark tests for comparing performance with and without SMT may be required in order to make the best choice.

Dynamic Allocations

For CPUs, the concept of dynamic allocations is that the hypervisor will associate physical CPUs with virtual CPUs (vCPUs) as the physical CPUs become available (are added to the system). This is an important feature in a cloud computing environment, where on any given hardware, virtual machines are often routinely started and stopped.

One potential drawback is that many cloud vendors will employ oversubscription methods, which often means that there are potentially more vCPUs than can be associated with the number of physical CPUs. Note that this is often also called *overcommitment*. See "Oversubscription" in Chapter 3, "High Availability and Scaling in Cloud Environments," for further details.

Oversubscription

See the "Oversubscription" section in Chapter 3.

Central Processing Unit (CPU)/ Virtual CPU (vCPU)

The CPU is a chip located on the main circuit board. It is placed into a special location called a *socket*. Its responsibility, as the name implies, is to process instructions provided by the operating system or applications running on the OS. The CPU is the brains of the computer or server.

The CPU will determine how fast computing operations will be performed. Unless you have access to a dedicated server in a cloud environment, you typically won't have any direct control over the CPU. Instead, the hypervisor will interact with the CPU and present a vCPU to your virtual machine.

When you create a virtual machine, one of the factors that will affect the cost of running the virtual machine will be how many vCPUs the hypervisor provides to the virtual machine. This number is a calculation of the CPU core count multiplied by the number of threads per core. For example, if the number of core CPUs is 8 and the thread count is 3, then the operating system costs would be for 24 vCPUs.

While "more is better" is true in the sense that more vCPUs will result in a faster virtual machine, you should also consider that more will end up in higher

costs. Recall the objective associated with this chapter: "Given a scenario, configure the appropriate compute sizing for a deployment." This means you need
to ensure that you pick a vCPU count that will allow your applications to run at
an acceptable speed while also not paying for too many vCPUs.

Configuring the appropriate compute size also might be a moving target
because the applications that are running on the virtual machine may require
more resources in the future. Performing benchmark tests on a regular basis
and comparing these tests to a baseline can help you determine if you need to
upgrade your system to more vCPUs.

Graphics Processing Unit (GPU)

Some applications require large amounts of processing power to be able to
display graphics. For example, you may have an application that takes an architect's blueprint and displays full renderings of the building. Video processing
also can take a large amount of compute power.

A GPU is a processor designed to handle graphics rendering data. In some
cases, this processor may not be needed for a cloud-based virtual machine
because you may not have any applications that display such data. However, in
some cases this may be an important feature. As a result, some cloud providers
now offer specific instance classes that have massive GPU processing power.
Examples include the AWS p2, p3, and p4 instance classes and Azure's NC-
Series instance classes.

Choose these instance classes with care because they will be expensive. You
should consider what the use case is to use one of these high-end instance
classes before launching a virtual machine on one of them.

Virtual

In a cloud computing environment, the hypervisor typically provides a virtual
GPU to virtual machines. Note that "shared" is a subobjective of the CompTIA
exam. When multiple virtual machines share the same physical system, the
virtual GPU is sharing the physical GPU.

Pass-through

In some cases, the hypervisor can be configured to provide pass-through access
to the GPU. This means that the virtual machine is provided direct access to
the GPU. In this situation, the virtual machine that is provided pass-through

access is the only virtual machine on that system that can use the GPU. This option, while providing more power and features to the virtual CPU, is also the most expensive option.

Clock Speed/Instructions per Cycle (IPC)

When choosing the hardware that a virtual machine will run on, you want to make sure you choose a CPU with a clock speed that will be able to handle the performance needs of the operating system and applications. The clock speed is normally provided in the documentation. For example, in looking at AWS Elastic Cloud Computer (EC2) documentation, you will see information like that highlighted in gray in Figure 14.4.

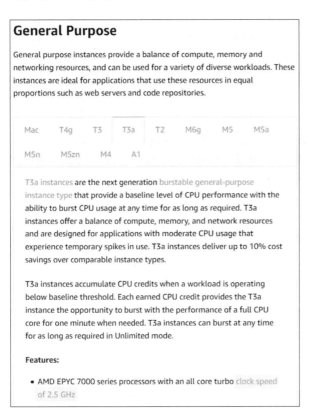

General Purpose

General purpose instances provide a balance of compute, memory and networking resources, and can be used for a variety of diverse workloads. These instances are ideal for applications that use these resources in equal proportions such as web servers and code repositories.

| Mac | T4g | T3 | T3a | T2 | M6g | M5 | M5a |
| M5n | M5zn | M4 | A1 | | | | |

T3a instances are the next generation burstable general-purpose instance type that provide a baseline level of CPU performance with the ability to burst CPU usage at any time for as long as required. T3a instances offer a balance of compute, memory, and network resources and are designed for applications with moderate CPU usage that experience temporary spikes in use. T3a instances deliver up to 10% cost savings over comparable instance types.

T3a instances accumulate CPU credits when a workload is operating below baseline threshold. Each earned CPU credit provides the T3a instance the opportunity to burst with the performance of a full CPU core for one minute when needed. T3a instances can burst at any time for as long as required in Unlimited mode.

Features:

- AMD EPYC 7000 series processors with an all core turbo clock speed of 2.5 GHz

FIGURE 14.4 **CPU Clock Speed Value**

The clock speed indicates how many cycles a CPU can handle in a second. A clock speed of 2.5 GHz means that the CPU can execute 2.5 billion cycles per second. This speed is a major component of how fast the CPU can perform calculations, but it isn't the only factor to consider.

Instructions per cycle (IPC) is, as its name implies, the number of instructions that the CPU can handle each cycle. The more IPCs, the faster the CPU can perform instructions. However, IPC is not often advertised by the cloud vendor and often not included in the specifications of the hardware vendor that manufactured the CPU. There are organizations that perform benchmark tests to determine the IPC of chips that can be used to determine the best choice when choosing an instance type.

Hyperconverged

To understand the concept of *hyperconverged*, let's focus on a single hardware component: storage. In a converged infrastructure (CI), storage devices that are used by virtual machines are directly attached to the physical server. This is referred to as *direct-attached storage (DAS)*. The primary advantage of this model is that access to storage tends to be very quick when compared to non-converged infrastructure where storage devices are often connected via the network (such as the storage-area network, or SAN, and network-attached storage, or NAS). The primary disadvantage is that this limits how much storage is available, although more can be added (adding more space is like adding more building blocks to the system).

In a hyperconverged infrastructure (HCI), storage is available to the entire node and controlled by software (a storage controller function). This is sometimes referred to as Storage as a Service.

Note that the terms *converged* and *hyperconverged* don't just apply to storage. Other hardware components are also part of CI and HCI. The primary advantage of CI and HCI is that they reduce the need for single-purpose, large physical systems. Combined with virtualization, they provide a more efficient use of system components.

Memory

When you're installing a virtual machine in the cloud, it is important to determine how much memory (RAM) the system will require. The amount of memory allocated to a virtual machine will have an impact on the cost of running the virtual machine.

Dynamic Allocation

Like the concept of dynamic allocations for CPUs (see the "Dynamic Allocations" section earlier in this chapter), dynamic allocation of memory means that RAM is provided to a virtual machine only as requested. For example, you may launch a virtual machine that is based on an instance that has 8 GB of RAM, but the hypervisor does not immediately reserve 8 GB of RAM for that virtual machine. Because the operating system requires more memory, it is dynamically allocated by the hypervisor, up to the maximum allowed by the instance type.

Ballooning

Imagine a situation in which a virtual machine is currently using 6 GB of RAM. Applications that require this RAM are currently running, but after a few hours the processing work is complete and the operating system no longer needs 2 GB of that RAM. The reason could either be that the application stopped or the application "returned" the RAM for the operating system to use.

However, in this case the operating system no longer needs that 2 GB of RAM at this time. Note that a driver on the virtualized operating system keeps track of what memory is actually in use, and the hypervisor can query this driver.

Now, another virtual machine requires more memory, but the hypervisor discovers there is no free RAM left to provide. After querying the other guest operating systems, the hypervisor discovers the 2 GB that is no longer needed in the original virtual machine. The hypervisor reclaims this memory in a process called *ballooning* and provides it to the second operating system.

Ballooning can be an advantage for cloud vendors because it is a technique that allows for oversubscription, but it can cause performance issues when there are a lot of guest virtual machines that use most of the memory allowed for their instance type.

Because of potential performance issues, you may consider spending more for a dedicated host. In a cloud environment, a dedicated host is one in which only your virtual machines will reside. This dedicated host provides you with more control and allows you to prevent any oversubscription. Of course, a dedicated host solution does cost more, so the cost must be weighed against the advantages.

CramQuiz

Answer these questions. The answers follow the last question. If you cannot answer these questions correctly, consider reading this section again until you can.

1. Which type of hypervisor communicates directly with the hardware?

   ○ **A.** Type 1

   ○ **B.** Type 2

   ○ **C.** Type 3

   ○ **D.** Type 4

2. Which of the following are types of hyperthreading? (Choose two.)

   ○ **A.** SMT

   ○ **B.** SHT

   ○ **C.** Temporal multithreading

   ○ **D.** Massive multithreading

3. Which of the following is a term associated with GPUs?

   ○ **A.** IPC

   ○ **B.** Clock speed

   ○ **C.** PASS-through

   ○ **D.** Hyperconverged

4. Which of the following have an impact on the performance of a CPU? (Choose two.)

   ○ **A.** Clock speed

   ○ **B.** IPC

   ○ **C.** Hyperjacking

   ○ **D.** Hyperconverged

5. Which of the following would describe an infrastructure where software is used to control access to storage devices?

   ○ **A.** CI

   ○ **B.** UCI

   ○ **C.** DAS

   ○ **D.** HCI

CramQuiz Answers

1. Type 1
2. SMT and temporal multithreading
3. Pass-through
4. Clock speed and IPC
5. HCI

What Next?

If you want more practice on this chapter's exam objectives before you move on, remember that you can access all of the CramQuiz questions on the companion website. You can also create a custom exam by objectives with the practice exam software. Note any objectives you struggle with and go to that objective's material in this chapter.

CHAPTER 15

Cloud Migrations

> **This chapter covers the following official CompTIA Cloud+ exam objective:**
>
> ▶ 3.5 Given a scenario, perform cloud migrations.
>
> (For more information on the official CompTIA Cloud+ exam topics, see the Introduction.)

Most organizations that are considering deploying resources in the cloud may consider migrating existing solutions from their on-premises environment to the cloud. This approach is very common in enterprise organizations where the networks and applications have been homegrown or bought off the shelf over the years and now it is time to transition to the cloud. Migrating solutions requires a great deal of consideration and planning because a bad migration can result in downtime and extra expense.

There also are born-in-cloud organizations in which the organizations do not have any legacy footprint and start their journey from cloud-native deployments and workloads.

This chapter will explore some of the different methods of migrating to the cloud. They will include physical-to-virtual, virtual-to-virtual, and even cloud-to-cloud migrations. Three types of resource migrations also will be explored: operating systems, storage, and database migrations.

CramSaver

If you can correctly answer these questions before going through this section, save time by skimming the ExamAlerts in this section and then completing the CramQuiz at the end of the section.

1. Besides manual and fully automated, what other method can be used to perform a physical-to-virtual migration?

2. Which open format can be used to create a virtual appliance?

3. Which term describes when a customer deploys a resource in the cloud that is dependent on software or features that are provided only by a specific cloud vendor?

4. True or false: A nonrelational database is also referred to as a SQL database.

Answers

1. Semi-automated
2. Open Virtualization Format (OVF)
3. Vendor lock-in
4. False

Physical to Virtual (P2V)

When planning to migrate your operations to the cloud, you will likely need to develop a strategy to transfer operating systems that reside on physical systems to the virtual environment provided by the cloud vendor. This process is referred to as a physical-to-virtual (P2V) migration.

There are three primary methods you can employ to perform a P2V migration:

▶ **Manual:** With this method, you deploy your cloud-based virtual machines, manually install any necessary software, and manually transfer any data from the physical OS to the virtual machine. For small migrations, this may be a reasonable solution, but this method does not scale well to large migrations.

▶ **Semi-automated P2V:** This technique makes use of a tool that aids in the process of migrating to a virtual machine. This process is semi-automated in the sense that a human is required to start the migration and may be required to answer questions during the migration process. Typically, these tools are provided by cloud vendors free of charge, and they do have the advantage of providing the user with some control of the migration process as it happens. Some of these tools also allow for hot migrations, in which the operating system is live while it is being migrated. However, in very large-scale migrations, semi-automated P2V tools can be very time-consuming to use.

▶ **Fully automated P2V:** A fully automated P2V also makes use of a tool, but this tool does not require any human interaction. In some cases, these tools may be able to explore a local network, find systems, and migrate the systems to the target state environment (this depends on the types of operating systems and how the network has been configured). A fully automated P2V works well in large migration deployments, but the software tool may cost money to use.

Virtual to Virtual (V2V)

You may already have virtual machines in your on-premises environment. If that is the case, the process of migrating these operating systems to a cloud infrastructure is called virtual-to-virtual (V2V) migration.

A V2V migration is often easier than a P2V migration because the host operating system is already in a virtualized state. There are also some standards in virtualization that help with this process. For example, the Open Virtualization Format (OVF) is a standard that isn't tied to any specific hypervisor. It provides a standard for the process of defining (packaging) virtual appliances (software that is run in a virtual environment). Many of the popular hypervisor vendors, including VMware, VirtualBox, Red Hat Enterprise Virtualization, and Oracle VM, provide support for OVF. For example, Figure 15.1 demonstrates the process of exporting a virtual machine in OVF format using VirtualBox.

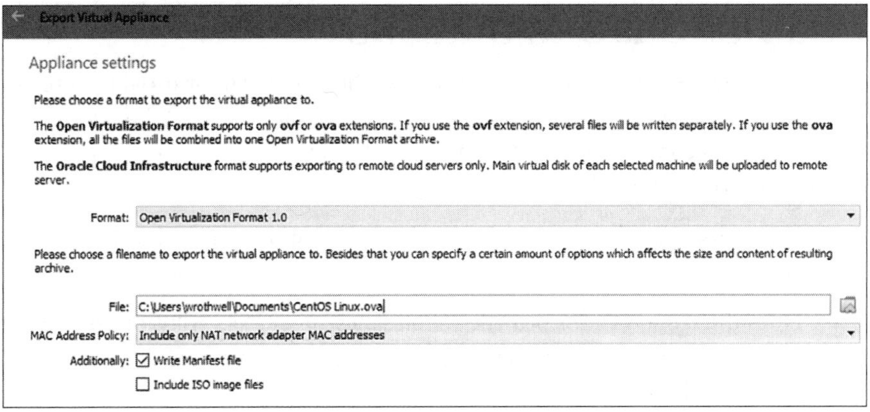

FIGURE 15.1   Exporting a Virtual Machine in OVF Format

Many cloud vendors provide support for importing virtual appliances that are in OVF format. Some vendors also provide tools to export virtual machines into a standard format, which can also be helpful for cloud-to-cloud migrations.

Cloud-to-Cloud Migrations

The concept of a cloud-to-cloud migration is that your organization decides to move resources from one cloud vendor to another. This move could be made for a variety of reasons, including cost, features, or security. This section will cover several topics that you should consider when performing a cloud-to-cloud migration.

Vendor Lock-in

One of the concerns about migrating to the cloud is the potential of *vendor lock-in* (also called *proprietary lock-in*). In this scenario a customer deploys a resource in the cloud that is dependent on software or features that are provided only by a specific cloud vendor.

The problem with vendor lock-in is that it eliminates the flexibility and options for customers who are migrating to the cloud. Vendor lock-in is sometimes the result of decisions made by the cloud vendor to employ a proprietary technology, such as a proprietary file format or encryption method. Although a customer may be able to migrate the resource to another cloud vendor, migration typically comes with a cost, either a financial or time-consuming cost.

PaaS or SaaS Migrations

Recall that with Platform as a Service (PaaS), the cloud vendor provides a platform (an operating system) that you use to deploy your software. There are many things to consider when planning a PaaS migration from one cloud vendor to another, including

▶ Is the language that your code is written for supported by the cloud vendor?

▶ Does the cloud vendor provide redundancy in its PaaS solution to prevent downtime? If so, what does the service-level agreement (SLA) provide for guaranteed minimum downtime?

▶ Does the cloud vendor provide a disaster recovery plan that meets the needs of the customer?

▶ Does the security of the cloud vendor's PaaS solution meet the needs of the customer? For example, is data encrypted at rest or in transit?

▶ What is the data backup policy for the cloud vendor's PaaS solution, and does this meet the needs of the customer?

▶ Does the cloud vendor's PaaS solution provide a Content Delivery Network (CDN)?

▶ Does the cloud vendor's PaaS solution meet all regulatory requirements that the customer is required to meet?

▶ Does the cloud vendor's support for its PaaS solution meet the needs of the customer?

Keep in mind that many of these concerns are related not only to PaaS migrations but are also concerns for other migrations, such as IaaS and SaaS. However, with PaaS the focus is on ensuring that the customer's software will function correctly on the cloud vendor's PaaS.

With Software as a Service (SaaS), the focus shifts to functionality and portability. For example, with SaaS the biggest factors and concerns typically include the following:

▶ Does the new vendor's SaaS solution provide the features that are required?

▶ Is it possible to migrate data from the existing SaaS solution to the new vendor's SaaS? If so, what is the process (manual, automated, semi-automated, and so on), and what are the associated costs for this migration?

▶ Does the new vendor's SaaS solution provide the capability to scale as required by the customer?

Access Control Lists (ACLs)

An access control list is used to determine who is able to access a specific resource within your cloud environment. For example, a network access control list (NACL) can include a list of IP addresses or IP networks that are permitted to access a VPC. Rules for NACLs are associated with network ports (or protocols) and either allow or deny access.

In terms of cloud-to-cloud migration, there are a few things to consider, including

▶ Does the new vendor provide an ACL solution that is similar to the functionality of the existing vendor's ACL solution?

> ▶ Is it possible to migrate the rules of the current ACL to the new vendor's ACL?

> ▶ Are there limitations to the new vendor's ACL solution that can result in security issues?

Firewalls

Firewalls provide a similar function to ACLs, but the functionality level is much higher than ACLs. There are also different types of firewalls that can implemented in the cloud. For example, a web application firewall (WAF) is a Layer 7 firewall designed to protect your cloud applications from web-based exploits. There are also various cloud-based firewall appliances, many of which can be deployed on different cloud vendor environments.

Because firewall rules are often complex, migrating from one cloud vendor to another can pose challenges. The wide variety of firewall solutions also tends to limit the chance of an automated solution migrating a firewall from one cloud environment to another.

Storage Migrations

Because storage migrations often involve massive amounts of data, much of which may contain proprietary information, the process of migrating storage solutions from on-premises to the cloud poses certain challenges. When planning for the migrating of storage, take the following issues into consideration:

> ▶ **Data integrity:** There needs to be a method to ensure that the original data is not corrupted during the migration process.

> ▶ **Monitoring:** You need to use a monitoring or logging solution to ensure all data is migrated.

> ▶ **Security:** For most data, it will be critical to ensure that the data is encrypted during transport.

> ▶ **Bandwidth:** Transferring massive amounts of data can take a great deal of time, even with large amounts of bandwidth. This transfer can also impact day-to-day business operations, so bandwidth throttling or data transfer scheduling can be used. Some vendors also provide alternative methods of transferring data, including shipping data using large storage devices or out-of-band data securely connected to the cloud.

▶ **Cost:** Depending on the storage solution, there may be a cost involved to transfer data into a cloud storage solution.

The rest of this section will cover specific considerations for block, file, and object migrations.

Block

On-premises block storage solutions are those that are stored on disk volumes. When migrating this sort of data, you should consider which cloud storage solution you want to migrate the data to. While storing the data in a cloud block storage solution might make sense, you may also consider storing the data in a file storage solution or even an object storage solution.

In terms of which solution would be easiest, typically a block-to-block migration would require the least amount of effort. This method also would allow you to maintain the same file system structure (such as NTFS, ext4, and FAT) as the original storage solution. Maintaining the same structure can be important if the data on the existing file systems is secured by file system features, like permissions.

A block-to-file migration solution is typically not much more complex than a block-to-block solution, but transferring individual files may be more time-consuming. However, transferring block data to object data will be more complex unless using a tool provided by the cloud vendor. It is important to note that features, such as file system permissions and the hierarchy of file systems (subdirectories or subfolder trees), are often lost in these sorts of migrations.

File

Because file storage solutions are being widely used on-premises and these solutions are network-based, transferring this data to a cloud solution is typically one of the easier migrations. Many cloud vendors also provide tools to make this migration process easy.

A file-to-block migration is not normally a viable or desired solution. However, a file-to-object migration is worth considering because object storage solutions may have benefits that file storage doesn't have (ACLs, capability to share via a URL, and so on).

Object

On-premises object-based solutions, like MinIO, Ceph, and LeoFS, can also be migrated to a cloud solution. The process of migrating this data to the cloud may seem simple, but object metadata, security, and access methods will complicate the process.

Database Migrations

When you're performing a database migration, there are several things to consider, including:

▶ **Scalability:** In most cases when you implement a cloud database solution, you associate the database with hardware (such as CPU, storage space, and network bandwidth). Although this hardware should fit the needs of your current database, you need to ensure that the hardware can be scaled to meet the future needs of your database solution.

▶ **Security:** Because your database will now be stored in the cloud, security may become even more of a priority.

▶ **Regulatory:** Any time that you are dealing with data, you may need to also adhere to compliance rules. These rules may originate from government regulatory agencies or third-party organizations, like banks. With your database now being stored in the cloud, you need to ensure that where and how the data is stored and maintained meet all regulatory requirements.

▶ **Architecture:** While all of these topics are important to consider when migrating a database solution to the cloud, the architecture of the database itself might be the most important. You might need to perform a heterogeneous migration where the source database architecture is different from the destination database.

▶ **Cost:** As with any cloud migration, cost must always be considered. This includes not only the cost of the database service that the vendor charges but also the costs of modifying software that uses the data and potentially needing to train employees on how to utilize the new database.

ExamAlert

Objective 3.5 is the only one on the CompTIA Cloud+ certification exam that addresses databases. This topic is only a very small part of the exam.

Relational

A *relational database* is one in which data is stored in tables, which consist of columns and rows. In many ways it is similar to a spreadsheet, but there are some key differences. The data within each row is referred to as a *record*. In a relational database there must be a column that contains a unique value. This value is called the *key*.

Relational databases are often called Structured Query Language (SQL) databases. SQL isn't really a database type, but rather a language that is used to create, modify, and query data in a relational database.

The relational part of relational databases is the feature that allows a connection (relation) between different tables in the database.

Here are some advantages of relational databases:

▶ They work well for structured data.

▶ The query times are typically very fast.

▶ Many software tools provide SQL functionality.

▶ The format of the database (rows and columns) is easy for users to conceptualize.

▶ There are many on-premises and cloud relational database management systems (RDBMS) solutions available.

Nonrelational

Nonrelational databases, also called *NoSQL databases*, employ a different method of storing data. There are four different types of nonrelational databases:

▶ **Document:** This database is used to store document types of data, which are normally encoded in a data format like JSON, XML, or YAML.

▶ **Columnar:** This database is similar to relational database, but with some key differences. For example, in a relational database, every record must have a value for every column. This is not a requirement for nonrelational databases.

▶ **Key-value:** A key is associated with a value in this type of database.

▶ **Graph:** In this type of database, complex relationships between data sets can be developed.

Here are some advantages of nonrelational databases:

▶ Very flexible structure

▶ Good for document-oriented data

▶ Great for Big Data situations

CramQuiz

Answer these questions. The answers follow the last question. If you cannot answer these questions correctly, consider reading this section again until you can.

1. Which of the following is not considered a P2V migration method?

   ○ **A.** Manual

   ○ **B.** Semi-automated

   ○ **C.** Fully automated

   ○ **D.** Semimanual

2. A(n) _____ is used to determine who is able to access a specific resource within your cloud environment.

   ○ **A.** ACL

   ○ **B.** Firewall

   ○ **C.** Vendor lock

   ○ **D.** SaaS

3. Which of the following is not a consideration when performing a storage migration?

   ○ **A.** Data integrity

   ○ **B.** Security

   ○ **C.** Bandwidth

   ○ **D.** User accessibility

CramQuiz Answers

1. Semimanual

2. ACL

3. User accessibility

What Next?

If you want more practice on this chapter's exam objectives before you move on, remember that you can access all of the CramQuiz questions on the companion website. You can also create a custom exam by objectives with the practice exam software. Note any objectives you struggle with and go to that objective's material in this chapter.

CHAPTER 16

Logging, Monitoring, and Alerting

This chapter covers the following official CompTIA Cloud+ exam objective:

▶ 4.1 Given a scenario, configure logging, monitoring, and alerting to maintain operational status.

(For more information on the official CompTIA Cloud+ exam topics, see the Introduction.)

This chapter explores three key topics: logging, monitoring, and alerting. In the "Logging" section you will learn about using collectors, categorizing logs by severity, performing log audits, and understanding different types of logs.

In the "Monitoring" section you will explore topics like baselines, thresholds, and tagging. You will also learn about log scrubbing and different types of monitoring, such as performance monitoring, resource utilization monitoring, and availability monitoring.

Lastly, in the "Alerting" section you will learn about common messaging methods and when you should disable alerts.

CramSaver

If you can correctly answer these questions before going through this section, save time by skimming the ExamAlerts in this section and then completing the CramQuiz at the end of the section.

1. SNMP version _____ provides key security features, such as authentication and encryption.

2. _____ is a feature in which metadata is applied to cloud resources.

3. True or false: You should disable alerts during software maintenance mode.

Answers

1. 3
2. Tagging
3. True

Logging

In this section you will learn about logging tools and techniques that are commonly used in a cloud environment.

Collectors

A *collector* is a tool that is designed to gather log messages in a central location. The most common tools for collecting data on a network are the Simple Network Management Protocol and the Syslog protocol.

Simple Network Management Protocol (SNMP)

Simple Network Management Protocol allows devices to send log messages to a central point of collection. SNMP utilizes two primary components: SNMP agents and the SNMP manager.

The role of an SNMP agent is to collect log messages from devices and send these messages to the SNMP manager. The SNMP manager stores these logs in a database, provides the means to query these logs, and can be configured to send alerts to end users.

See the following section for a quick comparison of SNMP and Syslog.

Syslog

The Syslog protocol enables devices (and operating systems, like Linux) to send log messages to a Syslog server (that is, a Syslog collector). Queries can be performed on the Syslog server to discover problems on the system, but the server can also be configured to send alerts to end users.

Note that there isn't any established rule that specifies what type of message would be associated with a severity level. This is left to the developers who create the alert messages on the device.

Syslog and SNMP perform similar functions, but there are a few key differences:

▶ If you are using version 3 of SNMP, there are some security features, including authentication. Syslog lacks security features.

▶ SNMP can gather messages either by polling devices or by having devices send messages via a trigger (called a *trap*). Syslog relies on the device to send the log messages.

▶ SNMP also provides some control functionality in which actions can take place on the device as the result of a log message. Syslog is designed to aid in troubleshooting by allowing for the monitoring of log messages.

Analysis

As you can probably imagine, on a busy network the number of logs generated can be staggering. It is difficult for a human to be able to keep up with all of the log entries. As a result, most organizations use tools that analyze log data.

A tool that analyzes log data will typically use a baseline to determine normal operation of network devices. By reviewing log entries, the analytic tool can determine whether there is an issue on the network or with a specific network device. In the event that the tool recognizes a possible problem, an alert should be sent to a human to investigate further. In some cases the tool may also take direct action to attempt to fix the problem.

Dozens of tools are available for both SNMP and Syslog. The following is just a small example of some popular SNMP analytic tools:

▶ SolarWinds Network Performance Monitor

▶ LogicMonitor

▶ Site24x7

▶ Spiceworks Network Monitor

Severity Categorization

One component of Syslog is the capability of devices to define a severity of the log message. The following severities are supported:

▶ 0—Emergency

▶ 1—Alert

- ▶ 2—Critical
- ▶ 3—Error
- ▶ 4—Warning
- ▶ 5—Notice
- ▶ 6—Informational
- ▶ 7—Debug

Audits

A *log audit* (also called a *log trail*) is a collection of logs that provide a sequence of events. This information is very useful in determining which steps may have resulted in a problem or error.

Types

Logs are often broken into categories called *types*. Examples of log types include

- ▶ Operating system logs
- ▶ Security logs
- ▶ Policy logs
- ▶ User-generated logs
- ▶ Data access logs
- ▶ Authentication logs
- ▶ Administrative action logs
- ▶ Application logs

Note that this isn't a complete list of log types because each cloud environment may also have additional log types.

The following sections will provide more details about some of these log types.

Access/Authentication

Typically, whenever a cloud resource is accessed, like reading data from a bucket or connecting to a database, an access log is created. There are some exceptions because many cloud vendors allow logging to be turned on or off for resources, but the point is that an access log details when a resource is accessed in some way. This can also include when access is denied to a resource.

Access doesn't always require authentication because some resources may be "world-accessible" or "world-readable." When authentication does take place, a log entry should be created. This typically is not something that can be turned off and should definitely also include failed login attempts.

System

A system log is one that is generated by an action on an operating system. Often these logs are also found on the operating system, but in some cases they may be sent to a log collector.

Application

An application log is a log entry that is created by some sort of cloud-based application. It may be an application that your organization creates, or it might be an application that is provided by the cloud vendor.

Automation

Log *automation* is the process of automatically performing an action based on a specific log entry. For example, if someone attempts to log in as the administrator on one of your systems and this attempt fails, you may want to automate the process of sending a text alert to your IT staff.

Trending

In terms of logging, *trending* is determining what is taking place in your cloud environment by viewing logs over a period of time. For example, if you are concerned that you might run out of space in a cloud storage resource, you can look at the daily reports of space utilization over a period of time (such as the past 30 days) to determine whether you need to upgrade to a larger storage device.

Monitoring

The line between logging and monitoring can be blurred at times because often the tool that is used for logging also provides the function of monitoring. Consider *logging* to be the recording of what is happening, while *monitoring* provides an idea of how your environment is behaving and can provide you with alerts based on criteria that you define.

This section will focus on the different monitoring features that you should be aware of, including understanding the purpose of baselines, thresholds, and tagging.

Baselines

A *baseline* is an established norm. Baselines are used to determine whether there may be a problem with a resource. Baselines are often established by analyzing data from logs over a period of time. Future activity is monitored to determine if a resource is functioning within the parameters of the baseline.

Thresholds

Thresholds are set to determine when an alert should be issued because an attribute of a resource has reached a maximum or minimum value. For example, performance of a web server running on a virtual machine might be important to ensure the web server is able to respond to client requests. This performance can be monitored by setting thresholds for key indicators, such as CPU utilization, free memory, and network performance. If the web server exceeds any of these thresholds, an alert would be issued, or an auto-scaling event (spanning another web server) could be implemented. Another example could be the threshold on cost of a cloud resource and an alert being sent to your email on reaching a predetermined limit.

Tagging

Tagging is a feature in which metadata is applied to cloud resources. This metadata typically includes key-value pairs. For example, a key could be "department," and the value could be "sales."

Tagging resources provides many advantages. For example, you could use tags to group together virtual machines to perform actions on all of the virtual machines. For instance, if you wanted to shut down a collection of virtual machines that were designed for a test of new database software, you could create a tag called "purpose" with a value of "database_test" for all of these resources. Then, to shut down all of these virtual machines, you could have the cloud management tool shut down all virtual machines with a value of "database_test" associated with the tag "purpose."

Tagging can also be used when monitoring resources. You may want to create a threshold rule that applies to all the organization's web servers. By applying the same tag value to all of these web servers, you can create a monitoring rule that applies to any resource with the tag value. This would also include any new resource that is created after you make the monitoring rule, assuming that it has the correct tag value.

Log Scrubbing

In some cases, sensitive information may be stored in logs. This is one of the reasons why your log data should be kept secure. But what if your log data is compromised? Wouldn't it be better if sensitive information wasn't stored in the logs?

You may not have a choice when it comes to what is initially stored in a log entry. Keep in mind that log information comes from a variety of sources, including applications and resources that may not provide you with the ability to customize what is logged. If you can modify what is sent to your logs and avoid placing sensitive data in the logs in the first place, this is the best course of action. When this approach isn't possible, log scrubbing is the next best solution.

Log scrubbing is using a tool to search for and remove sensitive information. For example, suppose a log entry includes a customer's Social Security number (hopefully, this would never happen!). You could use a log scrubbing tool to look for a number that matches the following pattern (N represents a single digit): NNN-NN-NNNN. If a value like this is matched, the log scrubbing tool can either delete it or replace it with a different value, such as "data removed."

Performance Monitoring

Performance monitoring is designed to determine if your cloud resources are reacting at an acceptable level or standard that is provided by an SLA definition. Cloud resources are often distributed, which can have an impact on performance. Additional cloud attributes may also have an impact on performance, including network security, hardware resources, and the configuration options of applications.

Application

Performance monitoring is often associated with a collection of tools called Application Performance Monitoring (APM). These APM tools can be used to determine how well the cloud resource is responding and help you determine where a bottleneck may be causing poor performance.

Infrastructure Components

Infrastructure components is a broad categorization of resources that can include the network itself, hardware components (CPU, memory, and so on), facilities (power, for example), and software. These are typically the sorts of components that can have an impact on performance and are the primary resources that are monitored with performance monitoring tools.

Resource Utilization

In the context of resource utilization, consider components like CPUs, memory, network bandwidth, and disk space to be the resources. The more resources your cloud infrastructure uses, the higher the costs of your cloud environment.

Resource utilization monitoring is designed to determine what parts of your cloud infrastructure are using these resources. The goal is to help you make better decisions of how to adjust your cloud environment to best optimize the resources that are available.

Availability

As you can probably imagine, many of the components of your cloud infra-structure need to be available almost 100 percent of the time. While 100 per-cent would be most ideal, there is almost always the chance of short periods of downtime. The goal is to keep this downtime as short as possible.

To determine whether a cloud resource is available, you can use monitoring tools to actively or passively check for this availability. The results should be compared to the uptime minimums that are defined in the cloud vendor's SLA (see "Service-Level Agreement (SLA)" in Chapter 4, "Solution Design in Support of the Business Requirements").

SLA-Defined Uptime Requirements

See the "Service-Level Agreement (SLA)" section in Chapter 4.

Verification of Continuous Monitoring Activities

Imagine a scenario in which you have opted to use a company to monitor the alarm system that you have installed in your house. You put your trust in this organization monitoring the status of your alarm to keep you and your house safe.

Now imagine that your alarm goes off one night and…nothing happens. No response from the alarm monitoring company, no police dispatched to your house, just no response at all. Clearly, this situation is something that you want to avoid, so you take care to pick a reputable company to monitor your alarm and ensure that it is routinely performing checks to verify that the alarm monitoring system is functioning correctly.

This same care needs to be established with the tools that you deploy to monitor your cloud infrastructure. This verification could include manual audit checks, alarms raised when a cloud resource is no longer providing data, or tools that run checks on your monitoring software.

Service Management Tool Integration

Service management, also called information technology service management (ITSM), is the means by which an organization provides IT services to its customers (which also include employees). When an organization uses the cloud to provide services, the monitoring solutions that are deployed need to be integrated with the service management tools to provide timely response times.

For example, suppose that an organization provides a service to its customers that is based on a cloud-based database. Clearly, this service becomes unusable if the database is no longer available. The tool that is used to monitor the database availability must be configured to "talk to" the ITSM software to provide IT support with accurate, up-to-the-minute information on the availability of the service.

Alerting

Alerting is one of the actions that monitoring tools can take when a threshold is reached or an error is encountered in your cloud environment. This section will explore some of the key components of alerting.

Common Messaging Methods

Where you send an alert can be as important as determining which alerts you want to send. Following are some of the common alert messaging methods that you typically find in cloud environments:

▶ SMS (that is, a text message to your mobile device)

▶ Email

▶ A messaging service, like AWS Simple Notification Service (SNS), PagerDuty, or Datadog

▶ A server via an API call

▶ A storage container, like a bucket

▶ A messaging tool, like Microsoft Teams or Slack

Enable/Disable Alerts

In some cases you should not have alerts enabled. For example, if a problem generates a massive number of alerts, you may want to disable the alert system until that problem is resolved.

Additionally, when a cloud service or resource is in maintenance mode (such as updating software or resolving bugs), disabling alerts prevents false warnings. It is very likely that software that is in maintenance mode will trigger alerts as the software is being worked on.

Maintenance Mode

See the preceding "Enable/Disable Alerts" section.

Appropriate Responses

Some alerts might just require additional research and monitoring, whereas others may require immediate action. Developing a solid response plan is just as important as determining which alerts to generate and where to send the alerts.

Included in developing a response plan is developing a policy for categorizing and communicating alerts. See the next section for more details.

Policies for Categorizing and Communicating Alerts

Not all alerts carry the same importance. For example, an alert indicating that a key database is no longer available should have a higher importance than an alert indicating that the same database may need more storage space in the near future.

You should develop a policy for categorizing alerts. This policy can be based on the level of importance of the alert or other criteria, like the following:

▶ The type of service or resource that is impacted by the alert (operating system, application, database, storage, network performance, and so on)

▶ Who should be notified based on the alert

▶ If the alert affects key customers or general overall service

▶ If the alert is related to a key service that impacts other resources or services

Once you have placed alerts into categories, your policy should be expanded to include how to communicate the alerts after they have been received. This includes determining when an alert needs to be escalated and who should be notified when this situation occurs.

CramQuiz

Answer these questions. The answers follow the last question. If you cannot answer these questions correctly, consider reading this section again until you can.

1. SNMP can gather messages either by polling devices or by having devices send messages via a(n) _____.

   ○ A. Trap

   ○ B. Alert

   ○ C. Notification

   ○ D. Push

2. Which of the following is the highest severity level of Syslog?

- ○ **A.** Critical
- ○ **B.** Emergency
- ○ **C.** Alert
- ○ **D.** Error

3. Log scrubbing is designed to remove what type of information?

- ○ **A.** Sensitive
- ○ **B.** Server
- ○ **C.** Redundant
- ○ **D.** Outdated

4. Which of the following is not normally a destination of an alert message?

- ○ **A.** Email
- ○ **B.** SMS
- ○ **C.** Phone call
- ○ **D.** Storage container

CramQuiz Answers

1. Trap
2. Emergency
3. Sensitive
4. Phone call

What Next?

If you want more practice on this chapter's exam objectives before you move on, remember that you can access all of the CramQuiz questions on the companion website. You can also create a custom exam by objectives with the practice exam software. Note any objectives you struggle with and go to that objective's material in this chapter.

CHAPTER 17

Operation of a Cloud Environment

This chapter covers the following official CompTIA Cloud+ exam objective:

▶ 4.2 Given a scenario, maintain efficient operation of a cloud environment.

(For more information on the official CompTIA Cloud+ exam topics, see the Introduction.)

This chapter focuses on several different areas that revolve around ensuring that the operation of the cloud environment is efficient. You will learn about different lifecycle features, including the concept of roadmaps. You will also learn about different topics related to patching and upgrading systems. Lastly, you will learn about the different features that dashboards and reporting provide to allow you to more efficiently manage a cloud environment.

CramSaver

If you can correctly answer these questions before going through this section, save time by skimming the ExamAlerts in this section and then completing the CramQuiz at the end of the section.

1. What type of roadmap describes when each version of a product will be provided?

2. If your organization is using software that is one version older than the most current stable release, you are using a(n) _____ release.

3. True or false: A blue-green upgrade method is exactly the same as an active-passive upgrade method.

Answers

1. Release roadmap
2. N-1
3. False

Confirm Completion of Backups

Backups are often performed automatically, and as a result, there is an assumption that the backup completed successfully. This assumption can result in a false sense of security because backups that didn't complete or had errors may result in the loss of data.

Consequently, there should be some sort of process in place to ensure that backups are completed successfully. In some cases, this process can be performed by the backup utility itself. If it is not something that can be handled by the backup utility, another process needs to be put in place to handle this task.

Lifecycle Management

In this section you will explore lifecycle management of cloud resources.

Roadmaps

In lifecycle management, roadmaps provide a timeline for the implementation of the product from start to finish. Roadmaps are also used to align the product with business goals and are designed to provide an easy way to visualize the lifecycle management of a project.

Each product may have multiple roadmaps because the visibility of the process may be different for different people. For example, executives may just need to see the "big picture," whereas implementers need to see every detail. Customers may also have a different roadmap because they will be focused on when features will be released. Roadmaps can often be grouped into one of the following categories:

▶ **Features roadmap:** This roadmap describes when features will be added to the product.

▶ **Release roadmap:** This roadmap describes when each version of the product will be released.

▶ **Portfolio roadmap:** This roadmap is a collection of product lifecycles and how they are related to one another.

▶ **Strategy roadmap:** This roadmap defines the overall high-level actions that must take place to meet the goals of the product during its lifecycle.

Old/Current/New Versions

A product's lifecycle management process must include how different versions of the product will be maintained and supported. For example, suppose the current release of a product is version 3.2. In this case, how is version 3.1 handled? Is it still supported by the organization? Is the product still being patched on a regular basis? What are the steps needed to migrate customers from 3.1 to 3.2? And, of course, you need to ask these same questions (and more) for version 3.0 and any previous version.

For new versions, you need to make decisions regarding new features and the migration process from older releases. How does the organization let the customer know about upcoming new features? What happens if a new feature is not available in the release it was originally planned for? Will some features of new versions also be implemented in older versions that are still supported (a process called *backporting*)?

Upgrading and Migrating Systems

Upgrading a system is the process of enhancing an existing system to provide more features or better performance. For example, you may opt to add more RAM to an existing system to increase available memory for an operating system.

Migrating a system is the process of moving a resource from one physical location to another. For example, instead of upgrading a system by adding more RAM, you could migrate the operating system to a new hardware platform that has more RAM than the original.

The same concepts apply in cloud computing. Operating systems are placed within virtual machines (VMs) in the cloud, and these virtual machines have underlying hardware components. In some cases, you may be able to enhance an existing virtual machine (like adding more virtual memory), but in other cases you might find migrating to a new virtual machine to be a better solution.

For example, if you need a faster or more powerful CPU, this isn't something that you just add to an existing virtual machine (at least not as a typical cloud vendor solution).

Note that upgrade versus migration doesn't just apply to virtual machines. Any cloud resource, including applications and database software, uses underlying hardware resources that may either be upgraded or require a migration to provide more power and flexibility.

Deprecations or End of Life

Most products will eventually reach a point where they no longer serve a useful purpose or no longer align with the organization's strategic or business needs. Typically, an organization takes one of two approaches:

▶ **Specify an end of life for the product:** This approach involves indicating when the product will no longer be supported and should no longer be used. It is also referred to as *sunsetting* a product.

▶ **Deprecate the product:** Using this approach, an organization indicates that the product should no longer be used and is unlikely to be supported in the future. Typically, a deprecated product is replaced with a newer product, but the organization isn't prepared to force customers to move to the new product. Consider *deprecated* to mean "it is still available, but the developer doesn't recommend you use it anymore."

Change Management

See "Change Management Failures" in Chapter 24, "Troubleshoot Deployment, Automation, and Orchestration Issues."

Asset Management

Asset management involves all of the processes that are involved in ensuring that an organization's assets, including physical, financial, and information-based assets, are managed in a structured manner. This way, the organization can make good business decisions because management is well aware of current assets and how they can be applied to current and future business needs.

Asset management involves several processes, including

▶ Planning the need for future assets

▶ Acquiring assets

▶ Operating the assets

▶ Maintaining the assets

▶ Securing the assets

▶ Disposing of the assets when no longer needed

Configuration Management Database (CMDB)

In a large organization, asset management can be a complex and complicated undertaking. To aid an organization, a Configuration Management Database (CMDB) is often employed. CMDB software not only stores data about assets but also provides insights or visibility into assets that the organization owns.

One challenge of cloud computing is that cloud assets are much more dynamic than traditional assets. For example, if you purchase a server for your data center (a traditional asset), this is a fairly easy asset to catalog in a CMDB. But a similar cloud-based resource would be a virtual machine, which could be deactivated and destroyed (and quickly rebuilt) at a moment's notice. As a result, a CMDB that manages cloud assets should have the capability to automatically catalog assets based on actions taken within the cloud environment.

Patching

Patching is the process of applying changes to software to resolve known problems. This section will cover several different types of patches that may be applied. Note that patching is also covered in the "Security Patches" section of Chapter 9, "Security Requirements," and the "Patching Failure" section in Chapter 24.

Features or Enhancements

While many patches are designed to fix an issue with a product, some patches are designed to provide additional features or enhancements to the software.

The addition of these features is typically performed in a full product upgrade, but in some cases a new feature may be requested by a customer and it needs to be implemented before the next upgrade cycle.

Fixes for Broken or Critical Infrastructure or Applications

One of the more common reasons a patch is deployed is to fix a problem in the product. Typically, this is referred to as a *bug fix*, and it is meant to be a temporary fix until the next update of the product.

Scope of Cloud Elements to Be Patched

Because cloud resources are often interrelated, a patch to one resource often requires patches to other resources. The scope of the cloud elements to be patched includes all of the cloud resources that need to be patched to successfully deploy changes.

Hypervisors

If you are working with a public cloud vendor, the vendor is responsible for maintaining patches for the hypervisor software. These patches may be applied without your knowledge, but if the patches can have an effect on your organization's virtual machines or provide additional features that you can utilize within your virtual machines, the vendor will often inform you about these patches.

If your virtual machines reside in a private cloud within your organization's data center, your organization is responsible for applying patches in a timely manner to the hypervisor software. Applying patches can be tricky because it is certainly possible that a hypervisor patch may cause problems with the virtual machines running on that hypervisor. You should consider performing tests before deploying patches on production systems. Consider following some of the principles discussed in the "Upgrade Methods" section later in this chapter, including deploying a blue-green deployment structure.

Virtual Machines (VMs)

Keep in mind that a VM is a virtual instance of an operating system on a hypervisor. Patching VMs in the cloud can pose challenges because the cloud environment doesn't typically include the means to patch operating systems. Patching the OS is almost always the responsibility of the cloud customer.

OS patches come from the OS developer, and there is typically a central location where you can learn about new patches. There are also automation tools that can be used to make the process of patching a large number of systems easier.

Also see the "Automation Activities" section in Chapter 19, "Automation and Orchestration Techniques," as well as the "Applications" section in this chapter.

Virtual Appliances

A *virtual appliance* is a type of virtual machine image. The difference between a virtual appliance and a standard virtual machine is that the virtual appliance has been preconfigured to perform a specific task (or set of tasks). This makes the process of patching more difficult because both the operating system and the applications of the virtual appliance will require patches on a regular basis.

Some vendors who create virtual appliances also provide patches for the appliance, but this isn't always the case.

Networking Components

When an organization uses a cloud vendor to deploy its cloud infrastructure, the networking components (routers, switches, and so on) are entirely the responsibility of the cloud vendor. If, however, your organization is implementing a private cloud on-premises, patching the network components is the responsibility of your organization.

Modern network components are complex and typically include a full operating system. As with any OS, the vendor who created the network component will release occasional patches. Typically, these vendors will have patch release announcements and may even have a regular patch release cycle.

Applications

In terms of patching applications, the scope will depend on the origin of the application as well as the responsibility level associated with the application. For example, if you are using a Software as a Service (SAAS) application, the cloud vendor or the application developer is 100 percent responsible for patching the application. It is important to review the service-level agreement (SLA) and other contracts to verify which organization is responsible for patching.

If the application is not SAAS, it will likely be the cloud customer's responsibility to patch (see "Cloud Shared Responsibility Model" in Chapter 1, "Different

Types of Cloud Models," for further details). This patch may be performed manually or via an automation tool.

Storage Components

A *storage component* is an underlying device where data is stored. It can include a magnetic hard drive, a solid-state drive, or a tape device. In terms of patching, the devices themselves may require occasional firmware updates (see the "Firmware" section next). Additionally, the software used by an operating system to access the storage device (called a *device driver*) may also need to be patched occasionally.

Firmware

Firmware is software that is designed to provide control over device hardware. In a public cloud, customers rarely have any control over the firmware that is being utilized by the physical hardware (exceptions can include when a customer leases the entire physical system for their use). As a result, the patching of firmware in a public cloud is almost always fully in the scope of the cloud vendor.

In a private cloud environment, where the control of the physical systems is in the hands of the organization using the private cloud, firmware is the responsibility of the organization.

Software

The terms *application* and *software* are often mistakenly used interchangeably, but these terms are not synonymous. An application is a type of software, but software encompasses all types of code that are executed on a system. Often to distinguish between application software and other types of software, the term *systems software* is used.

In terms of the scope of software patching in a cloud environment, systems software and application software are similar. The biggest difference is that application software is more often SAAS, and the patching falls under the responsibility of the cloud vendor or the application developer. Systems software is more often not SAAS and it is the responsibility of the cloud customer to ensure the software is properly patched.

Operating System (OS)

See the "Virtual Machines (VMs)" section earlier in this chapter.

Policies

Just because a patch is released doesn't mean that it should be immediately applied. Patches are often temporary fixes and may cause more problems than they fix. Some patches are also minor and unnecessary, at least in terms of the business goals of your organization.

Your organization should have policies on which patches to apply and how they should be applied. For example, you might have a policy that patches are first deployed in a testing environment and tests are performed before releasing in a development environment.

You should also consider which versions of software you wish to deploy. Some organizations opt to have the latest version installed, whereas others tend to stay one version behind. See the following "N-1" section for more details.

N-1

For the term *N-1*, *N* refers to the most recent stable release of software, whereas *N-1* refers to the previous most recent stable release of the software. There are advantages and disadvantages to always upgrading to the latest release versus staying one release behind the most current release, including:

▶ **Features:** The N release typically has newer features that the N-1 release does not.

▶ **Compatibility:** The N-1 release tends to be more compatible with other existing or older software, whereas the N release might work better if you have updated other related software.

▶ **Security:** The N-1 release tends to require less security patching than the N release because the code is more mature and more of the bugs have been worked out.

Rollbacks

A *rollback* is a method of undoing the steps taken during a patch. In some cases a patch may not permit a rollback. In these situations you should make sure you test the patch in a testing environment and make sure you back up all related data before patching a live system. You should also have another plan in place to recover the software, which could include performing a full backup on all software before implementing the patch.

Impacts of Process Improvements on Systems

For organizations to grow, meet new demand, and keep pace with competitors, they implement process improvement methods. *Process improvement* is a business practice in which an organization's business process is reviewed and analyzed to discover changes that would result in better performance, improved customer experience, reduced costs, and other results that would benefit the organization.

Process Improvement can have an effect on cloud systems in several different areas, including

▶ Changes in policies that can affect the accessibility, security, and performance of cloud resources.

▶ Changes in which cloud resources are used within an organization. This can be a minor change (switching from one software to another) or major (changing cloud vendors).

Upgrade Methods

In this section you will learn different upgrade methods that your organization may incorporate when upgrading resources in the cloud.

Rolling Upgrades

Rolling upgrades (also called *continuous delivery*) is the process of frequently providing updates to software. With this upgrade method, there are no specific release points (although it is common for rolling upgrades to happen nightly), but rather when the developer is ready, a new upgrade is released.

One advantage of a rolling upgrade is that new features are more rapidly released to customers. However, rolling upgrades may be more susceptible to bugs.

Most developers that provide rolling upgrades also provide traditional "release point" upgrades. For example, the popular Firefox web browser provides a nightly rolling upgrade but also provides regular standard releases.

Blue-Green

See "Blue-Green" in Chapter 4, "Solution Design in Support of the Business Requirements."

Canary

See "Canary" in Chapter 7, "OS and Application Security Controls."

Active-Passive

An active-passive upgrade is similar to a blue-green upgrade. With an *active-passive* upgrade, the upgrade is deployed to the active environment, and the passive environment is not changed.

If any problems occur in the active environment because of the patching, the passive environment is treated temporarily as the active environment. When the problems are worked out in the original active environment, the original passive environment is again treated as passive, and the original active environment is used again as the actual active environment.

If, after testing and a specific period of time, the active environment seems to be functioning properly, the patch is applied to the passive environment.

This upgrade is different from a blue-green upgrade system in which the two systems "flip-flop" between upgrades as active and passive.

Development/QA/Production/DR

You may have several similar environments that will have upgrades applied to them at different times. For example, instead of relying on a single deployment of a web server, you will likely want to have multiple deployments, each with a specific purpose. These deployments include the following:

▶ **Development environment:** You create or test new code for the software here.

▶ **Quality assurance (QA) environment:** This environment must mirror your production environment as closely as possible. You use this environment to test upgrade procedures before deploying them on a production environment.

▶ **Production environment:** In this environment customers use the software.

▶ **Disaster recovery (DR) environment:** This environment is very close to the production environment. If the production environment is not available for some reason, the DR environment should be able to take over the role of the production environment.

Dashboard and Reporting

A *dashboard* is a web-based infographic that provides you with insights into your cloud environment. The graphics can include charts, graphs, or text that displays information about the current status of cloud resources and components or information over a period of time. Figure 17.1 provides an example of some of the types of data representations you could place on a dashboard.

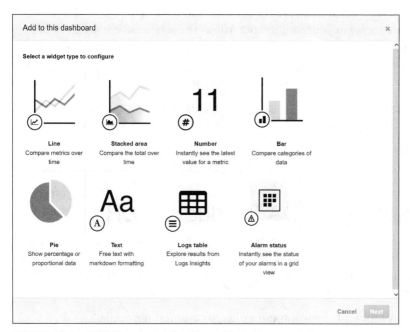

FIGURE 17.1   AWS Cloudwatch Dashboard Data Representations

Note that in addition to dashboards, most cloud vendors provide other reporting methods, including the following:

▶ **Alarms or alerts:** A method to proactively warn you about a possible problem. See "Alerting" in Chapter 16, "Logging, Monitoring, and Alerting," for more details.

▶ **Logs:** A place where you can see details about events that took place in your cloud environment. See "Logging" in Chapter 16 for more details.

▶ **Metrics:** Methods of looking at data results over a period of time with the goal to determine a course of action to take. For example, web server statistics can show that there is a spike in traffic every three months when your organization launches a new version of a popular product. You could use this information to proactively scale up your web servers 12 hours before the press release that announces the new version and then scale down the web servers 48 hours later.

In this section you will learn about different features of dashboards and the data that can be reported.

Tagging

Tags are metadata that can be applied to resources. For example, you could have a tag called "department" that can be set to values like "sales," "development," or "production."

Tags are useful for reporting because you can create reporting rules like "Show me all of the virtual machines that have a value of 'sales' for the tag named 'department.'" This information is critical when you need insights into which department, project, or individual is responsible for resources (and how much that is costing your organization).

See "Tagging" in Chapter 16 for more details regarding this topic.

Costs

Using the cloud can result in lowering your organization's operating costs, but if you aren't careful regarding how your resources are utilized (and how many resources there are), a cloud environment may end up costing your organization a lot of money. There are horror stories of organizations that were not aware of active resources and were hit with a large charge when their end-of-month bill arrived.

Reviewing a dashboard daily that shows the current costs incurred for the month can greatly reduce the chance of a large surprise bill at the end of the month. Most cloud vendors also make it easy to set alerts if your current costs exceed an amount.

Chargebacks

Imagine you have a large organization with different departments, each of which is financially responsible for its own resource utilization within your cloud infrastructure. Although you could have separate cloud accounts for each department and have the cloud vendor bill each individual department, there are some reasons why this is a bad choice, including

▶ **Higher overall costs:** Most cloud vendors will reduce costs the higher your volume of utilization is. In other words, a single account (or multiple accounts grouped together for billing purposes) with 1,000 virtual machines would pay less overall than 15 separate accounts with a total of 1,000 virtual machines.

▶ **Less visibility:** Even if each department is financially responsible for cloud resources, your IT department still needs to be able to see what is going on in the organization in terms of cloud utilization.

▶ **Less control:** IT departments want to provide standard controls (such as availability and security) across the entire organization. Having multiple separate cloud accounts makes this very difficult.

As a result of these drawbacks, most organizations will either have a single cloud account or group together accounts under one billing account. To handle the financial responsibility of each department, the IT department can use a system called a *chargeback* in which it internally bills each of the other departments.

Showbacks

Review the preceding "Chargeback" section to understand that concept first. Now suppose an IT department wants the advantages of a single billing account that incorporates several department cloud accounts, but corporate policy doesn't allow for chargebacks. In this case the IT department will likely utilize a *showback*, which makes resource utilization and costs for each department visible but does not result in an actual charge to the department.

Elasticity Usage

In cloud computing, the term *elasticity* refers to the ability to increase resource capability (scale up) or decrease resource capability (scale down) according to demand.

For example, consider an application that accepts point-of-sale data (credit card charges), validates the data, and then sends data to a database. The store where this data is coming from is open from 8 a.m. to 8 p.m. each day, and there is an increase in sales from 5 p.m. to 7 p.m. Additionally, the store has big sales on holidays and a monthly sale on the 15th of every month.

As a result, this application requires little to no compute capacity during the hours of 8 p.m. to 8 a.m. It needs normal compute capacity from 8 a.m. to 5 p.m. and increased capacity from 5 p.m. to 8 p.m., on holidays, and on the 15th of each month. This is a generalization, of course, and the required capacity can vary greatly based on new product lines, when customers receive their own paychecks, and other factors.

The best solution therefore might be to schedule compute capacity based on the hours of the sales and the previously mentioned factors, but also to monitor the activity on the server and have the compute capacity automatically scale up or down as required. You can also take a look at the metrics over time to determine how often the capacity scales (the elasticity usage) to better determine normal versus high-volume capacity needs.

Connectivity

Imagine you have a critical cloud resource, like a database, that needs to always be available. How would you know if the resource was no longer responding? You could rely on the feedback from users, but that approach isn't ideal because user feedback often takes time to reach the correct people. Ideally, you would monitor connectivity to key systems by using a dashboard or an alerting system.

Latency

Network *latency* is a measurement of how long it takes for a network packet to travel from the sender to the receiver. Large latency values have a major impact on the performance of services, as well as the user experience.

Because of the impacts of latency, having an easy way to discover latency issues is important. Some cloud vendors allow you to monitor latency and display this information on dashboards.

For more information regarding latency, see "Latency" in Chapter 18, "Optimize Cloud Environments."

Capacity

Capacity refers to the amount of availability of a specific resource, such as network bandwidth, storage space, or compute power. Monitoring capacity is one of the more common features of dashboards.

Incidents

Another feature often found on dashboards is incidents. *Incidents* are like alerts that indicate when an action has taken place.

Health

A health dashboard will provide you with an idea of if there are any issues for resources or services. Cloud vendors typically provide a health dashboard that indicates how the vendor's services are functioning, like AWS's Service Health Dashboard shown in Figure 17.2.

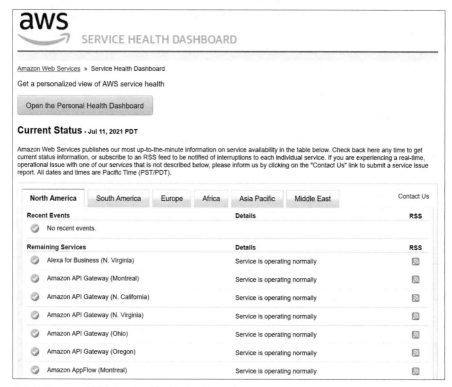

FIGURE 17.2   AWS Service Health Dashboard

Cloud vendors also provide a health dashboard that is specific to your organization's cloud account, like AWS's Personal Health Dashboard shown in Figure 17.3.

FIGURE 17.3   **AWS Personal Health Dashboard**

Overall Utilization

Overall utilization is a "big picture" visualization found on dashboards. This information gives you an idea of how a resource or service is being used and how to plan for future utilization patterns based on current patterns.

Availability

See the "Availability" section in Chapter 16.

CramQuiz

Answer these questions. The answers follow the last question. If you cannot answer these questions correctly, consider reading this section again until you can.

1. Which roadmap is used to define the overall high-level actions that must take place to meet the goals of the product during its lifecycle?

    ○ **A.** Strategy

    ○ **B.** Portfolio

    ○ **C.** Release

    ○ **D.** Features

2. Asset _____ involves all of the processes that are involved in ensuring that an organization's assets, including physical assets, financial assets, and information-based assets, are managed in a structured manner.

- ○ **A.** Management
- ○ **B.** Control
- ○ **C.** Tagging
- ○ **D.** Inventory

3. Which of the following systems would typically be the responsibility of the cloud vendor to patch? (Choose two.)

- ○ **A.** Virtual machines
- ○ **B.** Operating systems
- ○ **C.** Applications
- ○ **D.** Firmware

4. Which of the following is normally a cloud reporting method?

- ○ **A.** Alarms
- ○ **B.** Logs
- ○ **C.** Metrics
- ○ **D.** Transaction reports

CramQuiz Answers

1. Strategy
2. Management
3. Applications and firmware
4. Transaction reports

What Next?

If you want more practice on this chapter's exam objectives before you move on, remember that you can access all of the CramQuiz questions on the companion website. You can also create a custom exam by objectives with the practice exam software. Note any objectives you struggle with and go to that objective's material in this chapter.

## CHAPTER 18

Optimize Cloud Environments

This chapter covers the following official CompTIA Cloud+ exam objective:

▶ 4.3 Given a scenario, optimize cloud environments.

(For more information on the official CompTIA Cloud+ exam topics, see the Introduction.)

Cloud computing provides many benefits, but a cloud environment that isn't optimized may come at a heavy cost...literally. Cloud resources and networks that aren't optimized can result in higher cloud usage costs, unresponsive systems, and frustrated users.

In this chapter you will learn about optimizing resources in a cloud environment. This will include optimizing computer, storage, and network resources.

CramSaver

If you can correctly answer these questions before going through this section, save time by skimming the ExamAlerts in this section and then completing the CramQuiz at the end of the section.

1. The concept of right-sizing is to best ensure that your instances are using the proper amount of _____.

2. _____ is a numeric value that represents how much data can be transferred across a network within a specific period of time.

3. Jumbo packets change the size of the network _____.

4. _____ is a data center type in which a vendor provides equipment and space to an organization.

Answers

1. Resources
2. Bandwidth
3. Payload
4. Colocation

Right-sizing

The concept of *right-sizing* is to best ensure that your instances are using an ideal amount of resources. For example, if you provision a virtual machine with a massive amount of RAM, but the virtual machine only ever uses a small amount of that RAM, this will result in a higher charge than needed (wasted money). Conversely, if you provision a virtual machine with a small amount of RAM, less than is needed by the virtual machine, applications on the virtual machine may not execute correctly. In both these cases, the size of memory used is not the right or appropriate amount.

Right-sizing is discussed in more detail in the "Scalability" section in Chapter 3, "High Availability and Scaling in Cloud Environments," along with the following sections:

▶ "Auto-scaling"

▶ "Horizontal Scaling"

▶ "Vertical Scaling"

▶ "Cloud Bursting"

Compute and Storage

The compute and storage topics were described in previous chapters. For the information pertaining to them, see the following locations:

▶ **Compute**

▶ **CPUs:** See the "Central Processing Unit (CPU)/Virtual CPU (vCPU)" section in Chapter 14, "Compute Sizing for a Deployment."

▶ **GPUs:** See the "Graphics Processing Unit (GPU)" section in Chapter 14.

▶ **Memory:** See the "Memory" section in Chapter 14.

▶ **Containers:** See the "Containers" section in Chapter 11, "Integrate Components into a Cloud Solution," and the "Containers" section in Chapter 3.

▶ **Storage**

  ▶ **Tiers:** See the "Tiers" section in Chapter 12, "Storage in Cloud Environments."

  ▶ **IOPS:** See the "Input/Output Operations per Second (IOPS) and Read/Write" section in Chapter 12.

  ▶ **Deduplication:** See the "Deduplication" section in Chapter 12, "Storage in Cloud Environments."

  ▶ **Compression:** See the "Compression" section in Chapter 12.

Network

In any IT infrastructure, the performance of the network is a critical component of ensuring smooth operations. Given the nature of cloud computing, network optimization becomes ever more critical. An organization's cloud resources are not just accessed through the network but are located in a network that isn't entirely within the organization's control.

In this section you will learn about several key components of a cloud network that may be optimized to provide better performance.

Bandwidth

Optimizing network bandwidth is a vast topic. *Bandwidth* is a numeric value that represents how much data can be transferred across a network within a specific period of time. Typically, this value is given in bits per second (or megabytes per second or gigabits per second).

In cloud computing, the bandwidth may be associated with a virtual private cloud (VPC) or with a specific resource. For example, when you create a relational database in AWS, you choose an instance type that includes a defined bandwidth value, as you can see in the Network Performance (Gbps) column in Figure 18.1.

Model	Core Count	vCPU*	CPU Credits/hour	Memory (GiB)	Network Performance (Gbps)
db.t3.micro	1	2	12	1	Up to 5
db.t3.small	1	2	24	2	Up to 5
db.t3.medium	1	2	24	4	Up to 5
db.t3.large	1	2	36	8	Up to 5
db.t3.xlarge	2	4	96	16	Up to 5
db.t3.2xlarge	4	8	192	32	Up to 5

FIGURE 18.1   AWS Database Instance Bandwidth

Optimizing bandwidth includes developing a good understanding of your bandwidth requirements as well as employing techniques to maximize available bandwidth. To understand your bandwidth requirements, you make use of monitoring tools and metrics to develop a baseline of the bandwidth your network or resources require. Because the CompTIA Cloud+ certification is vendor neutral and these tools are often vendor specific, details regarding these tools are not covered in this book. However, you should realize that all cloud vendors provide monitoring tools, and there are third-party tools available as well from the ISV marketplace.

Developing a bandwidth baseline takes time. Metrics are collected over a specific period of time and analyzed to determine how much bandwidth is required for the various IaaS, PaaS, or SaaS applications. As demand grows, the required bandwidth may also increase, so employing monitoring tools and reviewing metrics is an ongoing process.

After you have determined your bandwidth needs, you could just make sure that your cloud network or resource has the necessary bandwidth. However, while this approach might be rightsizing the network in its current form, it isn't really an optimized network, which means you could be paying for more bandwidth than is really required. There are techniques you can use to reduce the need for bandwidth, including the following:

▶ **Optimize the flow of the traffic:** With this technique you are seeking methods of limiting how much network traffic occurs within your cloud network. For example, if you have a database that is heavily used by a web server, placing these two resources within the same subnet, rather than on separate subnets, will limit the traffic on your overall network.

▶ **Utilize network shaping:** By prioritizing network traffic, you can ensure that more important network traffic is not impacted by traffic volume.

One method is to use bandwidth throttling, where network access for specific resources is limited.

► **Use load balancing:** By placing collections of servers on different network segments or subnets, you can use load balancers to spread out the traffic between different networks, limiting the bandwidth usage on any specific network.

► **Schedule updates during off-peak hours:** Updates often require bandwidth to download the updates from the Internet or internal update servers to the servers in the VPC/VNet. In some cases, especially if you have multiple resources, the amount of bandwidth used can have an impact on network performance. For resources that you are responsible for updating, schedule the updates to occur when network traffic is typically low. You can determine this period by using the metrics that your network monitoring tools have generated.

Network Interface Controllers (NICs)

Physical network interface controllers have a wide range of parameters that can be configured to optimize how the NICs send data across the network. While there are parameters that are common to most NICs, individual vendors will sometimes also have parameters that are specific to those vendors' NICs. As an example of some common optimization parameters, consider the following:

► **Jumbo packets:** These packets change the size of the network payload. Changing the payload size provides better performance in networks that have massive chunks of data being transported.

► **Receive buffers:** These buffers use memory to store incoming network packets, limiting the chances of dropped packets (which could result in having the packets resent on the network, increasing the load on the network).

While knowing that you can modify NIC settings to improve performance, there are a few things you should consider:

► In some cases, such as jumbo packets, the NICs for all of the devices in the network, including the router, need to be customized. For example, the maximum transmission unit (MTU) value would need to be adjusted.

► Changing NIC parameters can have the opposite effect than what is intended. For example, jumbo packets may increase bandwidth utilization in a network in which the payload of the packets is small. Using monitoring tools and metrics is important to determine the effect of changing these parameters.

▶ A change in a parameter that is designed to optimize network utilization may adversely affect another component of the network (such as security).

▶ In a cloud environment, you often don't have access to NIC parameters because the cloud vendor provides a virtual NIC (or vNIC), not a physical NIC, to your instances. Some vNICs do have optimization parameters, but they may be different from the standard NIC parameters.

For more information about vNICs, see the "Virtual Network Interface Controller (vNIC)" section in Chapter 13, "Cloud Networking Solutions."

Latency

Network latency is a measurement of how long it takes for a network packet to travel from the source to the destination. Higher latency values have a major impact on the performance of services, as well as the user experience. There are several components of network latency, including:

▶ **Transmission delay:** A delay on the sender's side before the packet is sent across the network.

▶ **Processing delay:** A delay on the receiver's side. When the packet arrives, before it is sent to the system, it needs to be processed (checked for errors, determine the destination port, and so on).

▶ **Queuing delay:** After processing, the packet is sent to a queue until the system is ready to use the packet. A large queue can result in an increase in latency.

Because the cause of latency can be on the sender or receiver side (and any system/router in between the two), reducing network latency can be a daunting task. In cloud computing the most common methods deployed to limit latency include the following:

▶ **Employ Multiprotocol Label Switching (MPLS):** Using MPLS provides for a more optimized routing method.

▶ **Use a directly connected network:** Most cloud vendors provide a directly connected network (at a cost, of course) in which private networks are connected directly to the cloud infrastructure. This dedicated network naturally results in less latency but may also be customized to reduce latency even further.

▶ **Utilize edge computing:** See the "Edge Computing" section later in this chapter.

Software-Defined Networks (SDNs)

Historically, networks consisted of physical devices (routers, switches, firewalls, and so on) with proprietary software that performed the necessary tasks. The use of proprietary network devices resulted in several limitations that software-defined networking, or SDN, is designed to overcome or mitigate.

The primary purpose of these networking devices is to forward (or not forward, depending on the rules of the device) data packets from one network to another. To perform these tasks, a network administrator needs to manage the devices, often having to use custom proprietary commands run directly on the network device. SDN decouples the network management operations (control plane) from the network forwarding (data plane), which provides several advantages, including:

▶ **Centralized network management:** SDN provides the means to use a single system to manage a collection of network devices, rather than having the management coupled with each individual network device.

▶ **Lower costs:** SDN offers open and decoupled systems that can operate with third-party software without requiring any high-cost proprietary connectors. APIs and SDKs can be used to develop integration capabilities. SDN devices can be offered as cloud-based services.

▶ **Agility:** One of the challenges of legacy network devices is that a change in the network structure resulted in having to modify one or more of the network devices (sometimes by manually logging in to the device and executing a command). SDN makes these changes easier and, in many cases, automatic.

Additional advantages of SDN include a more holistic approach to managing the network, more granular security, fewer hardware expenditures, and more consistency.

Edge Computing

Consider a scenario in which a software program (the client) gathers some data and then sends the data to a cloud-based resource for processing. After processing, the data is returned to the software program. Depending on the location of the cloud-based resource, this method of processing the data can delay how long it takes for the client to receive the processed results (that is, increasing latency). *Edge computing* is a method that limits latency in scenarios like this by moving the computing process closer to the client.

CDN

See the "Content Delivery Network (CDN)" section in Chapter 13.

Placement

The placement of cloud resources can have a big impact on how optimized your cloud infrastructure is. In this section you will learn about the four components of resource placement: geographical, cluster placement, redundancy, and colocation.

Geographical

The geographic location of your cloud resources is important because resources that are close to your users will result in less latency and a better user experience. This concept was already covered in detail in the following sections:

▶ The "Edge Computing" section in this chapter

▶ The "Content Delivery Network (CDN)" section in Chapter 13

▶ The "Regions and Zones" section in Chapter 3

Cluster Placement

In a cloud environment, a *cluster* is two or more resources that provide the same functionality. These resources run in parallel, providing several benefits, including the following:

▶ **Redundancy:** In the event that one resource becomes unavailable, the other resource or resources can still provide the service to the client.

▶ **High availability:** A single resource may become bogged down with client requests. By having a cluster of resources, the service is more available.

▶ **Resilience:** Because there are multiple resources, a cluster can be designed to recover in the event of a failure quicker than a single resource.

The resources in a cluster should be placed geographically close to each other (at least within the same zone). Clustered resources normally need to either communicate with each other or communicate with a shared resource (like a database), and keeping the cluster in the same geographic area limits latency. However, to gain the benefit of redundancy, you should not put clusters on the same physical system or network because an outage that affects that system or network might mean the entire cluster becomes unavailable.

Redundancy

Redundancy is the condition that exists when one or more systems can be used to replace a failed system. There are many areas in cloud computing in which redundancy is utilized. For example, think of hardware redundancy, like the RAID devices covered in Chapter 12. Other cloud-based systems that often employ redundancy include databases, web servers, and even entire networks.

Colocation

If your organization decides to deploy a private cloud infrastructure, one challenge that it will face is providing resources in different geographic locations. Larger organizations may have offices with data centers in different parts of the world, but smaller organizations are less likely to have remote data centers readily available.

Colocation is a data center type in which a vendor provides equipment and space to an organization. The data center is often shared with other organizations, reducing the overall cost without having to have the organization pay up front for capital expenses.

Device Drivers and Firmware

Although a large percentage of the CompTIA Cloud+ certification exam focuses on public cloud solutions, some topics are more related to private cloud infrastructures. For example, in a public cloud, customers rarely have any control over the device drivers or firmware that is being utilized by the physical hardware (exceptions can include when customers lease the entire physical system for their use). In a private cloud environment, where the control of the physical systems is in the hands of the organization using the private cloud, device drivers and firmware become more relevant.

This section will provide a short introduction to the concepts of device drivers and firmware. Actual optimization techniques will vary greatly depending on which device drivers (and devices themselves) and firmware are used. The focus of the CompTIA exam is the difference between generic, vendor, and open-source device drivers and firmware.

It is important to first understand the difference between a device driver and firmware. *Firmware* is software that runs on the device itself in the chip or hardware platform rather than on an operating system. For example, consider firmware on a BIOS in a PC.

A *device driver* is software that runs on the operating system and enables the operating system to communicate with the device for which the device driver was designed. For example, think of a device driver for a sound card installed in a PC.

Generic

A generic device driver or firmware is software that isn't written for a specific device, but rather for a class of devices. For example, there are generic device drivers for network cards.

An alternative to generic device drivers and firmware, including why you might use generic software versus vendor software, is explained in the next section.

Vendor

Vendor device drivers and firmware, also known as original equipment manufacturer (OEM) device drivers and firmware, are software programs written by the vendor that manufactures the hardware device. Typically, these software programs are more ideal than generic software because they provide specific features for the hardware and are typically more closely integrated with the functionality of the hardware.

There are a few reasons to consider a generic device driver or firmware over a vendor-provided device driver or firmware:

▶ It is possible that the vendor may lock or disable a feature on the device that might be unlocked with generic software.

▶ Vendor software is normally *closed source*, which means you can't view the source code. You may consider an open-source generic driver. More detail on open source is provided in the next section.

Open Source

Software developers write code (called *source code*), which is then converted into the code that is executed by the hardware during a process called *compiling*. *Open-source software* is any software in which you are able to view the original source code. *Closed-source software* is any software in which you can't see the source code. For example, Linux comes in open-source and closed-source formats. RedHat Linux is an example of a commercial and closed-source OS, whereas SUSE Linux is an open-source OS.

There are some advantages to open-source software, including:

▶ By being able to see the code, you can be well aware of the actions that the software takes. You are able to discover suspect code that may cause errors or create security concerns.

▶ In many cases, the organization that created the open-source code grants you the ability to modify the code to suit your needs. Note that this is a license feature and not a requirement of open-source software.

There are some disadvantages to open-source software, including:

▶ Some open-source software is not supported by a specific organization. Support and documentation are often community-based.

▶ Open-source software may include components that may not be as fully tested as some paid, closed-source software programs.

CramQuiz

Answer these questions. The answers follow the last question. If you cannot answer these questions correctly, consider reading this section again until you can.

1. Which of the following is not considered a method of maximizing bandwidth?

○ **A.** Optimize the flow of the traffic.

○ **B.** Utilize network shaping.

○ **C.** Disable network access during off-peak hours.

○ **D.** Use load balancing.

2. Network _____ is a measurement of how long it takes for a network packet to travel from the sender to the receiver.

- ○ **A.** Bandwidth
- ○ **B.** Latency
- ○ **C.** Optional throughout
- ○ **D.** None of these answers are correct

3. Which of the following is used to optimize routing?

- ○ **A.** Edge computing
- ○ **B.** Direct connect network
- ○ **C.** MPLS
- ○ **D.** SDN

CramQuiz Answers

1. Disable network access during off-peak hours
2. Latency
3. MPLS

What Next?

If you want more practice on this chapter's exam objectives before you move on, remember that you can access all of the CramQuiz questions on the companion website. You can also create a custom exam by objectives with the practice exam software. Note any objectives you struggle with and go to that objective's material in this chapter.

CHAPTER 19

Automation and Orchestration Techniques

This chapter covers the following official CompTIA Cloud+ exam objective:

▶ 4.4 Given a scenario, apply proper automation and orchestration techniques.

(For more information on the official CompTIA Cloud+ exam topics, see the Introduction.)

As you continue your journey into learning about the cloud, you will discover that the process of automation is often critical to the success of any organization that uses cloud resources. In fact, automation is often one of the main reasons that organizations choose to migrate to the cloud. Automation enables tasks and processes to occur without the need of any human interaction. Automation speeds up the provisioning of instances, prevents human input errors, and reduces the cost of deploying a solution or product.

In this chapter you will learn about some key automation topics, including Infrastructure as Code (IaC), configuration management, and orchestration scripting. You will also explore continuous integration/continuous deployment (CI/CD) and secure scripting.

Cramsaver

If you can correctly answer these questions before going through this section, save time by skimming the ExamAlerts in this section and then completing the CramQuiz at the end of the section.

1. What are the two different approaches to IaC?

2. True or false: Continuous deployment is a process that extends continuous integration to deploy new releases as they are made available on the main branch.

3. In version control, what is the process of creating a new development branch called?

4. In configuration management, the _____ is the configuration file that is used to configure the instance.

Answers

1. Declarative and imperative/procedural

2. True

3. Checkout

4. Playbook

Infrastructure as Code (IaC)

Imagine a scenario in which your manager tells you that you need to deploy some virtual machines (VMs) in your organization's cloud infrastructure so that the organization's developers have a testing platform for the code they are writing. Initially, the developers will need 100 virtual machines, all of which have similar components, but some components in each virtual machine need to be different (such as user accounts, passwords, software installation, and storage space size).

You are also informed that as the project progresses, the developers will need additional virtual machines, again all similar to one another but with a few customizations. You start to realize that just creating these virtual machines might become a full-time task. In addition to the time it will take to manually configure each virtual machine, you are concerned that you might make mistakes along the way, resulting in misconfigured systems that will cause headaches for the developers. Fortunately for you, there is a better solution.

Infrastructure as Code (IAC) is a process in which you can use configuration files or scripts to deploy and manage systems, including virtual machines and containers. Many public cloud vendors provide a native IaC solution. There are third-party IaC solutions as well.

Note

There may be some confusion over the differences between Infrastructure as Code, configuration management, and orchestration. In fact, the lines that separate these three concepts are often blurred. Review the "Configuration Management" and "Orchestration Sequencing" sections in this chapter for more details.

Infrastructure Components and Their Integration

There are generally two primary IaC approaches: declarative and imperative. For systems that use declarative IaC, the configuration file contains a collection of data that defines the components of a resource. For example, if you're creating a declarative IaC configuration file for an AWS S3 bucket that is created by AWS Cloud Formation, values like the type of resource and bucket name would be defined like the following:

```
S3Bucket:

  Type: AWS::S3::Bucket

  Properties:

  BucketName: mybucket
```

In an imperative approach you describe how the resource is to be created. For example, the AWS command-line interface (CLI) enables you to create code that defines a resource using the imperative approach, like the following example that defines an AWS S3 bucket:

```
$ BUCKET="mybucket"

$ if ! 'aws s3api list-buckets --query Buckets[*].Name |
grep $BUCKET > /dev/null'; then aws s3api create-bucket
--bucket $BUCKET; else echo "This bucket exists"; fi
```

In a nutshell, the preceding code defines a variable called BUCKET and sets the value of this variable to mybucket. Then it checks to see whether a bucket called mybucket already exists. If it does, an error message is displayed ("This bucket exists"). If the bucket doesn't exist, it will be created.

For the CompTIA Cloud+ certification exam, don't get too hung up on the specifics of the code. The important point to remember is that a *declarative approach* describes what resource to create without stating how to reach the end state, whereas the *imperative approach* describes how to create the resource with all steps to reach the end state.

Continuous Integration/Continuous Deployment (CI/CD)

Many software vendors utilize a traditional software release approach in which software is released at specific intervals. For example, an organization may have a yearly release cycle, so each year a new major release of the software occurs. During the year there might also be minor releases or bug fix releases, depending on potential flaws or security holes that are discovered in the software. The advantage of this method of releasing software is that normally the organization gets time to test the software before it is released, which should result in a more stable program/product. However, the disadvantage of this release method is that it can take up to a year before new features are released, which may allow competitors to capture more market share if their software is released more often.

Continuous integration (CI) and *continuous deployment (CD)* are two processes that, when combined, result in rapid and continuous release of software. The two terms are often confused, likely because the word *continuous* appears in both terms. The differences between the two are as follows:

▶ *Continuous integration* is a process followed by developers (typically software developers). A software program that uses a version control utility (see the "Version Control" section in this chapter) employs a main branch of development that is used when the software is released to customers. Developers don't work directly on the main branch, but rather on their own branch. When the continuous integration process is used, developers merge the changes in their branch back into the main branch as often as possible (not exactly continuously, but that is the goal), and the changes are validated through some automated testing process. This results in the main release branch being continuously validated and updated.

▶ Although continuous integration means the main branch of development is often updated, it doesn't mean that customers have access to these changes. *Continuous deployment* is a process that extends continuous integration to deploy new releases as they are made available on the main branch (after testing has occurred). A similar process, called *continuous delivery*, also is used to deploy new releases rapidly, but this process requires a human to approve the release.

Version Control

One of the biggest headaches that developers must deal with is different versions of source code. Sometimes you just need to "go back" to a previous version of code (or roll back to a previous stable release). Maintaining these versions manually can be cumbersome, error prone, and time-consuming.

Compounding the problem is that multiple programmers work together on a single piece of source code. A large program can have tens of thousands of lines of code with different programmers responsible for different portions of the code.

Version control software can handle the complicated task of maintaining different versions of source code. The most popular version control system used today is called Git. Git utilizes repositories to store the different versions of the files that the developers are generating. Typically, a "central" repository contains all of the changes that have been committed to the main project. Additionally, each developer has his or her own copy of this central repository stored locally on his or her own system.

Here are some key version control terms:

▶ **Clone:** To create a local repository from the central repository, a clone process is performed. This process results in all of the central repository being duplicated on the local system (including all branches).

▶ **Branch:** The main branch contains the most recent release version of the project. Each developer typically creates a separate branch, which is a duplicate of the main branch (or another branch) at the time the developer's branch was created. Additional branches may be made for specific reasons, such as for bug fixes or the need to develop a new feature.

▶ **Checkout:** To create a new branch, a developer uses a process called a *checkout*. This process will create a new branch, using the name provided by the developer. Typically, this new branch is a copy of the main branch at the time the new branch was created, but branches can be made from any other branch.

▶ **Merge:** A merge is the process of combining changes made to a file in one branch with a different version of the same file in another branch. In some cases a merge may be performed automatically, but if there are complex differences between the two versions of the file, a human may need to manually perform the merge.

Configuration Management

To understand configuration management, consider the topic of Infrastructure as Code. The purpose of IaC is to use computer-readable configuration files, in conjunction with an IaC tool, to deploy an instance, like a virtual machine or storage device.

Configuration management is a slightly different process in which existing instances are modified, often based on a computer-readable configuration file in conjunction with a configuration management tool. For example, configuration management may be used to create a user account, install software, or modify the network settings on a virtual machine.

Popular configuration management tools include Chef, Puppet, Ansible, and SaltStack. Most major cloud vendors also provide their own configuration management tools.

It is important to note that configuration management and IaC perform similar operations, and many tools will act as both an IaC and a configuration management tool.

> **Note**
>
> There may be some confusion over the differences between Infrastructure as Code, configuration management, and orchestration. In fact, the lines that separate these three concepts are often blurred. Review the "Infrastructure as Code" and "Orchestration Sequencing" sections in this chapter for more details.

Playbook

In configuration management, the *playbook* is the configuration file that is used to configure the cloud resource. As with IaC, some configuration management tools, like Chef and Ansible, employ a procedural playbook in which the playbook contains instructions on how to perform the tasks needed to configure the instance. Other configuration management tools, like Puppet and SaltStack, use a declarative style that describes the desired end result.

Containers

See "Containers" in Chapter 11, "Integrate Components into a Cloud Solution," and "Secret Management" in Chapter 5, "Identity and Access Management."

Automation Activities

Automation is the process of performing tasks to achieve a desired outcome without requiring any human intervention. In cloud computing, automation is a crucial part of a successful deployment because many tasks must take place in a timely fashion, which isn't possible if they always need to be performed by a human.

You have already seen examples of automation in this chapter:

▶ During the continuous integration of CI/CD, the testing process that occurs during the merge is automated.

▶ During the continuous deployment of CI/CD, deployment happens automatically without the need for a human to start the task.

This section will cover some additional automation activities that are typically found in a cloud infrastructure.

Routine Operations

Many different types of routine operations can be automated in the cloud. For example, you could automate the process of creating resources as needed, like storage devices. Or you could automate the collection of metric data and have this data sent to a software tool that will analyze the data. Other routine operations could include the following:

▶ Backing up data of a critical system

▶ Automating changes to firewall rules

▶ Sending notifications of updates or system changes to users or customers

Updates

Consider a situation in which you have dozens (or even hundreds) of Linux virtual machines in your cloud infrastructure. Each of those operating systems needs to have updates applied routinely. Using an automation process, you could push out updates to all of the operating systems without needing any human interaction.

Scaling

See "Auto-scaling" in Chapter 3, "High Availability and Scaling in Cloud Environments."

Shutdowns

Having compute devices, like virtual machines and containers, running results in an expense to the organization. If you are aware of compute devices that don't need to be running during specific periods of time (like the weekends), you can automate the shutdown of these instances to save the organization money.

Restarts

There are sometimes reasons to restart a compute device. For example, if you install a new kernel on a Linux-based virtual machine, the operating system requires a reboot for the new kernel to take effect. If you have automated the process of updating your organization's Linux virtual machines, you will likely want to also automate the restart process when the updates include a new version of the kernel.

Create Internal APIs

An *application programming interface (API)* is a method to allow two applications to communicate. A client application sends an API request across the network, and the server performs operations based on this client request. Many of the systems that you communicate with use APIs to perform tasks (even if you are not aware that APIs are being used).

APIs can be created automatically on the server side by using automation tools. This capability is important when new servers are created automatically, such as through a scaling process.

Secure Scripting

One of the challenges in working with automation is that you will often be creating scripts (programs) to perform automation, configuration, and orchestration tasks. These scripts may end up being standard language scripts, like Python, or scripts that are specific to a cloud vendor.

This section will focus on some of the security concerns that you must consider when writing automation scripts.

No Hardcoded Passwords

Although automation scripts don't require humans to run, they will likely be executed by users who didn't create the script for either testing purposes or in situations in which they want to manually start a process. For example, if you have an automation script that starts a virtual machine, users may want to use that script to create a virtual machine for their own purposes.

Typically, these users will need to be able to view the script to execute it. For this reason, the script should never contain any passwords. The script uses these passwords to gain elevated privileges (see the following "Use of Individual Service Accounts" section), and if a user is able to see the password, that user may be able to gain this elevated privilege manually and perform unauthorized actions.

Instead of hardcoding passwords, consider using a password vault or key-based authentication. See the following "Password Vaults" and "Key-Based Authentication" sections for more details.

Use of Individual Service Accounts

When the script is executed, it should take on a service account (or service role) to perform its actions. This service account would have privileges that a regular user, like the user running the script, doesn't have.

Password Vaults

Because you don't want to store passwords within scripts, an alternative called a password vault can be used instead. With a password vault, a cloud-based service stores passwords (and other secrets, like keys) and provides them as needed to scripts or other processes. The script can be configured to ask the password vault to provide the password to authenticate and perform the required actions.

Also see the "Secret Management" section in Chapter 5.

Key-Based Authentication

See the "Public Key Infrastructure (PKI)" section in Chapter 5.

Orchestration Sequencing

Recall that Infrastructure as Code is the process of using a configuration file to deploy an instance. This process works well if you want to deploy a single instance (or a collection of similar instances) that are unrelated to other instances, but what if you need to deploy an entire system of instances that are related to one another?

For example, suppose you need to deploy a virtual machine that runs software that generates data. This software is then sent to a database, and the results are accessible via a website. This means you need to deploy three instances: a virtual machine, a database server, and a web server. In fact, you may need to deploy these instances in a specific order for the entire system to work correctly.

This process of deploying instances that relate to one another in a specific order is called *orchestration sequencing*. With orchestration, you can deploy that database server first, then gather information about it (like its IP address), and use that information to deploy the virtual machine so the VM sends information to the database. Then you can have the orchestration process deploy the web server and have the web server connect to the database to display the information.

Many IaC tools include orchestration sequencing, but some do not.

> **Note**
>
> There may be some confusion over the differences between Infrastructure as Code, configuration management, and orchestration. In fact, the lines that separate these three concepts are often blurred. Review the "Infrastructure as Code" and "Configuration Management" sections in this chapter for more details.

CramQuiz

Answer these questions. The answers follow the last question. If you cannot answer these questions correctly, consider reading this section again until you can.

1. Which IaC approach would the following file be?

```
S3Bucket:
    Type: AWS::S3::Bucket
    Properties:
    BucketName: mybucket
```

   ○ **A.** Orchestration
   ○ **B.** Declarative
   ○ **C.** Imperative
   ○ **D.** Configuration management

2. Which IaC approach would the following file be?

```
$ BUCKET="mybucket"
$ if ! 'aws s3api list-buckets --query Buckets[*].Name |
grep $BUCKET > /dev/null'; then aws s3api create-bucket
--bucket $BUCKET; else echo "This
```

    ○ **A.** Orchestration

    ○ **B.** Declarative

    ○ **C.** Imperative

    ○ **D.** Configuration management

3. Software is automatically deployed to the customer based on whenever a change is made on the main branch. This is an example of which of the following?

    ○ **A.** Continuous integration

    ○ **B.** Continuous deployment

    ○ **C.** Continuous delivery

    ○ **D.** None of these answers are correct

4. To create a local repository from the central repository, a _____ process is performed.

    ○ **A.** Duplication

    ○ **B.** Copy

    ○ **C.** Sync

    ○ **D.** Clone

CramQuiz Answers

1. Declarative

2. Imperative

3. Continuous deployment

4. Clone

What Next?

If you want more practice on this chapter's exam objectives before you move on, remember that you can access all of the CramQuiz questions on the companion website. You can also create a custom exam by objectives with the practice exam software. Note any objectives you struggle with and go to that objective's material in this chapter.

CHAPTER 20

Backup and Restore Operations

This chapter covers the following official CompTIA Cloud+ exam objective:

▶ 4.5 Given a scenario, perform appropriate backup and restore operations.

(For more information on the official CompTIA Cloud+ exam topics, see the Introduction.)

Careers in IT have been made and destroyed because of data loss. Failures to develop and adhere to a backup strategy have had severe impacts on organizations as well as those responsible for ensuring data is not lost.

This chapter focuses on backup and restore operations. You will learn about different backup types, including incremental, differential, full, synthetic full, and snapshots. You will also learn about backup objects, targets, and policies.

Lastly, you will learn about restore methods, including in-place, alternate location, and restore files.

CramSaver

If you can correctly answer these questions before going through this section, save time by skimming the ExamAlerts in this section and then completing the CramQuiz at the end of the section.

1. Which backup type will back up all data that has changed since the last full or incremental backup?

2. True or false: File-system backups should include the file data but not the file metadata.

3. Which backup target is considered faster: tape or disk?

4. Which term matches the following definition?

How long the recovery process should take from the moment that you have been made aware of the loss.

Answers

1. Incremental

2. False

3. Disk

4. Recovery time objective (RTO)

Backup Types

When you plan a backup strategy, it is important to understand the different backup types. Some types provide quicker backup times but may take longer to restore. Other types are slower to perform the backup but provide a simpler and quicker restore process. In this section you'll learn these different backup types and explore the advantages and disadvantages of each.

Incremental

An *incremental backup* includes all files that have changed since the last incremental or full backup.

Incremental backups provide several advantages:

▶ Each backup takes less time than a full backup and, in most cases, a differential backup.

▶ Incremental backups are normally smaller than full and differential backups, so they take up less storage space.

However, there are some disadvantages:

▶ Restoring from incremental backups can be time-consuming. First, the full backup must be restored and then each incremental backup until the incident that caused the loss of data.

▶ Finding a specific file from an incremental backup can be difficult because the file can be in different locations.

Differential

A *differential backup* archives any files since the last full backup. Differential backups don't take into account files that were backed up with previous differential or incremental backups.

Differential backups provide several advantages:

- ► All of the source data is located in two backups (the full and differential), making it easier to find files than with incremental backups.

- ► Restoring from a full backup is quicker than other incremental methods.

However, there are some disadvantages:

- ► A differential backup can be a time-consuming process compared to incremental backups.

- ► Normally, more storage space is used for differential backups than incremental backups.

- ► If the backup is performed remotely, a differential backup will use more bandwidth than incremental backups.

Full

With a *full backup*, everything from the source is backed up. This can include files that haven't changed since previous backups.

Full backups provide several advantages:

- ► All of the source data is located in one backup, making it easier to find.

- ► Restoring from a full backup is quicker than other backup methods.

However, there are some disadvantages:

- ► A full backup can be a very time-consuming process.

- ► Normally, much more storage space is used for full backups than other methods.

- ► If the backup is performed remotely, a full backup will use much more bandwidth than other methods.

Synthetic Full

Suppose you performed the following backups:

▶ Monday: Full backup

▶ Tuesday: Incremental backup (all files that have changed since the full backup on Monday)

▶ Wednesday: Full backup (all files that have changed since the incremental backup on Tuesday)

Now it is Thursday morning and the file system that you have backed up has become corrupted. You need to recover the file system so it has everything that was on the file system when you did the Wednesday backup. To ensure this happens correctly, you need to perform the following steps:

▶ Recover the full backup that was created on Monday.

▶ Recover the incremental backup that was created on Tuesday.

▶ Recover the above it says a full backup was created Wednesday.

Performing these recoveries can take a fair amount of time. When the data on the file system is mission critical, recovery time becomes even more important. In these cases you may want to consider an synthetic full backup. A *synthetic full backup* is actually like an incremental backup in that it takes less time to back up the file system, but the result is more like a full backup because it merges the results of the incremental backup with the last full backup to create the synthetic full backup.

The advantage of this method is that the incremental backup process is still quick, but after those changes have been applied to the previous full backup, a new full backup can be used to more quickly recover the file system.

Snapshot

Many backup utilities take the following approach to backing up a file system:

1. Record the metadata for the files being backed up.

2. Record the metadata for the directories being backed up.

3. Back up the directories (which really is the list of files that belong in each directory).

4. Back up the files' contents.

The problem with this technique is when live (mounted) file systems are backed up. Between backing up the metadata and the file data, it is possible that changes can take place in the file system.

It is best to unmount the file system before backing it up, but unmounting isn't always possible on production machines. So instead you can make use of a snapshot. A *snapshot* provides a "frozen image" of the file system at the moment that the snapshot was created. By backing up the frozen image, you ensure a good (error-free) backup.

Note that a snapshot is typically used on virtual machines, not other data structures like databases.

Backup Objects

In this section you'll explore different types of data that you may consider backing up. How you back up the data depends on the type of data. The type of data is often referred to as the *data object*.

Application-Level Backup

Many applications have associated data that may need to be backed up separately. For example, a web server includes web page files that may need to be backed up more often than the rest of the operating system.

Most backup utilities allow you to back up either individual directories (folders) or files. In most cases applications store all of their data within a specific directory structure, but if the files are spread out, you need to adjust the backup utility to include all file and directory locations for the application data.

> **Important Note**
>
> If you utilize both a file-system backup and an application-level backup and the file system needs to be recovered, it is important that both the file-system backup and the configuration backup are restored in the correct order. This will likely be the file system restore first and application-level restore second, but you should review the timestamps of the backups to ensure the correct order is followed (older backups should be restored first).

File-System Backup

One of the most common types of backups is a *file-system backup*. This sort of backup backs up not only the data (files) but also the structure of the data and the data's metadata. The structure of the data is the directory or folder structure of the data. The metadata is anything about the file besides the file's content or the file's name. Examples of metadata include the following:

- ▶ File ownership
- ▶ File type
- ▶ Permissions
- ▶ Date/timestamps
- ▶ Data block location

Database Dumps

A *database dump* is created when a utility like mySQLdump is used to duplicate the database, either to create a backup or to populate a second instance of the database. It is important to realize that a database dump is specific to the relational database management system (RDBMS), so a database dump of one RDBMS can't be restored to a different RDBMS. Instead, a migration tool is needed.

A database dump can also be used to back up just the schema or metadata of the database. For example, you may want to create a test database that contains the format of an existing database but not the actual data in the database.

Configuration Files

On an operating system, configuration files are used to configure either applications or features of the operating system. For example, on Linux-based systems the /etc/passwd and /etc/shadow files are used to configure user accounts.

While these files will be backed up as part of file-system backups, they often need to be backed up more regularly. For example, an operating system firewall may have dynamic rules created whenever the system recognizes a hacking attempt. These rules may be added throughout the day. If you rely on a file-system backup to back up the file system once a week—say on Sunday evening—many of these rules may be lost if the file system needs to be recovered mid-week.

Backup Targets

Where you direct the data backup is another important consideration when creating a backup strategy. In this section you will explore the advantages and disadvantages of backing up to tape, disk, or object storage.

Note that disk (block) storage and object storage are covered in the "Block" and "Object" sections, respectively, of Chapter 12, "Storage in Cloud Environments." The focus of this chapter will be how these storage devices are used to store backups.

Tape

Tape devices have been used to store data for decades (in fact, the magnetic tape was invented in 1928 to record sound). Tapes provide a good medium for backups because they are affordable and reliable. They also are a good medium for long-term storage.

Tapes do have some disadvantages, however. They are slower than other devices, like disk devices. This means that the backup process is typically slower. They also tend to have a lower amount of available storage per tape, meaning multiple tapes may be required to perform a backup or restore. In many modern cloud-based data centers that use tape devices, tapes in the tape drive are switched out with a robotic arm, but if this capability isn't available for the data center, the manual process of changing tapes is cumbersome and labor intensive.

Tapes are also much more portable than disk devices because they are, by their design, removable and relatively small. This means they may be more vulnerable to theft. However, strong physical security combined with encryption of the backup can mitigate most of this risk.

Tapes also are not as good to recover specific data from the backup, like a single file. The reason is that the tape must be moved to the correct spot and that process takes time.

Disk

Normally, disk backup devices are compared to tape backup devices. When comparing the two, consider that disk devices are often much faster than tape devices and can almost always hold much more data. Disk devices are also more expensive than tape devices, especially SSD disks.

Disk devices are very good at quickly finding and recovering specific bits of data. The verification process (when the backup data is verified to be error free) is quicker and more efficient on disk backups. Disk backups also typically scale better, but at a higher cost.

Object

Objects are typically stored on disk devices, so they have some of the same advantages and disadvantages as disk backup devices. However, object-based backups have some unique advantages. One advantage is that object storage normally can use a retention schedule. Most object storage solutions allow for old data to be migrated to less expensive storage options and, eventually, removed completely.

Backup and Restore Policies

Random backups don't serve any real business purpose. It is important to ensure you have a very well-planned backup strategy as well as policies in place regarding how and where the backups are stored. This section will cover these topics as well as restore policies that you should create for your organization.

Retention

The idea of retention is to define how long backups should be stored before they are deleted. While keeping backup data indefinitely might sound like a good plan, storing massive amounts of data is costly.

How long should you retain data? There is no rule that fits all scenarios. You should consider the following factors when creating a retention policy:

- ▶ How critical is the data to the organization?
- ▶ At what point does old data no longer provide any value?
- ▶ What are the costs associated with retaining old data?
- ▶ Are there any compliance regulations that must be followed in regard to storing old data?

You should start by putting data into different categories. These categories will include data that is governed by compliance regulations, data that is confidential or proprietary in nature, and data that is required for business needs.

The actual categories you create are up to you (except for compliance regulation and any policies that have been created by your organization's board of directors).

After you categorize the data, you need to consider the following:

▶ How long will the data be retained?

▶ How and where will it be stored?

▶ When the data reaches its end of life, how will the data be destroyed?

▶ How soon can the data be recovered?

Schedules

A *schedule* is how often you back up your data and what type of backup you will perform. For example, consider the following weekly plan for backing up a file system:

▶ Sunday @ 10 p.m.—Full backup

▶ Tuesday @ 10 p.m.—Incremental backup

▶ Thursday @ 10 p.m.—Incremental backup

When you schedule backups will depend on factors such as how often the data changes. For example, the preceding backup schedule would not work if massive changes were taking place on the file system each day. In that case, a daily backup or backups performed throughout the day would make more sense.

Location

Keep in mind that you want to keep your backups secure. Doing so means ensuring that the data is secure from theft and secure from damage. Therefore, storing your backups in a secure location is a critical component of a backup strategy.

In addition to security, you should also consider where to store your backups in relation to where the original data is stored. For example, suppose you are backing up servers in your data center and you decide to keep your backups in the server room. If a fire breaks out in the server room, you risk losing not only your original data, but all of the backup data. For this reason, many organizations consider storing backups offsite, like in a cloud environment.

Service-Level Agreements (SLAs)

If you are using a cloud vendor to manage your backups, you should be aware of the service-level agreement regarding backups. The SLA should contain provisions for the uptime percentage of the storage that is used by the backup, which can vary based on whether you are using georedundant storage. To see a sample SLA for a cloud storage service, take a look at the following SLA for Azure Backup: https://azure.microsoft.com/en-us/support/legal/sla/backup/v1_0/.

Note that you might not be using a cloud vendor's backup solution but still be using the cloud vendor to store your backups. For example, you might use AWS Buckets to store your backups instead of using AWS's backup service. In this case, you should review the SLA for AWS S3 so that you are aware of the agreement and provisions provided by the SLA.

Recovery Time Objective (RTO)

Suppose an instance's data has become corrupted and you have been notified that you need to recover this data using backup data. How long should the recovery process take from the moment that you have been made aware of the loss? This is the definition of the *recovery time objective*. After the recovery is complete, you will need to document how the recovery process went, including if the process was completed in more than the RTO value. This information is especially important for any business-critical data or any data that falls under the governance of regulatory compliance.

Note that RTO is a value that might be covered under an SLA when you are using a vendor to manage or store your backups. See the preceding "Service-Level Agreements (SLAs)" section.

Recovery Point Objective (RPO)

The *recovery point objective* is designed to determine what is an acceptable amount of data loss when a data disaster occurs. It is almost impossible to ensure that there is no data loss when a data disaster occurs, but it is important to define what amount of data can be lost without having an undesirable effect on business operations.

RPO is described in terms of time, not actual amount of data. For example, your organization may consider a 12–24-hour RPO acceptable for data loss in a noncritical file system, but only a 1–4-hour RPO for data stored in a specific database table.

Mean Time to Recovery (MTTR)

The *mean time to recovery* is the average time it takes to recover from a failure. The MTTR value is often a component of an SLA or a maintenance contract when you are using a vendor to manage or store your backups. See the earlier "Service-Level Agreements (SLAs)" section.

Typically, the lower the MTTR, the higher the maintenance costs will be. Also note that the *R* in MTTR is sometimes associated with the words *replace*, *repair*, *respond*, or *resolve*, depending on the context that it is used in.

3-2-1 Rule

The *3-2-1 rule* is that the following should be followed:

▶ There should be three copies of data.

▶ There should be at least two different media types.

▶ At least one copy of the data should be stored offsite.

This rule is designed to best ensure that your data is not at risk of being lost.

Restoration Methods

A *restoration method* is essentially how the data is restored. In this section you'll learn several methods that you should consider when developing a backup strategy.

In Place

With an *in-place restoration*, the data is restored in its entirety, back to the original location. This type of restoration is common when the loss of an entire file system or database is affecting business operations and the restoration must be made as quickly as possible.

There are, however, potential drawbacks to performing an in-place restoration. A corrupted backup or a backup that is out of date might result in further problems after the restoration. If the in-place method is used to partially recover data, it could end up overwriting existing data that is valid and more up to date. In these cases, it would make sense to consider an alternate location, which is covered in in the next section.

Alternate Location

With an *alternate location restoration*, the data is restored in a different location than where the original data was stored. This technique allows you to review the data to ensure it is complete, not corrupted, and has timestamps that indicate it is recent enough to be considered good data. After the data is verified, it can then be copied to the original location.

The biggest advantage of this technique is the verification of the data. However, this technique can take time, and this may cause further issues because the data will not be available for business purposes for a longer period of time. If speed is important, you should consider the in-place method, described in the preceding section.

Restore Files

In some cases, restoring everything may not be required. For example, if a user accidently deletes a file, only the file needs to be recovered, not all of the data of the backup.

For this reason, you should have a method available to restore individual files instead of restoring the entire backup.

Snapshot

A *snapshot restore* is normally a bit different from other restore methods because many of the existing files are left alone and only the files that are different in the snapshot are restored. In other words, a snapshot restore is very selective and not used to fully restore all of the files in the file system or directory.

CramQuiz

Answer these questions. The answers follow the last question. If you cannot answer these questions correctly, consider reading this section again until you can.

1. Which backup type is considered the most time-consuming?:
   - ○ **A.** Synthetic full
   - ○ **B.** Differential
   - ○ **C.** Incremental
   - ○ **D.** Full

2. Which file metadata is not included in the list of metadata that should be backed up when performing a file-system backup?
   - ○ **A.** File ownership
   - ○ **B.** File type
   - ○ **C.** File status
   - ○ **D.** File permissions

3. Which backup target is considered slow?
   - ○ **A.** Disk
   - ○ **B.** Object
   - ○ **C.** Tape
   - ○ **D.** None of these answers are correct

4. The _____ is the average time it takes to recover from a failure.
   - ○ **A.** SLA
   - ○ **B.** MTTR
   - ○ **C.** RTO
   - ○ **D.** RPO

CramQuiz Answers

1. Full
2. File status
3. Tape
4. MTTR

What Next?

If you want more practice on this chapter's exam objectives before you move on, remember that you can access all of the CramQuiz questions on the companion website. You can also create a custom exam by objectives with the practice exam software. Note any objectives you struggle with and go to that objective's material in this chapter.

CHAPTER 21

Disaster Recovery Tasks

This chapter covers the following official CompTIA Cloud+ exam objective:

▶ 4.6 Given a scenario, perform disaster recovery tasks.

(For more information on the official CompTIA Cloud+ exam topics, see the Introduction.)

This chapter builds on Chapter 20, "Backup and Restore Operations," by exploring the process of performing disaster recovery tasks. You will learn about failovers, failbacks, replication, and standby sites. You will also learn about the documentation involved in disaster recovery and the geographical requirements you should consider when choosing a data center.

CramSaver

If you can correctly answer these questions before going through this section, save time by skimming the ExamAlerts in this section and then completing the CramQuiz at the end of the section.

1. When a(n) _____ system is available and an organization switches over to this system, this is called a failover.

2. In a(n) _____ standby site, the site is always available for immediate failover.

3. A(n) _____ includes all of the resources and tools needed to perform all of the operations of your disaster recovery plan.

4. True or false: The political climate for an area should not be a consideration when choosing the geographic location of a data center.

Answers

1. Redundant
2. Hot
3. Disaster recovery (DR) kit
4. False

Failovers

Many organizations have redundant systems if one system fails. Some examples include

▶ Hardware redundancy in the event that a hardware device fails

▶ Application redundancy if an application crashes or is no longer available via the network

When a redundant system is available and an organization switches over to the redundant system, this is called a *failover*. In some cases, this failover may happen automatically. For example, a monitoring process may recognize when the original system is not responding and then invoke the failover process.

In most cases, once a failover occurs, the reason for the failure should be explored; this process is also known as a *root cause analysis*. Ideally, when the problem is discovered and fixed, the system should revert back to using the original.

Failback

After a failover occurs, it is important to restore the original system and revert the service back to the original system. This process is called *failback*.

It is important to implement a failback operation in a timely manner because normally the redundant system isn't designed for long-term use. For example, it may have fewer hardware resources available. Think of the redundant system like a spare tire in a car; while the spare will work in a pinch, it isn't normally designed to completely replace a regular tire. This isn't always the case, but consider that redundant systems can double the costs for the resource if they are as fully functional as the original.

Restore Backups

For more information on restoring backups, see the "Restoration Methods" section in Chapter 20.

Replication

In Chapter 20, we discussed recovery point objectives (RPOs). This discussion was related to how important it was to have timely backups to ensure that an organization is able to meet its RPO objectives. That discussion covered only backing up data in a timely manner, which is important in situations when data is corrupted or lost.

But what if an entire instance or resource is lost? For example, what if a virtual machine that hosts a critical web server crashes and can't be recovered? In these situations, you should have one or more redundant instances in place so that you can use a redundant instance as a fallback (see the earlier "Failback" section).

To have a valid redundant resource, you need to replicate the active resource often enough to support your RPO. For example, if that critical web server has an RPO of 6–12 hours, you must ensure you use a replication method that updates the redundant systems at least every 12 hours.

Note that some cloud vendors offer replication for some products automatically. Databases, for example, are often considered to be mission-critical resources. As a result, cloud vendors often provide an automatic replication option for database resources.

On-Premises and Cloud Sites

When dealing with mission-critical cloud-based resources, you may consider having a standby site available to quickly resume operations. This standby site can be defined as either hot, warm, or cold. In this section you'll learn the difference between the three types.

Hot

In a *hot standby site*, the site is always available for immediate failover. This type of standby site provides the quickest availability and is used in situations in which downtime must be avoided at all costs. There are some disadvantages of a hot site:

▶ To replicate the active site as accurately as possible, the replication process may be complex and time-consuming to manage.

▶ The hot site itself must be managed, typically by a dedicated support team.

▶ The cost of maintaining a hot site is higher than maintaining warm or cold sites.

If the hot site is on-premises, the organization needs to provide all of the hardware components and the dedicated team to manage the site. Given that a standby site should be in a different geographic location than the active site to allow for recovery from natural disasters, an on-premises hot site can be very costly for an organization.

A cloud-based hot site is typically managed by a cloud vendor or partner. This type of hot site may result in lower costs if a facility that is shared by other clients is used. However, most organizations prefer a hot site to be physically separated from other clients, so the cost of a cloud hot site can also be high.

Warm

While a *warm site* isn't immediately available for failover, it should be available fairly quickly. Given the complexity of the active site, this may be anywhere from hours to up to a day. Warm sites are more cost effective than hot sites and, for many situations, have a reasonable delay before the site is available. Because a warm site is not always active, the replication process may result in some lost data or application configuration. Also, a warm site isn't normally available for testing, so it may not be as reliable as a failover as a hot site is.

A warm on-premises site may be hosted in the data center of a branch office for an organization. A branch office can be ideal because it should have IT staff on hand to handle the rest of that data center's needs. Warm cloud standby sites are typically shared with other customers to reduce costs.

Cold

A *cold standby site* is one that needs to be provisioned before it is available. The hardware should be available, but backups must be used to restore services. This type of standby site has not only the lowest cost but also the highest downtimes.

Cold on-premises standby sites are rare because they require dedicated hardware to be always available. This hardware would just be sitting there, waiting for a disaster to occur. More likely, a cloud vendor would provide a disaster recovery team to aid an organization in recovering its site.

Requirements

Several requirements topics were covered in Chapter 20. The information for the pertinent sections is provided in the following sections in that chapter:

▶ **RPO:** See "Recovery Point Objective (RPO)"

▶ **RTO:** See "Recovery Time Objective (RTO)"

▶ **SLA:** See "Service-Level Agreements (SLAs)"

Corporate Guidelines

Most large organizations (and many smaller ones) have well-established corporate guidelines related to IT operations. This includes recovery rules that must be followed when establishing disaster recovery tasks.

Before developing any recovery policies, make sure you are aware of your organization's corporate guidelines. This includes not only the procedures and rules you must follow when performing recovery operations but also what reports need to be created after the recovery process is complete.

Corporate guidelines will often also mandate how the recovery process is documented. See the following section for more details.

Documentation

In the middle of a disaster recovery is not the time to try to figure out what your organization needs to do to recover. Well-thought-out plans should be put in place, and every step of the recovery should be well documented. In this section you'll explore some key components to disaster recovery documentation.

Note that this documentation is governed by the organization's business continuity plan (BCP). The BCP is a document that describes how the organization will be able to function during a disaster or an emergency.

DR Kit

A disaster recovery (DR) kit includes all of the resources and tools needed to perform all of the operations of your disaster recovery plan. Exactly what is in the kit depends on your infrastructure, but it could include essential user names and passwords, contract information for key individuals, and software licenses.

Playbook

In disaster recovery a playbook provides the step-by-step tasks that need to be performed to conduct the disaster recovery process. The playbook should be very specific and should make clear who is responsible for which tasks. The playbook should include many of the components discussed in this chapter and the topics from Chapter 20. This includes defining the RTOs, methods to monitor the recovery process, and how to utilize the DR kit.

Network Diagram

When you're dealing with complex network structures, especially in the cloud, having a network diagram can be critical when recovering all or parts of a network structure. A network diagram illustrates where all of the different components of the network reside, including network configuration settings (IP address, subnet, and so on).

Many tools are available for creating network diagrams. For example, Figure 21.1 displays the Lucidchart online tool, which has a free mode available in the event that you want to try it out (https://www.lucidchart.com/).

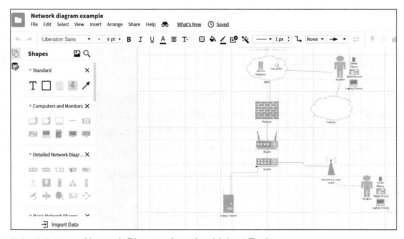

FIGURE 21.1   Network Diagram from Lucidchart Tool

Geographical Data Center Requirements

Choosing a data center is a process that includes many requirements, but the location of the data center is often one that has the biggest impact. Following are some of the most important requirements for determining the geographic location of a data center:

▶ How close is the data center to the organization's business offices and customers?

▶ What is the local climate?

▶ How geographically stable is the location?

▶ Is the location prone to extreme weather?

▶ How stable is the political climate for the area where the data center is located?

▶ What local IT talent is available?

▶ How stable is the infrastructure in the area, particularly power and network access?

CramQuiz

Answer these questions. The answers follow the last question. If you cannot answer these questions correctly, consider reading this section again until you can.

1. What is the process of migrating from a standby system back to the standard active system called?

   ○ **A.** Failback

   ○ **B.** Site restore

   ○ **C.** Reverse failover

   ○ **D.** Return

2. To have a valid redundant resource, you need to replicate the active resource often enough to support your _____.

   ○ **A.** RPO

   ○ **B.** RTO

   ○ **C.** SLA

   ○ **D.** None of these answers are correct

3. Which standby site is typically the least costly overall?

- ○ **A.** Hot
- ○ **B.** Cold
- ○ **C.** Warm
- ○ **D.** None of these answers are correct

4. In disaster recovery a _____ is the step-by-step tasks that need to be performed to conduct the disaster recovery process.

- ○ **A.** Playbook
- ○ **B.** DR kit
- ○ **C.** Site recovery plan
- ○ **D.** Restore plan

CramQuiz Answers

1. Failback

2. RPO

3. Cold

4. Playbook

What Next?

If you want more practice on this chapter's exam objectives before you move on, remember that you can access all of the CramQuiz questions on the companion website. You can also create a custom exam by objectives with the practice exam software. Note any objectives you struggle with and go to that objective's material in this chapter.

CHAPTER 22

Troubleshooting Methodology

This chapter covers the following official CompTIA Cloud+ exam objective:

▶ 5.1 Given a scenario, use the troubleshooting methodology to resolve cloud-related issues.

(For more information on the official CompTIA Cloud+ exam topics, see the Introduction.)

In this chapter you will learn about the troubleshooting methodology, which consists of six well-defined steps that you should follow when troubleshooting issues. You also will learn how to apply this troubleshooting methodology to resolve cloud-related issues. When taking the CompTIA Cloud+ exam, you should expect to see scenarios related to troubleshooting and which steps are being used in a particular scenario.

CramSaver

If you can correctly answer these questions before going through this section, save time by skimming the ExamAlerts in this section and then completing the CramQuiz at the end of the section.

1. What is the first step of the troubleshooting process?
2. What is the second step of the troubleshooting process?
3. What is the third step of the troubleshooting process?
4. What is the fourth step of the troubleshooting process?

Answers

1. Identify the problem
2. Establish a theory
3. Test the theory
4. Establish a plan of action

Always Consider Corporate Policies, Procedures, and Impacts Before Implementing Changes

Considering corporate policies, procedures, and impacts before implementing changes might seem like common sense. In the heat of the moment when you're troubleshooting a problem, however, and other people are pressuring you for an answer, this commonsense advice is often ignored. Unfortunately, not following this advice can lead to other problems, including the loss of your job.

You may be wondering what sort of scenario would result in not considering corporate policies, procedures, and impacts? For example, consider a scenario in which a user is attempting to access an S3 bucket in your company's AWS environment.

By looking at the permissions of the bucket, you can see that the user should have the ability to read the contents of this bucket. The user claims that he can't view the contents and asks you to change the permissions to include the write permission. He says he needs access immediately and feels granting write access will also allow him to read (view) the contents of the S3 bucket.

Your company has a policy that to gain write permissions on an S3 bucket, a user must fill out a request form. You mention this policy to the user, who you now realize is a senior manager, and he says, "We don't have time for that. Just give me write access now."

As you can see, you are now in a difficult position. You want to help the user, but taking the action that he is requesting will break company policy. The policy is in place for a reason: to prevent unauthorized access to corporate data that is stored in S3 buckets. Although you may be tempted to give in to the user's demands, it is best to follow the corporate policy to the letter. You might be able to expedite the user's request, but following the policy is important to ensure additional problems are avoided.

While some may consider troubleshooting to be a mysterious art form, it is really based on very specific steps that you should follow. Here's a summary of these steps:

1. Identify the problem.

2. Establish a theory.

3. Test the theory.

4. Establish a plan of action.

5. Verify full system functionality.

6. Document the findings.

For the rest of this chapter, you will explore what actions to take in each of these steps.

1. Identify the Problem

The first step to the troubleshooting methodology is to identify the problem. In this step you want to gather information to determine the cause of the problem. This step includes actions like the following:

▶ Question the user, identify user changes to the computer, and perform backups before making changes.

▶ Inquire regarding environmental or infrastructure changes.

ExamAlert

Consider that the exam objective that this chapter covers is "Given a scenario, use the troubleshooting methodology to resolve cloud-related issues." Because the Cloud+ exam is designed to be vendor-neutral, this means that you will not be asked to perform actual troubleshooting steps. Instead, you will be given information about a scenario and asked a question like "What step of the troubleshooting process is being described?"

Throughout the rest of this chapter, we will use a scenario to help you further understand what actions are performed in each step of the troubleshooting process. To avoid specifics about any particular cloud vendor, the steps will be somewhat generic.

Scenario: You have been contacted by a user who maintains a web server in your corporate cloud environment. This user indicates that the web server is no longer responding. You will be using your troubleshooting skills to solve this problem.

Step 1: Identify the problem. You start by asking the user a series of questions (the answers to these questions are in italics after the question):

▶ When was the last time you were able to access this web server? *Last Tuesday morning.*

▶ Where did you try to access the web server (home, in the corporate network, some other location)? *In the corporate network.*

▶ Are there other applications on the server? If so, are they still accessible? *No other applications that I am aware of.*

▶ Did you try to access the web server using its name or its IP address? *I used the web server name.*

▶ Have changes been made recently to the web server? *Not that I know of.*

▶ Have changes been made recently to the operating system where the web server is installed? *Not that I know of.*

2. Establish a Theory of Probable Cause (Question the Obvious)

In this step you need to conduct external or internal research based on symptoms and then establish a theory of the probable cause of the problem. Depending on the problem, this step may require you to take any of the following actions:

▶ Review documentation for the software/system.

▶ Test multiple techniques to work around the problem.

▶ View log files.

▶ View internal change orders (changes made to the system).

▶ If there is a similar system or software available (and working), attempt to compare the two (configuration files, settings, log entries, etc.)

Scenario, Step 2: Establish a theory of probable cause. You have researched the problem and have discovered that you can access the web server via a **ping** using its IP address, but not by the web server's name. The **ping** command uses an ICMP network packet to determine if a device is reachable via the network. Your theory is that a change to the internal DNS server has resulted in the IP address-to-name lookup process to fail.

3. Test the Theory to Determine Cause

You may be tempted to immediately fix the problem after you have established a theory; however, there is another step to take before you try to fix the problem. You should test your theory before trying to fix anything. This step includes the following:

▶ After the theory is confirmed, determine the next steps to resolve the problem.

▶ If the theory is not confirmed, reestablish a new theory or escalate the problem to a higher level of support.

Scenario, Step 3: Test the theory to determine cause. To test the theory that the DNS server is to blame, you attempt to access the web server using a web browser and the IP address of a web server, and you get a response. You verify that the response is correct with the user who notified you of the problem. You also contact the team that is responsible for the DNS service in your organization and ask if any recent changes have been made to the DNS service. The response: The DNS server was updated Wednesday morning.

4. Establish a Plan of Action to Resolve the Problem and Implement the Solution

When you feel confident that you have determined the cause of the issue, it is time to establish a plan of action to resolve the problem. The reason this plan of action is important is that the steps you take might not really solve the issue, and as a result, you may need to "back out" of the steps that you took. If you just take the steps without planning them first, undoing any actions that you take will be very difficult.

Additionally, this plan of action will make it easier to document this issue. One of the steps of documenting a troubleshooting process is to describe the actions that you took to solve the problem.

Scenario, Step 4: Establish a plan of action. Working with the DNS team, you develop a plan in which a new DNS entry will be added for the web server. After this change takes place, you will test the functionality by first trying to connect to the web server using its name and the **ping** command. If this is successful, you will then attempt to access the web server using its name via a web browser.

5. Verify Full System Functionality and, if Applicable, Implement Preventive Measures

A solution may produce additional problems. For example, if a solution to accessing a web server is to open a hole in the company firewall, this solution may result in additional, unintended access. To the best of your ability, you should test to verify that your solution does not cause additional problems.

Scenario, Step 5: Verify full system functionality. You have notified the user that the problem seems to be fixed and asked the user to verify. While discussing this solution with the user, you ask the user to share his screen and walk through using the website to ensure it is fully functional. Because there are no other applications hosted on this system, this step completes your verification of a fully functional system.

6. Document the Findings, Actions, and Outcomes Throughout the Process

If you have worked with computers for a while, you most likely have had the following happen to you: You run into a problem, take the time to research and troubleshoot the problem, and fix the problem only to have it crop up again sometime later. If you are like most people, you will vaguely remember the problem and maybe parts of the solution, but in many cases, you will have to troubleshoot the problem from scratch.

Our brains are just not good at documenting solutions to problems that we have seen only once. This is one of the reasons that you should document all issues, including your findings, any actions you took, and the outcome to those actions. If you document as you go, this is really an easy process. If you wait until the end of these steps, you are likely to forget parts of the troubleshooting steps you took.

Scenario, Step 6: Document the findings. You have been gathering documentation during the troubleshooting process. Your company has a tool that takes this information and stores it in a database so others can access the information. You use the tool to upload your findings, and your job is now complete.

CramQuiz

Answer these questions. The answers follow the last question. If you cannot answer these questions correctly, consider reading this section again until you can.

1. You are troubleshooting a problem and think you know what the problem is. What step of the troubleshooting process are you currently in?
    - ○ **A.** 2. Establish a theory
    - ○ **B.** 3. Test the theory
    - ○ **C.** 4. Establish a plan of action
    - ○ **D.** 5. Verify full system functionality

2. You are troubleshooting a problem and are collecting information from the user who reported the problem. What step of the troubleshooting process are you currently in?
    - ○ **A.** 1. Identify the problem
    - ○ **B.** 2. Establish a theory
    - ○ **C.** 3. Test the theory
    - ○ **D.** 4. Establish a plan of action

3. You are troubleshooting a problem and have just confirmed that your solution has worked. What step of the troubleshooting process are you currently in?
    - ○ **A.** 1. Identify the problem
    - ○ **B.** 3. Test the theory
    - ○ **C.** 5. Verify full system functionality
    - ○ **D.** 6. Document the findings

4. You are troubleshooting a problem and have just confirmed that your solution has worked. What is the next step of the troubleshooting process?
    - ○ **A.** 1. Identify the problem
    - ○ **B.** 3. Test the theory
    - ○ **C.** 5. Verify full system functionality
    - ○ **D.** 6. Document the findings

CramQuiz Answers

1. 2. Establish a theory
2. 1. Identify the problem
3. 5. Verify full system functionality
4. 6. Document the findings

What Next?

If you want more practice on this chapter's exam objectives before you move on, remember that you can access all of the CramQuiz questions on the companion website. You can also create a custom exam by objectives with the practice exam software. Note any objectives you struggle with and go to that objective's material in this chapter.

## CHAPTER 23

Troubleshoot Security Issues

This chapter covers the following official CompTIA Cloud+ exam objective:

▶ 5.2 Given a scenario, troubleshoot security issues.

(For more information on the official CompTIA Cloud+ exam topics, see the Introduction.)

The focus of this chapter is the troubleshooting of security issues. It is a broad topic and builds on many topics that were covered in previous chapters. You will learn about privileged accounts, troubleshooting authentication, and authorization, and you'll gain an understanding of security groups.

This chapter will also explore keys and certificates, including how to handle expired, revoked, or compromised keys and certificates.

CramSaver

If you can correctly answer these questions before going through this section, save time by skimming the ExamAlerts in this section and then completing the CramQuiz at the end of the section.

1. _____ is the process in which a regular user account gains privileged access.

2. What is the range of server-side REST error codes?

3. A(n) _____ security group is a set of rules that allows or blocks access to resources for specific users or other cloud-based resources.

4. True or false: FTP is a secure protocol.

Answers

1. Escalation
2. 500–599
3. Directory
4. False

Privilege

Recall from Chapter 5, "Identity and Access Management," that with privileged access a user is granted rights that allow for escalated access to a resource. This access is not something granted to a regular user account in most cases but is reserved for individuals who need to have more administrative control over a resource.

Managing privileged access poses several challenges. Most organizations follow a Least Privilege policy in which user accounts are given only the access that users need. The goal is to prevent users from having access to privileged operations that they are not required to have, but this can result in problems in which a user ends up with not enough access.

A user may end up having problems with privileged access for many reasons, which are covered next.

Missing

An account or role may be missing the privileged credentials altogether. To determine if this is the case, review access logs, group memberships, and account permissions using the Identity and Access Management (IAM) or the logging dashboard.

Incomplete

There may be several steps or components to providing privileged access to a resource. In this situation, each case is different, and there isn't a single troubleshooting method to resolve the problem. As with missing privileged credentials, review access logs, group memberships, and account permissions. Also consult the documentation regarding how to set up the privileged access to determine if a step was skipped.

Escalation

Privilege escalation is the process in which a regular user account gains privileged access. The method used to perform the escalation can vary quite a bit. For example, a user working on a Linux virtual machine might use the **su** or **sudo** command to escalate his or her account to gain privileged access. Or, if the user is working with cloud-based accounts, security or IAM policies could be used to escalate the user account. Because there are so many methods to escalate user account privileges, there isn't any single troubleshooting technique to determine the cause of errors. Consult log files and review the documentation for the escalation process to start the troubleshooting process.

Keys

Access to cloud resources may be granted via keys rather than the traditional username/password combination. Note that this topic will be covered in more detail in the "Keys and Certificates" section later.

Authentication

Recall from Chapter 5 that identification occurs when a user provides some sort of value, such as a username, to indicate who he or she is. By itself, identification isn't enough to grant access to the system; the process of authentication must also be used. Authentication occurs when the user proves his or her identity by using another piece of information, such as a password or an access token.

In terms of troubleshooting authentication problems, consider the following:

▶ Review security and access log files because often entries in the log files indicate the reason authentication fails.

▶ Attempt to replicate the failure, where possible, in a nonproduction setup. In some cases, the cause of the failure is with the user making a mistake during the authentication process. This can include providing the wrong username/password combination or "fat fingering" the username or password. Users also might be trying to log in to the wrong resources. You might spend hours trying to troubleshoot an authentication problem only to discover it is a simple user error.

▶ Leverage cloud-native and third-party troubleshooting tools.

▶ Consider resetting the password or issuing new access keys.

▶ If the user is logging in via a web browser, consider having the user clear the browser cookies. Cookies can contain old, outdated information that can impact the authentication process.

▶ If using multifactor authentication (MFA), verify that all authentication components are working correctly.

Authorization

Recall from Chapter 5 that after a user has been identified and authenticated, that user is granted access to resources within the system. This is the process of *authorization* when an authenticated user is either allowed or denied access to resources based on predetermined rules.

In terms of troubleshooting authorization problems, consider the following:

▶ Verify that the resource that the user is being authorized to access is functioning properly and is accessible via the network. Note that the resource that provides the authorization may be different from the resource that the authorization is being provided to access.

▶ For token-based authorization, verify that the token hasn't expired.

▶ Verify that the account has been correctly configured for access to the resource.

▶ Verify that the user is currently authenticated. Many authentication methods have a timeout value. If the user isn't currently authenticated, the authorization method will fail.

▶ Many authorization methods use application programming interface (API) calls via a protocol like representational state transfer (REST). Standard error codes can indicate the source of an error. Error codes 100–199 are for informational purposes and are not normally used for troubleshooting problems. Error codes 200–299 are successful responses. Error codes 300–399 are for times when an API call is redirected to another resource. Normally, error codes 400–499 (client-side errors) and 500–599 (server-side errors) are used to troubleshoot API problems. See Table 23.1 for some of the most common REST error codes.

TABLE 23.1 **REST Error Codes**

Code	Meaning
400	Bad request
401	Unauthorized
403	Forbidden
404	Not found
405	Method not allowed
500	Internal server error
501	Not implemented
502	Bad gateway
503	Service unavailable

Security Groups

In a cloud environment, a *security group* is used to control who can access a resource. Two types of security groups are covered here: network security groups and directory security groups.

Network Security Groups

A *network security group* is designed to provide protection to a network (VPC). These groups act like virtual firewalls for your cloud-based network. To troubleshoot a network security group, you follow many of the same steps as you would use with a standard firewall:

► Verify the problem applies to network access to your cloud-based network, not a problem with the resource itself that you are attempting to access.

► Verify that access is available within your cloud-based network.

► Determine whether there have been any recent changes to your network security group rules.

► Review the log file(s) for the network security group.

► Review the rule(s) for the network security group.

► Monitor network traffic while testing new configurations.

Note that errors related to network security groups could be either that access is blocked when it should be allowed or access is allowed when it should be blocked.

Directory Security Groups

A *directory security group* is a set of rules that allows or blocks access to resources for specific users or other cloud-based resources. The basic troubleshooting operations are similar to network security groups, but you are testing access based on users rather than connections from outside your network coming into your network.

Keys and Certificates

In cloud computing, keys provide an alternative method of authentication. Instead of providing a traditional username and password, an authentication key is provided instead. Keys are not normally used when users manually log in to a cloud environment but are leveraged when placing API calls to perform an action on a resource.

One of the problems with IT security revolves around the concept of trust. For example, suppose you want to connect to your bank online, and you type the bank's URL in a browser. Your browser gets a response from a remote server, but how can you ensure that remote server is actually your bank and not a server that hijacked your connection attempt?

The solution to this issue is a digital certificate. When the browser connects to the server, the server issues a signature that is tied to a digital certificate. The web browser then consults a third-party organization called a certificate authority (CA) to verify the signature. The trust is built between the client system and the server by using the CA for verification. Public CAs are available for certificate signing.

You may encounter several issues when troubleshooting keys and certificates, including the ones described next.

Expired

Both keys and certificates can be set to expire after a specific period of time. This issue is much more common with certificates because setting an expiration date for a certificate is a default option. An expired key or certificate is no longer valid and will require issuing a new key or certificate.

Revoked

An administrator may decide to revoke a key or certificate either because he or she believes the access is no longer needed or because the key or certificate may have been compromised. A revoked key or certificate is no longer valid and will require issuing a new key or certificate.

Trust

Trust is more of a certificate issue than a key issue. For a certificate to be used, the client system must trust the CA. Typically, this is a configuration option on the client system. For example, in a web browser you can go to your settings and specify which CA servers the web browser will trust.

Compromised

A compromised key or certificate can pose a serious security risk. For example, if a key is compromised, the result can be unauthorized access to resources. If a certificate is compromised, the result can be a server hijacking and stealing sensitive information. Troubleshooting compromised keys or certificates can be challenging unless reported by the individual who allowed the compromise. For compromised keys, running audits that look for specious user activity can help. For compromised certificates, user complaints or the lack of traffic to a server can indicate a problem.

Misconfigured

Any misconfigured resource is likely to cause problems. Resources that rely on keys or certificates will not work correctly if the keys or certificates are not configured correctly. To troubleshoot this issue, review log files, double-check the configuration documentation to ensure all steps were followed correctly, and always remember to test a configuration after you have completed the setup process.

Misconfigured or Misapplied Policies

For more information on misconfigured or misapplied policies, see "Policies" in Chapter 7, "OS and Application Security Controls."

Data Security Issues

This section will focus on data security issues that you will face within a cloud environment.

Unencrypted Data

See "Encryption" in Chapter 8, "Data Security and Compliance Controls in Cloud Environments."

Data Breaches

If you pay attention to the news, you are probably aware of the rise in data breaches that have been reported by major organizations. Hackers are becoming more sophisticated and finding more ways to access organizations' classified information.

To limit having to troubleshoot data breach issues, first focus on keeping the data as secure as possible. Securing the data includes following many of the policies and procedures that were covered in Chapter 8, including segmenting data, limiting access to data, and developing a good records management policy.

You should also consider the following steps to help troubleshoot when a data breach occurs:

▶ Use tools to determine whether a data breach has occurred.

▶ Have a plan in place in the event of a data breach.

▶ Do not hesitate to engage a third-party organization to help you mitigate the data breach.

▶ Contact law enforcement immediately because the sooner the crime is reported, the better law enforcement officers can provide aid.

Misclassification

See the "Classification" section in Chapter 8.

Lack of Encryption in Protocols

Protocols that lack encryption create the risk of data being stolen during transport. This issue can be mitigated if data is encrypted before transport using a separate utility, but it is normally better to avoid using protocols that lack encryption. As a result, you should avoid using the following protocols in your cloud environment:

▶ File Transfer Protocol (FTP)

▶ Telnet

▶ Network File System (NFS)

▶ Simple Network Management Protocol (SNMP)

▶ HTTP

There may be some exceptions to the "don't use these protocols" rule. For example, modern organizations widely use FTP to share files as read-only to anonymous users. And within the confines of a protected network, some organizations use SNMP and NFS in specific situations, but they should never be used outside the company network.

Insecure Ciphers

Some ciphers are no longer considered to be secure because the algorithm used to perform the encryption is vulnerable to hacking attempts. Be aware of ciphers that the encryption industry now considers to be insecure and avoid using these ciphers:

▶ DES encryption cipher

▶ 3DES encryption cipher

▶ RC4 encryption cipher

▶ AES with CBC encryption cipher

Exposed Endpoints

An *endpoint* is any device or resource that is designed to be the destination in a network communication. Many endpoints are designed to be exposed to entities outside your network. For example, your web server and email server are endpoints that you want to be connected to the Internet. These endpoints should have a security plan in place to allow only the intended access to the endpoint.

However, many endpoints are not supposed to be exposed outside your network. For example, consider a database resource that stores sensitive company data. As a result, it is important to make sure these endpoints are secured behind a firewall or a similar security appliance.

Misconfigured or Failed Security Appliances

Note that the topics of this Cloud+ exam objective are covered in Chapter 6, "Secure a Network in a Cloud Environment," and Chapter 7, "OS and Application Security Controls," as follows:

> ▶ **IPS:** In the "Host-Based IDS (HIDS)/Host-Based IPS (HIPS)" section in Chapter 7

> ▶ **IDS:** In the "Host-Based IDS (HIDS)/Host-Based IPS (HIPS)" section in Chapter 7

> ▶ **NAC:** In the "Network Access Control (NAC)" section in Chapter 6

> ▶ **WAF:** In the "Web Application Firewall (WAF)" section in Chapter 6

Unsupported Protocols

An *unsupported protocol* is one that your organization has decided will not be permitted to be used. The reason for not using it could be security related or because the protocol does not support the organization's business requirements.

Some tools, like port scanners, can be used to determine which protocols are being used on a cloud resource within your cloud infrastructure. For more details, see "Packet Capture" and "Packet Analyzer" in Chapter 25, "Troubleshoot Connectivity Issues and Common Performance Issues."

External/Internal Attacks

A lot of security experts spend a great deal of time and effort trying to ward off *external attacks*. Tools and procedures covered in previous chapters, specifically Chapters 6–10, address many of these external attacks and how security experts attempt to prevent these attacks as well as troubleshoot issues that arise from these attacks.

However, *internal attacks*, which are attacks launched by valid users within the organization, must also be considered. A level of trust must be given to internal users, but this level of trust often makes it easier for an internal user to launch an attack.

Following are some procedures and tools that you can utilize to troubleshoot and limit internal attacks:

▶ Clearly document what actions are permitted and which actions are not permitted.

▶ Make users aware of their security responsibilities. For example, users should not walk away from their workstations unless they first lock their computer.

▶ Impose strict security requirements, including strong passwords.

▶ Secure internal resources, including the network.

▶ Use auditing tools to provide greater insight to user activity.

CramQuiz

Answer these questions. The answers follow the last question. If you cannot answer these questions correctly, consider reading this section again until you can.

1. Which of the following is a method that a user can use to escalate his or her account on a Linux-based system?

   ○ **A.** resolve

   ○ **B.** upvar

   ○ **C.** sudo

   ○ **D.** rise

2. Which REST error code indicates the request is not authorized?

   ○ **A.** 400

   ○ **B.** 401

   ○ **C.** 402

   ○ **D.** 403

3. Which of the following is not considered an issue related to keys and certificates?

   ○ **A.** Expired

   ○ **B.** Revoked

   ○ **C.** Locked

   ○ **D.** Compromised

4. Which of the following are considered insecure ciphers?

- ○ **A.** DES encryption cipher
- ○ **B.** 3DES encryption cipher
- ○ **C.** AES with CBC encryption cipher
- ○ **D.** All of these are insecure ciphers

CramQuiz Answers

1. sudo

2. 403

3. Locked

4. All of these are insecure ciphers

What Next?

If you want more practice on this chapter's exam objectives before you move on, remember that you can access all of the CramQuiz questions on the companion website. You can also create a custom exam by objectives with the practice exam software. Note any objectives you struggle with and go to that objective's material in this chapter.

CHAPTER 24

Troubleshoot Deployment, Automation, and Orchestration Issues

This chapter covers the following official CompTIA Cloud+ exam objectives:

▶ 5.3 Given a scenario, troubleshoot deployment issues.

▶ 5.6 Given a scenario, troubleshoot automation or orchestration issues.

(For more information on the official CompTIA Cloud+ exam topics, see the Introduction.)

In this chapter you will learn some of the troubleshooting techniques used during deployments, automation, and orchestration. Recall that deployment is the process of implementing cloud resources. Automation is the process of making deployments streamlined by handling most or all of the deployment tasks automatically, without manual intervention. And orchestration is the process of deploying a collection of resources that are related to each other. (See "Automation Activities" and "Orchestration Sequencing" in Chapter 19, "Automation and Orchestration Techniques," if you don't recall the details of these topics.)

Note that CompTIA chose to make troubleshooting deployment issues a separate objective from troubleshooting automation or orchestration issues, but they are merged together in this chapter because of how closely related these topics are.

CramSaver

If you can correctly answer these questions before going through this section, save time by skimming the ExamAlerts in this section and then completing the CramQuiz at the end of the section.

1. True or false: DNS issues can affect network performance.

2. True or false: Configuration scripts can be in different formats, like JSON and YAML.

3. True or false: Tags are used exclusively for creating cost reports.

4. True or false: The regional location within a cloud vendor's system has no effect on how the configuration of an orchestration tool functions.

Answers

1. True

2. True

3. False

4. False

Connectivity Issues

Regardless of whether you are using an on-premises or vendor-based cloud infrastructure, connectivity issues can have a major impact on cloud performance. Some cloud vendors provide tools to help you determine if a network issue is related to connectivity. For example, Google Cloud provides Connectivity Tests.

For the Cloud+ exam, the primary focus is to know how to troubleshoot cloud service provider (CSP) or Internet service provider (ISP) outages. That is the main focus of the next section.

Cloud Service Provider (CSP) or Internet Service Provider (ISP) Outages

The cloud service provider is the vendor that provides the cloud services. To troubleshoot connectivity issues with a CSP, consider the following:

▶ Most CSPs have a publicly available website that describes which services are functioning properly and which services have issues. See Figure 24.1

for an example of the AWS Service Health Dashboard. This site is a critical first step in troubleshooting connectivity issues to rule out the possibility of an unresponsive cloud service.

▶ If you are not able to access one of your cloud resources, verify that you are able to connect to other resources within the same cloud environment or network. You should determine if the connectivity issue is related to a specific resource or to all of your resources to narrow down the issue.

▶ If you can connect to where the resource is configured in the CSP environment, you should verify that the resource is configured correctly.

▶ Review cloud network configurations to determine that a network configuration isn't the cause of the problem. This includes IP settings and security appliance settings, like NAC or WAF settings.

▶ Don't hesitate to reach out to your support team at the CSP. Most organizations pay good money to have 24/7 support, and when you're having connectivity issues, that is one of the times to take advantage of the support the CSP provides.

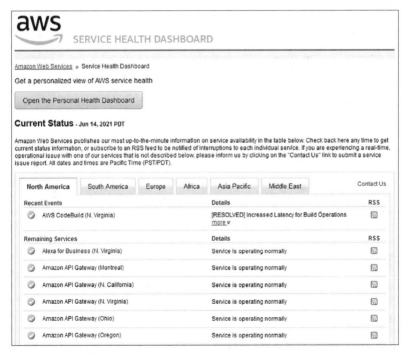

FIGURE 24.1   **AWS Service Health Dashboard**

Of course, the traditional network connectivity troubleshooting steps, tactics, and tools should also be used when troubleshooting connectivity issues with a cloud service provider. You should always consider a networking issue within your own network or with your Internet service provider.

Outages related to issues with your organization's ISP will be easier to troubleshoot. The reason is that an outage with your ISP will have an impact not just on accessing your cloud resources but also on other network-based activity in your organization.

As with any network connection issue, the connection problems may not be something that your ISP controls. Check internal networking configurations and applications, such as firewalls and routers, to ensure that they are configured correctly. Contact your ISP immediately if connectivity issues persist.

Performance Degradation

In terms of networking, *performance degradation* refers to a decrease in response speed on the network. Network performance degradation can be caused by a number of different problems, including

▶ Increased bandwidth usage

▶ Poor physical connections

▶ Malfunctioning networking devices

▶ DNS issues

▶ ISP issues

▶ Quality of service (QoS) issues

Network performance degradation is often tied to an issue referred to as latency, which will be discussed in more detail next.

Latency

Network latency refers to delays in communication across a network. There are several metrics that you can use to determine if you have a latency issue, including the following:

▶ **Round-trip time:** This is the time it takes for a packet to be sent to another system and the response time of the return packet. Note that in this case the network packets should not require processing on the server because just the time to traverse the network is being evaluated.

▶ **Server response time:** This metric measures the delay caused by the application as well as the time it takes to traverse the network between the client and the server. Comparing this value to the round-trip time provides a better understanding of the cause of the problem because it can either be the network itself or a server response issue.

▶ **Jitter:** This is a value that describes a difference in the delay between packets. A high jitter value can indicate a network issue related to irregularities in packet flow.

Configurations

As previously mentioned, configuration errors in a network can have an impact on the performance of the network. Configuration errors can be the result of users manually configuring network resources, but they can also be the result of scripts, which are often used to automate the implementation of networks. Scripts will be covered in more detail next.

Scripts

Scripts provide a powerful function of automating the process of implementing a resource. They are often used to implement the complex components that make up a cloud network, including the IP address settings, security groups, WAFs, and other cloud network resources.

Although scripts are great for automation processes, they can result in hard-to-troubleshoot errors. When troubleshooting scripts, consider the following:

▶ Whenever possible, test scripts fully in a testing or development environment before deploying them in a production environment.

▶ Scripts may fail because of changes made by the cloud vendor. A cloud vendor may release new features for a resource or change existing feature options.

▶ Some vendors provide tools to validate scripts before you use them. Take advantage of these tools if they exist.

▶ Scripts are sensitive to syntax errors. In many cases, standard formats (JSON, YAML, and so on) are used, and these formats have syntax validators that you should use to discover errors.

▶ Don't rely on third-party organizations to create your scripts unless you have a strong support contract. If no one in your organization understands the scripts you are using, when a script fails, you won't have a way to troubleshoot it.

Applications in Containers

For more information on using applications in containers, see "Containers" in Chapter 3, "High Availability and Scaling in Cloud Environments."

Misconfigured Templates

For details about handling misconfigured templates, see "Templates" in Chapter 11, "Integrate Components into a Cloud Solution."

Missing or Incorrect Tags

A *tag* is metadata that is associated with a cloud resource. Tags are used for a variety of purposes, including

▶ Creation of cost reports

▶ Access control

▶ Automation operations

▶ Operational support

▶ Security risk management

Note that tags are typically key-value pairs. For example, you might have a key named "department" and a value named "sales" for a specific resource. Or you might have a key called "location" and a tag value named "US" for a resource.

When applied correctly, tags provide a huge benefit. However, when a resource is missing a tag or has an incorrect tag, this can result in problems. For example, consider a scenario in which a tag named "stage" is used to remove all of the resources that make up a cloud network. You perform an operation in which you want to delete all resources with a value of "test" for the tag named "stage." If some of the resources in that network don't have this key-value combination, they won't be removed. Failure to remove them could cause issues with other resources in your cloud infrastructure, and it could result in additional charges to your cloud account for resources that are still active but not being used.

Insufficient Capacity

Lacking capacity can create issues in cloud resources because the resources will not be able to handle demands placed on the resources. All of the topics discussed in this section were covered in detail in earlier chapters. As a result, see the following:

- **Scaling configurations:** See "Scalability" in Chapter 3 and "Right-sizing" in Chapter 18, "Optimize Cloud Environments."

- **Compute:** See "Compute" in Chapter 3 and "Virtualization" in Chapter 14, "Compute Sizing for a Deployment."

- **Storage:** See "Storage" in Chapter 11 and "Storage System Features" in Chapter 12, "Storage in Cloud Environments."

- **Bandwidth issues:** See "Performance Degradation" and "Latency" in this chapter, and "Bandwidth" in Chapter 18.

- **Oversubscription:** See "Oversubscription" in Chapter 3.

Licensing Issues

Licensing can be a complicated topic in cloud computing because licenses are based on different usages, such as per-user, socket-based, and subscription based. It is important to understand which license is being used, what limits are imposed based on the license, and how to best determine which license is best for your situation.

These issues were covered in a previous chapter. To refresh your memory, see "Licensing" in Chapter 2, "Capacity Planning."

Vendor-Related Issues

When deploying in a cloud environment, you may be faced with issues that originate from the vendor. This section will focus on these issues.

Migrations of Vendors or Platforms

Recall from Chapter 15, "Cloud Migrations," that vendor issues can be related to different platforms between vendors (or your on-premises solution); for example, those which can result in vendor lock-in. You might also face issues such as different storage or database solutions being provided by vendors that you are migrating to.

Integration of Vendors or Platforms

Recall that the "Integration" section of Chapter 4, "Solution Design in Support of the Business Requirements," covered the topic of performing requirement analysis for the integration. It is during this analysis that you first troubleshoot potential problems with integrating your on-premises solutions with the cloud solutions that you are deploying.

Integration, however, is not a one-time function. In the future you will be adding, removing, and replacing on-premises solutions, and they will likely need to integrate with your existing cloud infrastructure. Additionally, whenever you remove, add, or modify an existing cloud resource, you will need to ensure that it doesn't have a negative impact on your on-premises infrastructure.

One way of troubleshooting potential integration problems is to deploy a blue-green environment in both your on-premises infrastructure and cloud infrastructure. Doing so allows you the opportunity to perform tests and troubleshoot issues before they are placed in a production environment. See the "Blue-Green" section in Chapter 4 for further details.

API Request Limits

An application programming interface (API) is a mechanism that is used to provide a well-known communication method between a client and a server. A client will issue an API request to a server, typically using representational state transfer (REST); see "Authorization" in Chapter 23, "Troubleshoot Security Issues."

One potential issue with API requests is that cloud vendors will limit how many API requests can be made. This number may be associated with billing costs because your license plans may limit how many API requests can be made in a specific period of time. For example, you may be limited to 50,000 API requests for a specific cloud resource.

What happens when you reach your limit? In most cases this results in further requests being refused. Refused requests can have a significant impact on your cloud performance if the server that the API is being sent to is mission critical.

In other cases, if you exceed your API limit, you may be charged for each request over the limit. Going over the limit can result in much higher than expected costs.

One way to avoid these problems with limits is to create an alert. *Alerts* are warnings that can be sent via email, text messages, or other means; they can warn you that you are approaching or have exceeded a limit. If you do implement alerts, make sure you have a plan of action in the event that an alert is sent. This plan should include ensuring that the right people are notified of the alert and what steps to take to mitigate the problems associated with reaching an API limit.

Cost or Billing Issues

With a subscription model, you typically don't need to pay for the resources that you have used until the end of the billing period (typically a month). If you are using a subscription model and you aren't careful, you might end up with a surprisingly large bill at the end of the billing period.

Cost isn't something to be taken lightly. Some smaller organizations have found themselves in a very difficult financial situation because of a surprise cloud vendor bill. Even larger organizations are sometimes caught off guard by a large bill.

As with API limits, the best way to troubleshoot this potential problem is to set up an alert. In this case, you can set up a billing alert that will warn you if you are close to or have exceeded a specified budget. Remember to have a good plan of action to handle this situation should it arise.

Also keep in mind that billing happens automatically, and in many cases, the bill is settled via a credit card charge. What happens if the charge exceeds the spending limit of the credit card? If the charge is declined, it can result in the immediate freeze of your cloud services. If your cloud resources are mission critical, a freeze on services can end up costing you even more money in lost revenue. Best practice to avoid this issue includes:

▶ Use a dedicated credit card for your cloud bills.

▶ Set a reminder for yourself to check the cloud bill and the available credit on your credit card a few days before the billing cycle ends.

▶ Routinely pay down or pay off the credit card balance.

Account Mismatches

When performing automation or orchestration operations, you will be providing account information to authenticate to the cloud environment. This may, at times, require providing information for multiple accounts when you are orchestrating operations because orchestration will involve creating several different resources that are related to one another.

These situations can become very complex, and it is possible that the wrong accounts may be used. This can result in some of the cloud resources failing during the orchestration process. To troubleshoot this issue, consider the following:

▶ Most automation and orchestration operations have log entries that indicate what failed and why. Consult these logs to determine whether an account mismatch is the problem.

▶ Attempting to create the failed resource manually using the account that was provided to the orchestration tool to determine whether an account mismatch is the problem.

▶ Utilize a blue-green environment to best ensure mission-critical operations are not affected by orchestration operations.

Change Management Failures

Every successful organization uses change to promote growth. This could be change in management, in the organization structure, and certainly, change in the IT infrastructure. The manner in which change is implemented is referred to as *change management*.

Change management is a complex discipline that includes several different models, including Lewin's Change Management Model and Kotter's 8-Step Change Model. Don't get too hung up on this topic because it is not a major part of the Cloud+ exam. You should at least know that there are four primary phases in the change management process:

▶ Understand the need for the change.

▶ Plan the change.

▶ Implement the change.

▶ Communicate the change with all impacted individuals and organizations.

The change management process will often have a powerful impact on orchestrating resources in the cloud. Often this impact will be positive, but in some cases it can result in time-consuming delays and even complete restarts of the orchestration project.

This is no simple problem to troubleshoot. The best solution is to ensure all phases in the change management process are completed fully and with great thought. Ensure multiple individuals (stakeholders) have input into the changes that are being made to best ensure that the changes will go as smoothly as possible.

Server Name Changes

This isn't likely to be a surprise: if you are referring to a server by name in an orchestration process and that server name changes, the orchestration process won't go as you planned it. Before implementing an orchestration operation, double-check all server names. If an orchestration process fails due to a server name change, the log files should indicate that the server is "unreachable" or provide a similar error.

IP Address Changes

For more information on IP address changes, see the preceding "Server Name Changes" section because an IP address change is very similar.

Location Changes

Consider this scenario: you are using an orchestration tool and have configured it perfectly so that it creates a series of resources exactly as you want. You have tested it, and it works perfectly. A colleague in your organization asks whether you would share your orchestration configuration, and you are happy to oblige.

The next day you get a message from this colleague in which she informs you that the orchestration process failed. After doing some research, you discover that the colleague used your orchestration configuration to implement resources in a different geographic region. This region didn't have support for some key resources that the region you created the orchestration configuration for did support.

Location changes can impact orchestration processes like this one. Different features are supported in different regions, or the limits for one region are different than those in another region. As a result, you can't just assume that an orchestration process that works in one region will automatically work in another. You should research the differences between the regions, update your configurations, and perform the same testing operations that you did when you created the original configuration.

Version/Feature Mismatch

Cloud vendors update the services that they provide at a fairly rapid pace. Although they will often keep a feature with a new version, sometimes features are removed (see "Deprecated Features" later in this chapter), add new features, or modify existing features.

For example, the cloud vendor you currently work with may now support older magnetic disk drives, which you use in one of your orchestration operations because of their lower costs. But what happens to that orchestration process in a couple of years when the cloud vendor decides to no longer support magnetic disk drives?

The best way to troubleshoot this problem is by being proactive and keeping up to date with changes in the vendor's features. When you notice upcoming changes, verify that they won't have an impact on your orchestration processes.

Automation Tool Incompatibility

The popularity of automation tools has exploded in recent years as automation has become more important in the IT industry. This increased popularity has led to a large increase in the number of automation tools that perform a variety of functions. For an idea of the functions that some of these tools offer, consider the following list:

- ▶ **Git:** A software version control tool

- ▶ **Gradle:** A software build tool

- ▶ **Jenkins:** A build management tool

- ▶ **Docker:** A tool for managing containers

- ▶ **Chef:** A configuration management tool

- ▶ **Ansible:** Another configuration management tool

This list is in no way complete. The number of automation tools that are available is a benefit in that they provide many options. However, in a cloud environment, this number poses a challenge to cloud vendors. Cloud vendors are not able to support a large number of options, so they often limit the options. This means if you are migrating to the cloud and are using an automation tool currently on-premises, you may need to also migrate to a different automation tool.

Migrating to a different tool is a bigger task than it may initially sound. Keep in mind that many of these automation tools have very specific features and configuration formats. For example, both Chef and Ansible can perform tasks like the automation of software on a remote system. How they do this is different, and even their configuration file formats (one is in JSON and the other is in YAML) are different.

Deprecated Features

When a developer of a tool, language, or utility decides to remove a feature from the product, the developer often decides to deprecate it rather than remove it completely. *Deprecated* means "we left it in there, but we don't recommend using it anymore and reserve the right to remove it in a future release." Sometimes a deprecated feature is slated to be removed in the next release, but in other cases it may be part of the product for many years.

In other words, it is important to realize when a feature that you are using has been deprecated. By reading the release notes of a product, you can determine which features are deprecated and put together a game plan on how you use the product to avoid the deprecated features.

API Version Incompatibility

As with any software program, the APIs used to interact with a server will change over time. This is normally the result of changes in the server software. As new features are added, new APIs are introduced. When a feature is changed, a new version of the API will be released. And when a feature is deprecated or removed from the server, the API will either be modified (often deprecated features result in a warning when used) or removed.

As with any change to software, it is important to keep up to date with changes. Included with the server's release note should be coverage of changes made to APIs. To avoid issues, review release notes and be sure that your API calls are for the correct version of the server's APIs.

Job Validation Issue

When an automation task is performed, it is referred to as a *job*. A job can be something simple, such as creating a user account, or sometimes more complex, such as deploying a web server and configuring extensions on the web server.

When you're working with automation tools, it is important that there is a process called *job validation*. This process is designed to ensure that the job was performed correctly. In some cases, job validation might be included with the automation tool that you are using. You may either receive a report at the end of the automation process or be able to see the validation results by looking at log files.

However, this feature isn't always available, so you may need to automate the job validation task yourself. Automating it may include writing some code that will determine if the job is functioning properly.

In any event, if the job validation process has an issue, this situation can pose even greater challenges. For example, the job validation process may indicate no problems when the task itself did fail. This result can lead to the false belief that the resource was deployed correctly.

While a failed deployment causes issues, those issues are likely to be noticed soon enough when users or other resources attempt to use the newly deployed resource or service. Perhaps even more frustrating is the situation that occurs when job validation indicates a failure, but the resource was deployed correctly. This situation can cost you time as you try to determine the cause of the problem when there isn't a problem in the first place.

If you are having issues with your job validation processes, it is important to migrate the automation process to a testing platform and determine the root cause. Only when the cause is found and a fix is in place should the automation tool be used again in a production environment.

Patching Failure

Patching systems is often a tedious and time-consuming (hence, also costly) process. As a result, automation processes are often used to patch the software and operating systems of cloud resources. Both cloud vendors and clients use automation tools to perform this task.

When this process fails, it can have serious negative impact. Recall that patches often include important security fixes, so if a patch process fails, it can result in a vulnerable system.

As previously mentioned, automation tools normally either generate a report or generate log files. Reviewing these reports or logs for failed patching operations is a critical component of automation. Remember that automation is designed to aid in the process of making changes, but it doesn't completely replace the responsibility of humans to ensure the security and functionality of cloud resources.

CramQuiz

Answer these questions. The answers follow the last question. If you cannot answer these questions correctly, consider reading this section again until you can.

1. Which is a value that describes a difference in the delay between packets?

   ○ **A.** Server response time

   ○ **B.** Jitter

   ○ **C.** Round-trip time

   ○ **D.** Juke

2. Which of the following are typical data formats for configuration scripts? (Choose two.)

  ○ **A.** JSON

  ○ **B.** XML

  ○ **C.** YAML

  ○ **D.** HTML

3. Which of the following is not a typical use of tags?

  ○ **A.** Access control

  ○ **B.** Automation operations

  ○ **C.** Authentication method

  ○ **D.** Security risk management

4. Which of the following are considered steps in change management?

  ○ **A.** Understand the need for the change.

  ○ **B.** Plan the change.

  ○ **C.** Implement the change.

  ○ **D.** All of these are steps in change management.

CramQuiz Answers

1. Jitter
2. JSON and YAML
3. Authentication method
4. All of these are steps in change management.

What Next?

If you want more practice on this chapter's exam objectives before you move on, remember that you can access all of the CramQuiz questions on the companion website. You can also create a custom exam by objectives with the practice exam software. Note any objectives you struggle with and go to that objective's material in this chapter.

CHAPTER 25

Troubleshoot Connectivity Issues and Common Performance Issues

This chapter covers the following official CompTIA Cloud+ exam objective:

▶ 5.4 Given a scenario, troubleshoot connectivity issues.

▶ 5.5 Given a scenario, troubleshoot common performance issues.

(For more information on the official CompTIA Cloud+ exam topics, see the Introduction.)

The bulk of this chapter will cover troubleshooting connectivity issues. This description will include common networking configuration issues and the tools that are commonly used to troubleshoot these networking issues.

CramSaver

If you can correctly answer these questions before going through this section, save time by skimming the ExamAlerts in this section and then completing the CramQuiz at the end of the section.

1. _____ are designed to protect a VPC, whereas _____ are used to protect virtual machines within a VPC.

2. With _____ a network connection is established between two VPCs.

3. What are some of the components that make up QoS?

4. You can see the gateways that the packet passes through by executing the _____ command.

Answers

1. Security groups, network ACLs
2. Peering
3. Bandwidth, latency, and jitter
4. tracert or traceroute

Network Security Group Misconfigurations

Recall that a network security group is designed to provide protection to a network (VPC). These groups act like virtual firewalls for your cloud-based network. However, they aren't designed to protect everything in the VPC, but rather just the virtual machine (VM) resources. To protect the entire VPC, you can create network ACLs (access control lists). Some additional differences are demonstrated in Table 25.1.

TABLE 25.1 **Security Group versus NACL**

Feature	Security Groups	NACLs
State	Stateful (incoming rules will be applied to outgoing rules automatically)	Stateless
Allow or deny	Only allow rules are permitted	Both allow and deny rules are permitted
Rule order	Does not apply	Rules are applied in the order that they appear in the rule list
Number of rule sets	Multiple security groups can be applied to a subnet	Only one NACL can be applied to a subnet

Access Control Lists (ACLs)

A misconfigured network ACL can end up blocking or allowing access to the resources, which is not the intention. Keep in mind that the order of the rules is important, so not placing rules in the correct order can result in unexpected results. For example, suppose you want to allow all systems from the 192.168.100.0/24 network to be allowed to connect to the subnet, but you don't want to allow machine 192.160.100.200 from that subnet to have any access. A rule set like the following would work to accomplish this goal (note that these are not actual rules, but verbal descriptions of the rules, and … represents "other rules that don't apply in this example"):

...

> Rule 27: Block 192.168.100.200
>
> Rule 28: Allow 192.168.100.0/24

...

However, the following rule set would not block 192.168.100.200:

...

> Rule 27: Allow 192.168.100.0/24
>
> Rule 28: Block 192.168.100.200

...

After a rule is applied to an inbound packet, none of the subsequent rules will be applied.

Inheritance

In some cases you may be able to inherit NACLs from other rule sets. If this is the case, understand fully what rules the inherited rule set provides. If it is true inheritance (sometimes it is just a copy of an existing rule set), understand that changes to the inherited rule set can impact your overall rule set. Typically, inherited rule sets are applied first, so this is another complication that you need to consider when using this feature.

Common Networking Configuration Issues

In any network environment, a large number of things can go wrong. In this section you'll learn about some of the common networking configuration issues that you may encounter.

Note that for any of the network categories found in this section, dozens of different issues can cause problems. It is important to note that this exam objective is about focusing on "common" networking issues that are based on "configuration," not all of the networking issues that can arise from multiple categories of problems.

Peering

Within your cloud network, you may encounter situations in which you want resources in one VPC to be able to communicate with resources in another VPC. This type of communication isn't normally configured by default.

If the resources have public IP addresses, they may be able to communicate, but this communication also might be blocked by security group rules or network ACL rules. The communication might also suffer lags because the network packets are routed toward the Internet first and then back into the security group, VPC, and then the destination resource.

With peering (often called *VPC peering* or *virtual network peering*), a network connection is established between two VPCs. This connection allows resources to communicate between the two VPCs, much like if they were on the same network. In this way, resources can use the cloud network instead of the Internet for communications.

In terms of troubleshooting, one common issue arises when one VPC becomes associated with the peering connection. Another issue to look for is if one of the VPCs is migrated to a different region, which will likely require establishing a new peering connection.

Incorrect Subnet, IP Address, and IP Space

Many of the cloud resources that are assigned an IP address make use of dynamic assignment via a DHCP server. This server is normally provided by the cloud provider (or, for on-premises solutions, managed by your organization). For some situations you may want to use static IP assignment in which you manually configure the IP address, subnet mask, and other network settings. This configuration is important to ensure a consistent IP address for servers.

However, whenever you manually configure IP settings, you run the risk of errors. You may provide the wrong address, subnet, IP space, or other networking configuration information. This can result in connectivity issues.

To troubleshoot such issues, verify the network settings and make sure they are correct for the network where the resource was placed. Try to connect to the system from outside the network using the tools described in the "Network Troubleshooting Tools" section later in this chapter, including the **ping**, **ipconfig/ifconfig/ip**, and **tracert/traceroute** commands.

Routes

A *route* is the way a resource communicates outside the local network. This communication is sent to a router (also called a *gateway*). An incorrectly configured route can result in not being able to send network packets outside the local network. Use the **route** command, which is described in the "Route" section later in this chapter, to see how to display the routes and make changes to the routes.

Default

In some cases, a resource might be in a network that has different routers connected to the network. For example, one router may provide access to another network within your infrastructure, whereas another router may provide access to the Internet. In this scenario, you would configure the resource's routing table to specifically send any network traffic destined for the internal network directly to a specific router. Then you would have a rule in the routing table that says, "Send all other network traffic (besides traffic on the local network that the resource is a part of) to the Internet router." In this case, the Internet router is referred to as the *default router*.

As with any routing issue, you should use the **route** command, which is described in the "Route" section later in this chapter, to help you troubleshoot issues with the default router.

Static

In static routing an administrator sets specific routers or gateways to route network traffic. A static route doesn't change after it has been set, unless the administrator manually changes the configuration.

The potential problem with static routing is that it creates a single point of failure. If the specified router becomes unresponsive, traffic to that network no longer works. To resolve this issue, troubleshoot issues with that router, which can include mechanical problems or a configuration change. Additionally, you can consider switching to dynamic routing.

Dynamic

In *dynamic routing* routing paths can change automatically based on algorithms that indicate the best routing path to take. While more complex than static routing, dynamic routing tends to be more robust because lost connectivity to a router results in a new routing path being chosen.

Dynamic routing is normally used in large network infrastructures and can be complex to implement and administer. When issues do arise, you should focus troubleshooting efforts on the routing protocol and use tools described in the "Ping" and "Tracert/Traceroute" sections in this chapter.

Firewall

A firewall is used to either permit or block network traffic based on conditions like the source IP of the network packet or the destination port of the network packet, for example. For further details, see "Firewall Software" in Chapter 7, "OS and Application Security Controls."

Incorrectly Administered Microsegmentation

Microsegmentation is a security feature that allows administrators to logically divide resources into groups and apply a different set of security rules to each group. In terms of firewalls, microsegmentation is the process of creating zones.

With a firewall zone, you can create firewall rule sets that apply to a specific logical area of the network. Zones provide more flexibility for the firewall administrator, but they can also make it more difficult to troubleshoot problems if you are not aware of how the zones are configured and which resources belong to which zones.

To troubleshoot, start by creating a network diagram that displays all of the resources in the network and which zone each resource belongs to. Verify that the zone rules are applied correctly for each resource that resides within that zone. To test connectivity though the firewall, use tools described in the "Ping" and "Tracert/Traceroute" sections in this chapter.

Network Address Translation (NAT)

Network Address Translation is a configuration setting found on a router that converts the private IP addresses of a network packet into public IP addresses.

The goal is to be able to send network packets from internal, private networks to the Internet without exposing the internal addresses. NAT was originally designed to overcome the lack of Internet-routable IP addresses that IPv4 provides, but it has other benefits.

There are several different forms of NAT:

▶ **DNAT (Destination NAT):** Used when you want to place servers behind a firewall and still provide access from an external network.

▶ **SNAT (Source NAT):** Used when you have an internal network with statically assigned private IP addresses. Using SNAT, you can funnel access to the Internet via a single machine that has a live IP address (an address that is routable on the Internet). This system is configured with SNAT, which is used to map internal addresses with external communication.

▶ **MASQUERADE:** Used when you have an internal network with dynamically (DHCP) assigned private IP addresses. Using MASQUERADE, you can funnel access to the Internet via a single machine that has a live IP address (an address that is routable on the Internet). This system is configured with MASQUERADE, which is used to map internal addresses to external communication.

Because most internal networks use DHCP to assign IP addresses, MASQUERADE is more common than SNAT. It is also easier to configure because SNAT requires you to create rules for each internal system.

NAT rules are often implemented on a router that acts as a firewall. The rules of the firewall perform the modification of the source and destination IP addresses in the metadata of the network packets. As a result, when you're troubleshooting issues with NAT, the configuration of the firewall that performs the NAT function should be the first place you look.

For details about VPNs, see "Virtual Private Networks (VPNs)" in Chapter 13, "Cloud Networking Solutions."

Load Balancers and DNS Records

For more details, see the "Load Balancers" and "Domain Name Service (DNS)" sections in Chapter 13.

VLAN/VxLAN/GENEVE and Proxy

For more information, see "Virtual LAN (VLAN)/Virtual Extensible LAN (VxLAN)/Generic Network Virtualization Encapsulation (GENEVE)" and "Proxy Servers" in Chapter 6, "Secure a Network in a Cloud Environment."

Maximum Transmission Unit (MTU)

When packets are sent on the network, there needs to be an agreement between the different nodes on the network as to the maximum size of the packet. As a result, an attribute called the *maximum transmission unit, or MTU*, is normally assigned to the network. The MTU tells the system that when it puts together network packets they should not exceed the size indicated by this value.

On most modern systems, this value is automatically assigned when the network interface (network interface card, or NIC) first connects to the network. A query is sent to the node attached to the local node to determine what the maximum packet size should be. This value can also be configured manually, but the risk with that is the value might not be the same as other nodes on the network.

The standard MTU size is 1500 bytes, but this value can be adjusted to provide better network performance. For troubleshooting, ensure that all nodes in the network are using the same MTU.

Quality of Service (QoS)

Quality of service is a term that is applied to networks to ensure that the overall performance of a network is within an acceptable range. QoS is closely related to other terms, including bandwidth, latency, and jitter. See "Network" in Chapter 18, "Optimize Cloud Environments," for more details on these terms.

Time Synchronization Issues

For more details on time synchronization issues, see the "Network Time Protocol (NTP)" section in Chapter 13.

Network Troubleshooting Tools

In this section you'll explore a collection of troubleshooting tools that you can use to determine the cause of networking issues. The examples provided are executed on a Linux-based system. In most cases these tools will also function on Windows or MacOS.

ping

The **ping** command is used to verify that a remote host can respond to a network connection:

```
[root@OCS ~]# ping -c 4 google.com

PING google.com (172.217.5.206) 56(84) bytes of data.

64 bytes from lax28s10-in-f14.1e100.net (172.217.5.206):
icmp_seq=1 ttl=55 time=49.0 ms

64 bytes from lax28s10-in-f206.1e100.net (172.217.5.206):
icmp_seq=2 ttl=55 time=30.2 ms

64 bytes from lax28s10-in-f14.1e100.net (172.217.5.206):
icmp_seq=3 ttl=55 time=30.0 ms

64 bytes from lax28s10-in-f206.1e100.net (172.217.5.206):
icmp_seq=4 ttl=55 time=29.5 ms

--- google.com ping statistics ---

4 packets transmitted, 4 received, 0% packet loss, time 3008ms

rtt min/avg/max/mdev = 29.595/34.726/49.027/8.261
```

tracert/traceroute

When you send a network packet to a remote system, especially across the Internet, it often needs to go through several gateways before it reaches its destination. You can see the gateways that the packet passes through by executing the **traceroute** command:

```
# traceroute onecoursesource.com

traceroute to onecoursesource.com (38.89.136.109), 30 hops max, 60
byte packets

 1  10.0.2.2 (10.0.2.2)  0.606 ms  1.132 ms  1.087 ms

 2  b001649-3.jfk01.atlas.cogentco.com (38.104.71.201)
0.738 ms  0.918 ms  0.838 ms

 3  154.24.42.205 (154.24.42.205)  0.952 ms  0.790 ms 0.906 ms

 4  be2629.ccr41.jfk02.atlas.cogentco.com (154.54.27.66)
1.699 ms  1.643 ms 1.347 ms

 5  be2148.ccr41.dca01.atlas.cogentco.com (154.54.31.117)
8.053 ms  7.719 ms  7.639 ms

 6  be2113.ccr42.atl01.atlas.cogentco.com (154.54.24.222)
18.276 ms 18.418 ms 18.407 ms
```

```
 7  be2687.ccr21.iah01.atlas.cogentco.com (154.54.28.70)
32.861 ms   32.917 ms   32.719 ms

 8  be2291.ccr21.sat01.atlas.cogentco.com (154.54.2.190)
38.087 ms   38.025 ms   38.076 ms

 9  be2301.ccr21.elp01.atlas.cogentco.com (154.54.5.174)
48.811 ms   48.952 ms   49.151 ms

10  be2254.ccr21.phx02.atlas.cogentco.com (154.54.7.33)
57.332 ms 57.281 ms   56.896 ms

11  te2-1.mag02.phx02.atlas.cogentco.com (154.54.1.230)
56.666 ms 65.279 ms   56.520 ms

12  154.24.18.26 (154.24.18.26)   57.924 ms 58.058 ms   58.032 ms

13  38.122.88.218 (38.122.88.218)   79.306 ms 57.740 ms 57.491 ms

14  onecoursesource.com (38.89.136.109)   58.112 57.884 ms 58.299 ms
```

Note that on some systems, like Microsoft Windows, the **traceroute** command is called **tracert**.

flushdns

DNS entries are often cached for a period of time. This can cause problems if the DNS records change. To remove the cached DNS entries in Microsoft Windows, execute the **ipconfig /flushdns** command.

ipconfig/ifconfig/ip

The **ifconfig** command displays basic IP network settings for devices:

```
[root@localhost ~]# ifconfig
enp0s3: flags=4163<UP,BROADCAST,RUNNING,MULTICAST>  mtu 1500
        inet 192.168.1.26 netmask 255.255.255.0  broadcast 192.168.1.255
        inet6 fe80::a00:27ff:feb0:dddc  prefixlen 64  scopeid 0x20<link>
        ether 08:00:27:b0:dd:dc  txqueuelen 1000  (Ethernet)
        RX packets 103224  bytes 17406939 (16.6 MiB)
        RX errors 0  dropped 0  overruns 0  frame 0
        TX packets 16408  bytes 3008229 (2.8 MiB)
        TX errors 0  dropped 0 overruns 0  carrier 0  collisions 0


lo: flags=73<UP,LOOPBACK,RUNNING>  mtu 65536
        inet 127.0.0.1  netmask 255.0.0.0
```

```
inet6 ::1  prefixlen 128  scopeid 0x10<host>

loop  txqueuelen 0  (Local Loopback)

RX packets 4891  bytes 257583 (251.5 KiB)

RX errors 0  dropped 0  overruns 0  frame 0

TX packets 4891  bytes 257583 (251.5 KiB)

TX errors 0  dropped 0 overruns 0  carrier 0  collisions 0
```

Table 25.2 describes important options for the **ifconfig** command.

TABLE 25.2   **Common ifconfig Options**

Option	Description
-a	Displays all interfaces, even interfaces that are currently down
-s	Displays output like the **netstat -i** command
-v	Turns on verbose mode

The **ifconfig** command can also be used to manually define network settings for a specific device. For example:

```
ifconfig enp0s3 192.168.1.26  netmask 255.255.255.0 broadcast
192.168.1.255
```

Note

These changes are temporary and will survive only until the next time the system is booted. Permanent changes are made within your system's configuration files, which vary from one distribution to another.

Note that on some systems, like Microsoft Windows, the **ifconfig** command is called **ipconfig**.

The newer **ip** command is designed to replace a collection of commands related to network interfaces. Table 25.3 describes some of the more important options.

TABLE 25.3   **Important ip Options**

Object	Refers to
addr	IPv4 or IPv6 address
link	Network device
route	Routing table entry

Table 25.4 describes some of the more important commands that can be executed.

TABLE 25.4 **Important ip Commands**

Command	Description
add	Adds an object
delete	Deletes an object
show (or **list**)	Displays information about an object

The following example displays network information for devices, much like the **ifconfig** command:

```
[root@OCS ~]# ip addr show
1: lo: <LOOPBACK,UP,LOWER_UP> mtu 65536 qdisc noqueue state UNKNOWN
    link/loopback 00:00:00:00:00:00 brd 00:00:00:00:00:00
    inet 127.0.0.1/8 scope host lo
      valid_lft forever preferred_lft forever
    inet6 ::1/128 scope host
      valid_lft forever preferred_lft forever
2: enp0s3: <BROADCAST,MULTICAST,UP,LOWER_UP> mtu 1500 qdisc pfifo_fast
state UP qlen 1000
    link/ether 08:00:27:b0:dd:dc brd ff:ff:ff:ff:ff:ff
    inet 192.168.1.26/24 brd 192.168.1.255 scope global dynamic
enp0s3
      valid_lft 2384sec preferred_lft 2384sec
    inet 192.168.1.24/16 brd 192.168.255.255 scope global enp0s3
      valid_lft forever preferred_lft forever
    inet6 fe80::a00:27ff:feb0:dddc/64 scope link
      valid_lft forever preferred_lft forever
```

nslookup/dig

The **nslookup** command is designed to perform simple queries on DNS servers:

```
[root@OCS ~]# nslookup google.com
Server:        8.8.8.8
Address:       8.8.8.8#53
```

```
Non-authoritative answer:
Name:   google.com
Address: 216.58.219.238
```

Although this command has often been referred to as obsolete or deprecated, it is still often used on modern distributions. The **nslookup** command is normally run without any options.

The **dig** command is useful for performing DNS queries on specific DNS servers. The format of the command is demonstrated here:

```
[root@OCS ~]# dig google.com

;  <<>> DiG 9.9.4-RedHat-9.9.4-38.el7_3 <<>> google.com
;; global options: +cmd
;; Got answer:
;; ->>HEADER<<- opcode: QUERY, status: NOERROR, id: 56840
;; flags: qr rd ra; QUERY: 1, ANSWER: 1, AUTHORITY: 0, ADDITIONAL: 1

;; OPT PSEUDOSECTION:
; EDNS: version: 0, flags:; udp: 512
;; QUESTION SECTION:
;google.com.                  IN      A

;; ANSWER SECTION:
google.com.       268      IN      A      216.58.217.206

;; Query time: 36 msec
;; SERVER: 192.168.1.1#53(192.168.1.1)
;; WHEN: Sun Mar 05 17:01:08 PST 2017
;; MSG SIZE rcvd: 55
```

To query a specific DNS server rather than the default DNS servers for your host, use the following syntax: **dig @server host_to_lookup**. Table 25.5 describes common options for the **dig** command.

TABLE 25.5 **Common dig Options**

Option	Description
-f *file*	Uses the content of *file* to perform multiple lookups; the file should contain one hostname per line.
-4	Performs only IPv4 queries.
-6	Performs only IPv6 queries.
-x *address*	Performs a reverse lookup (returns the hostname when provided an IP address).

netstat/ss

The **netstat** command is useful for displaying a variety of network information. It is a key utility when troubleshooting network issues. Table 25.6 describes common options for the **netstat** command.

TABLE 25.6 **Common netstat Options**

Option	Description
-t or **--tcp**	Displays TCP information
-u or **--udp**	Displays UDP information
-r or **--route**	Displays the routing table
-v or **--verbose**	Turns on verbose mode; displays additional information
-i or **--interfaces**	Displays information based on a specific interface
-a or **--all**	Applies to all
-s or **--statistics**	Displays statistics for the output

For example, the following command will display all active TCP connections:

```
[root@OCS ~]# netstat -ta
Active Internet connections (servers and established)
Proto Recv-Q Send-Q   Local Address            Foreign Address State
tcp        0      0 192.168.122.1:domain      0.0.0.0:* LISTEN
tcp        0      0 0.0.0.0:ssh               0.0.0.0:* LISTEN
tcp        0      0 localhost:ipp             0.0.0.0:* LISTEN
tcp        0      0 localhost:smtp            0.0.0.0:* LISTEN
```

```
tcp6       0       0 [::]:ssh              [::]:* LISTEN

tcp6       0       0 localhost:ipp         [::]:* LISTEN

tcp6       0       0 localhost:smtp        [::]:* LISTEN
```

The **ss** command is used to display socket information. Without any options, it lists all open sockets. For example:

```
[root@OCS ~]# ss | wc -l
160
[root@OCS ~]# ss | head
Netid  State   Recv-Q Send-Q  Local Address:Port       Peer Address:Port
u_str  ESTAB   0      0       /var/run/dovecot/anvil 23454966    * 23454965
u_str  ESTAB   0      0       /var/run/dovecot/anvil 23887673    * 23887672
u_str  ESTAB   0      0       /run/systemd/journal/stdout 13569  * 13568
u_str  ESTAB   0      0                     * 13893             * 13894
u_str  ESTAB   0      0                     * 13854             * 13855
u_str  ESTAB   0      0                     * 13850             * 13849
u_str  ESTAB   0      0                     * 68924             * 68925
u_str  ESTAB   0      0                     * 17996             * 17997
u_str  ESTAB   0      0       /var/run/dovecot/config 9163531    * 9163871
```

Useful options for the **ss** command include those described in Table 25.7.

TABLE 25.7 **Common ss Options**

Option	Description
-lt	Lists open TCP sockets
-lu	Lists open UDP sockets
-lp	Lists the process ID that owns each socket
-n	Doesn't resolve IP addresses to hostnames or port numbers to port names
-a	Displays all information
-s	Displays a summary

route

The **route** command can be used to display a routing table:

```
[root@OCS ~]# route
Kernel IP routing table
Destination  Gateway      Genmask         Flags Metric  Ref Use Iface
default      192.168.1.1  0.0.0.0         UG    100     0   0   enp0s3
192.168.0.0  0.0.0.0      255.255.0.0     U     100     0   0   enp0s3
192.168.1.0  0.0.0.0      255.255.255.0   U     100     0   0   enp0s3
```

This information can also be displayed with the **ip** command:

```
[root@OCS ~]# ip route show
default via 192.168.1.1 dev enp0s3 proto static metric 100
192.168.0.0/16 dev enp0s3 proto kernel scope link src 192.168.1.24
metric 100
192.168.1.0/24 dev enp0s3 proto kernel scope link src 192.168.1.26
metric 100
192.168.122.0/24 dev virbr0 proto kernel scope link src 192.168.122.1
```

The **route** command can also be used to modify the default router:

```
route add default gw 192.168.1.10
```

To add a new router, execute the following command:

```
route add -net 192.168.3.0 netmask 255.255.255.0 gw 192.168.3.100
```

This command will send all network packets destined for the 192.168.3.0/24 network to the 192.168.3.100 router. These changes are temporary and will survive only until the next time the system is booted. Permanent changes are made within your system's configuration files, which vary from one distribution to another.

arp

The **arp** command is used to view the Address Resolution Protocol (ARP) table or make changes to it. This table is used on a local network to keep track of which IP addresses are associated with Media Access Control (MAC) addresses, because within a local network, MAC addresses are used to communicate between network devices. Note that MAC addresses are often referred to as *hardware addresses*.

When executed with no arguments, the **arp** command displays the ARP table:

```
# arp
Address        HWtype  HWaddress         Flags Mask    Iface
192.168.1.11   ether   30:3a:64:44:a5:02   C             eth0
```

In the event that a remote system has its network card replaced (or if a virtual network device has been assigned a new MAC address), you might need to delete an entry from the ARP table. You can accomplish this by using the **-d** option to the **arp** command:

```
# arp -i eth0 -d 192.169.1.11
```

After the address is removed from the ARP table, there should be no need to add the new address manually. The next time the local system uses this IP address, it will send a broadcast request on the appropriate network to determine the new MAC address.

curl

The **curl** command allows for noninteractive data transfer from a large number of protocols, including

- ▶ FTP
- ▶ FTPS
- ▶ HTTP
- ▶ SCP
- ▶ SFTP
- ▶ SMB
- ▶ SMBS
- ▶ Telnet
- ▶ TFTP

In the following example, data from the http://onecoursesource.com URL is downloaded to the local system:

```
# curl http://onecoursesource.com
<!DOCTYPE HTML PUBLIC "-//IETF//DTD HTML 2.0//EN">
```

```
<html><head>

<title>301 Moved Permanently</title>

</head><body>

<h1>Moved Permanently</h1>

<p>The document has moved <a href="http://www.onecoursesource.
com/">here</a>.</p>

</body></html>
```

Packet Capture

When you're troubleshooting network issues or performing network security audits, it can be helpful to view the network traffic, including traffic that isn't related to the local machine. The **tcpdump** command is a packet capture utility, and it enables you to view local network traffic.

By default, the **tcpdump** command displays all network traffic to standard output until you terminate the command. Running this command could result in a dizzying amount of data flying by on your screen. You can limit the output to a specific number of network packets by using the **-c** options:

```
# tcpdump -c 5

tcpdump: verbose output suppressed, use -v or -vv for full protocol
decode

listening on eth0, link-type EN10MB (Ethernet), capture size 65535
bytes

11:32:59.630873 IP localhost.43066 > 192.168.1.1.domain: 16227+ A?
onecoursesource.com. (37)

11:32:59.631272 IP localhost.59247 > 192.168.1.1.domain: 2117+ PTR?
1.1.168.192.in-addr.arpa. (42)

11:32:59.631387 IP localhost.43066 > 192.168.1.1.domain: 19647+ AAAA?
onecoursesource.com. (37)

11:32:59.647932 IP 192.168.1.1.domain > localhost.59247: 2117
NXDomain* 0/1/0 (97)

11:32:59.717499 IP 192.168.1.1.domain > localhost.43066: 16227 1/0/0 A
38.89.136.109 (53)

5 packets captured

5 packets received by filter

0 packets dropped by kernel
```

Packet Analyzer

Wireshark is an amazing network capture and analyzer tool that provides both graphical user interface (GUI) and text-based user interface (TUI) tools. To start the GUI tool, execute the **wireshark** command. The output should be similar to Figure 25.1.

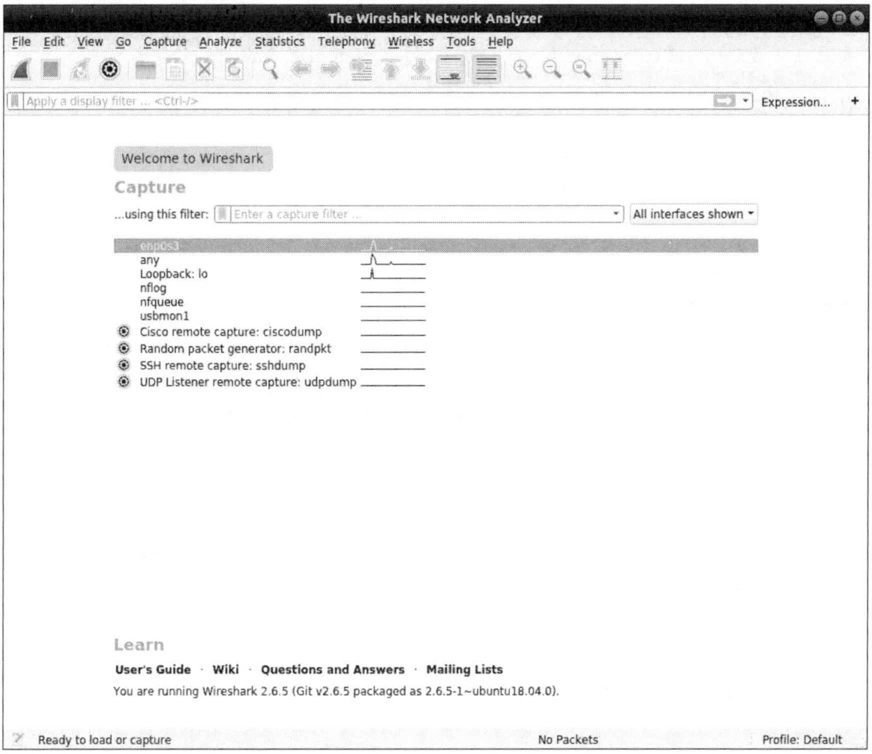

FIGURE 25.1   **The wireshark Command**

To view network traffic, you need to start a capture. Click **Capture + Start**. You can also limit what is captured by setting filters and options (click **Capture + Options**).

To use the TUI-based form of Wireshark, execute the **tshark** command as the root user:

```
# tshark
Capturing on 'enp0s3'
    1 0.000000000    10.0.2.15 → 68.105.28.11 DNS 81 Standard query
0xeec4 A google.com OPT
```

```
    2 0.001031279    10.0.2.15 → 68.105.28.11 DNS 81 Standard query
0x3469 AAAAgoogle.com OPT

    3 0.017196416 68.105.28.11 → 10.0.2.15    DNS 109 Standard query
response 0x3469 AAAA google.com AAAA 2607:f8b0:4007:800::200e OPT

    4 0.017265061 68.105.28.11 → 10.0.2.15    DNS 97 Standard query
response 0xeec4 A google.com A 172.217.14.110 OPT

    5 0.018482388    10.0.2.15 → 172.217.14.110 ICMP 98 Echo (ping)
request  id=0x122c, seq=1/256, ttl=64

    6 0.036907577 172.217.14.110 → 10.0.2.15    ICMP 98 Echo (ping)
reply    id=0x122c, seq=1/256, ttl=251 (request in 5)

    7 1.021052811    10.0.2.15 → 172.217.14.110 ICMP 98 Echo (ping)
request  id=0x122c, seq=2/512, ttl=64

    8 1.039492225 172.217.14.110 → 10.0.2.15    ICMP 98 Echo (ping)
reply    id=0x122c, seq=2/512, ttl=251 (request in 7)
```

OpenSSL Client

Secure communication over SSL is an important component of cloud-based networking. To troubleshoot SSL issues, you may need to make use of the **openssl client** utility. For example, to test an SSL connection, you can execute the following command:

```
openssl s_client -connect <hostname>:<port>
```

Replace <hostname> with the SSL server's hostname and <port> with the network port that the server is listening on.

Resource Utilization

As previously mentioned, you'll notice several redundancies in the CompTIA Cloud+ objectives. This section is a good example because many of these topics were covered in previous chapters:

▶ **CPU, GPU, and Memory:** Chapter 14, "Compute Sizing for Deployment"

▶ **Storage and I/O:** Chapter 12, "Storage in Cloud Environments"

▶ **Capacity:** Chapter 17, "Operation of a Cloud Environment"

▶ **Network Bandwidth and Latency:** Chapter 18, "Optimize Cloud Environments"

▶ **Replication:** Chapter 21, "Disaster Recovery Tasks"

▶ **Scaling:** Chapter 3, "High Availability and Scaling in Cloud Environments"

Application

Application configuration consists of providing resources to the application so that the application is able to perform its tasks. In this section you'll learn about two troubleshooting categories of application configuration: memory management and service overload.

Memory Management

Like all compute operations, applications need memory to store information. When you deploy an application in a cloud environment, you also assign a specific amount of memory to the application. This requirement might not meet the needs of the application, however.

Because most cloud environments provide tools to monitor memory usage for an application, the way you troubleshoot this sort of problem is to view the metrics for memory utilization. You can also set warnings when memory utilization reaches a specific value to receive advance warning of potential problems.

Adding more memory for the application might seem like an easy solution, but remember that memory, like most cloud resources, comes at a cost. You might also want to consider optimizing the application so that it doesn't require much memory. This task might be something that you can do in a configuration file for the application, but also might require working with the developers who maintain the application.

Service Overload

An application service overload can be the result of the application using more CPU or vCPU resources than it has been allocated. As with memory resources, most cloud environments allow you to monitor vCPU utilization.

Troubleshooting this issue is similar to troubleshooting a lack of memory: determine whether the application can be modified to use less vCPU resources or allocate more vCPU resources.

Incorrectly Configured or Failed Load Balancing

To learn more about incorrectly configured or failed load balancing, see the "Load Balancers" section in Chapter 13.

CramQuiz

Answer these questions. The answers follow the last question. If you cannot answer these questions correctly, consider reading this section again until you can.

1. In which of the following cloud components is the order of the rules unimportant?
   - ○ **A.** Network ACL
   - ○ **B.** Firewall
   - ○ **C.** Security group
   - ○ **D.** The order of the rules is important in all of these components.

2. Which type of NAT is used when you want to place servers behind a firewall and still provide access from an external network?
   - ○ **A.** DNAT
   - ○ **B.** SNAT
   - ○ **C.** MASQUERADE
   - ○ **D.** FWALL

3. The standard MTU size is _____ bytes.
   - ○ **A.** 700
   - ○ **B.** 2100
   - ○ **C.** 1400
   - ○ **D.** 1500

4. Which of the following can be used to display basic IP network settings for devices? (Choose all that apply.)
   - ○ **A.** ipconfig
   - ○ **B.** ifconfig
   - ○ **C.** if
   - ○ **D.** ip

CramQuiz Answers

1. Security group
2. DNAT
3. 1500
4. ipconfig, ifconfig, and ip

What Next?

If you want more practice on this chapter's exam objectives before you move on, remember that you can access all of the CramQuiz questions on the companion website. You can also create a custom exam by objectives with the practice exam software. Note any objectives you struggle with and go to that objective's material in this chapter.

Glossary of Essential Terms and Components

A

Access control list (ACL) A list that defines access privileges to a network resource by defining rules in terms of IP address, ports, source, destination, and/or protocol.

Access key ID An IAM credential that you can use to authenticate to a cloud resource.

Active logging A common intelligence gathering tool used during the forensics process.

Address Resolution Protocol (ARP) A protocol that allows the resolution of a device's assigned IP address into its MAC hardware address.

Administrative control A control based on business and organizational processes and procedures.

Advanced Encryption Standard (AES) A symmetrical 128-bit fixed-block encryption system that has a key size of 128, 192, or 256 bits and replaces the legacy DES standard.

Advanced persistent threat (APT) A threat that is rooted in the capability to infiltrate a network and remain inside while going undetected. This access often provides the means for a more strategic target or defined objective, including the capability to exfiltrate information over a long period of time.

Agile   An SDLC model that breaks development into cycles. The Agile model combines iterative and incremental process models.

Annual loss expectancy (ALE) The expected cost per year arising from a risk's occurrence. It is calculated as the product of the single loss expectancy (SLE) and the annualized rate of occurrence (ARO).

Annual rate of occurrence (ARO) The number of times a given risk will occur within a single year.

Antivirus   A software program used to protect the user environment that scans for email and downloadable malicious code.

Application logging   A major focus of security in a more web-based world, with exploits such as cross-site scripting and SQL injections now an everyday occurrence.

Application programming interface (API)   A connection between computers or between computer programs.

Asymmetric key   A pair of key values (one public and the other private) used to encrypt and decrypt data, respectively. Only the holder of the private key can decrypt data

encrypted with the public key; this means that anyone who obtains a copy of the public key can send data to the private key holder in confidence.

Attribute Based Access Control (ABAC)   A logical access control model recommended as the preferred access control model for information sharing among diverse organizations by the Federal Identity, Credential, and Access Management (FICAM) Roadmap.

Auditing   The tracking of user access to resources, primarily for security purposes.

Authentication   The process of identifying users.

Authentication header (AH) A component of the IPsec protocol that provides integrity, authentication, and antireplay capabilities.

Authorization   The process of identifying what a given user is allowed to do.

Auto-scaling   An AWS service that adjusts compute capacity to maintain desired performance.

Availability zone   A fault isolation area in one AWS region that is composed of one or more data centers. Multiple availability zones are connected to independent Internet, power, uplink, and other providers to mitigate the possibility of a failure affecting more than one availability zone at a time.

B

Baseline or baselining   Measure of normal activity, used as a point to determine abnormal system and network behaviors.

Black box   A test conducted when the assessor has no information or knowledge about the inner workings of the system or knowledge of the source code.

Block cipher   A way to transform a message from plain text (unencrypted form) to cipher text (encrypted form) one piece at a time The block size represents a standard chunk of data that is transformed in a single operation.

Block storage   Data records stored in blocks on a storage-area network.

Blowfish   A block cipher that can encrypt using any size chunk of data and perform encryption with any length encryption key, up to 448 bits.

Bot   Short for *robot*; an automated computer program that needs no user interaction. Bots allow hackers to take control of a system. Many bots used together can form a larger botnet.

Botnet   A large number of computers (bots) that forward transmissions to other computers on the Internet. You might also hear a botnet referred to as a *zombie army*.

Bring your own device (BYOD)   A policy allowing employees to use personal mobile devices for access to enterprise data and systems.

Brute-force attack   An attack that relies on cryptanalysis or algorithms capable of performing exhaustive key searches.

Bucket   The storage unit for an S3 object.

Buffer overflow   An attack that occurs when the data presented to an application or service exceeds the storage space allocation that has been reserved in memory for that application or service.

Business continuity plan (BCP)   A plan that describes a long-term systems and services replacement and recovery strategy, designed for times when a complete loss of facilities occurs. A business continuity plan prepares for automatic failover of critical services to redundant offsite systems.

Business impact analysis (BIA)   The process of determining the potential impacts resulting from the interruption of time-sensitive or critical business processes.

Business partner agreement (BPA)   A type of contract that establishes the responsibilities of each partner.

C

Caching   Temporarily storing frequently used data closer to the final data destination (server or client).

cat   A command-line file manipulation command to read files sequentially and used to concatenate files.

CDN   Content delivery network; a system of distributed servers (network) that deliver pages and other web content to a user, based on the geographic locations of the user.

CER   A common certificate extension. A CER file is used to store X509 certificates.

Certificate authority (CA)   A system that issues, distributes, and maintains current information about digital certificates. Such authorities can be private (operated within a company or an organization for its own use) or public (operated on the Internet for general public access).

Certificate policy   A statement that governs the usage of digital certificates.

Certificate revocation list (CRL)   A list generated by a CA that enumerates digital certificates that are no longer valid and the reasons they are no longer valid.

Certificate signing request (CSR)   A request to apply for a digital certificate.

Chain of custody   The documentation of all transfers of evidence from one person to another, showing the date, time, reason for transfer, and signatures of both parties involved in the transfer. Chain of custody also refers to the process of tracking evidence from a crime scene to the courtroom.

Challenge Handshake Authentication Protocol (CHAP)   A widely used authentication method in which a hashed version of a user's password is transmitted during the authentication process.

CI/CD   Continuous integration/ continuous delivery (or deployment); a practice that focuses on the toolchain that can automate the delivery of software in a fast, iterative manner.

Cipher   A method of encrypting text. The term *cipher* also refers to an encrypted message (although the term *cipher text* is preferred).

Cipher Block Chaining (CBC)   A commonly used mode that provides for confidentiality only, not integrity.

CLI   Command-line interface; a tool to access a service or feature in a terminal or command-line session.

Cloud Access Security Broker   A Gartner-created term describing a cloud cybersecurity layer focused on visibility, compliance, data security, and threat protection.

Cloud Security Alliance (CSA)   A nonprofit organization that provides security best practices for cloud-based services and computing.

Cloud-native application   An application designed and built to run in the cloud.

Cold site   A remote site that has electricity, plumbing, and heating installed, ready for use when enacting disaster recovery or business continuity plans. At a cold site, the company enacting the plan supplies all other equipment, systems, and configurations. Compare this with hot and warm sites.

Compensating control An alternate control that is intended to reduce the risk of an existing or potential control weakness.

Compute To perform calculation, computation, and transformation of incoming data or requests.

Computer/cyber incident response team (CIRT) The team of experts who respond to security incidents. Also referred to as a CSIRT (computer security incident response team).

Containers Technology that packages applications and services together with their runtime environment enabling them to be run anywhere.

Corrective control A control that is reactive and provides measures to lessen harmful effects or restore the system being impacted.

Cross-site request forgery (XSRF) A web attack that exploits existing site trust, such as unexpired banking session cookies, to perform actions on the trusting site using the already existing trusted account.

Cross-site scripting (XSS) Malicious executable code placed on a website that allows an attacker to hijack a user session to conduct unauthorized access activities, expose confidential data, and log successful attacks back to the attacker.

Cryptographic module Any combination of hardware, firmware, or software that implements cryptographic functions such as encryption, decryption, digital signatures, authentication techniques, and random number generation.

Cryptography A process that protects information by disguising (encrypting) it into a format that only authorized systems or individuals can read.

Crypto-malware Malware that is specifically designed to find potentially valuable data on a system and encrypt it.

curl A command-line tool that enables you to get and send data using URLs.

CVE Common Vulnerabilities and Exposure; a list of publicly known vulnerabilities that provides descriptions and reference.

CVSS Common Vulnerability Scoring System; a standard that provides a severity rating.

Cyber kill chain A framework to track the steps or phases that an attacker goes through as part of an intrusion.

D

Data Encryption Standard (DES) A block cipher that uses a 56-bit key and 8 bits of parity on each 64-bit chunk of data.

Data exfiltration The unauthorized transfer of data. A more basic definition is data theft.

Data loss prevention (DLP) Security services that identify, monitor, and protect data during use, storage, or transfer between devices. DLP software relies on deep inspection of data and transactional details for unauthorized access operations.

Data sensitivity   The classification scheme of data among organizations.

Decryption   The process of turning cipher text into plain text.

Defense-in-depth   A term rooted in military strategy that requires a balanced emphasis on people, technology, and operations to maintain information assurance (IA).

Denial of service (DoS)   A type of attack that denies legitimate users access to a server or services by consuming sufficient system resources or network bandwidth that it renders a service unavailable.

DER   The binary form of a PEM certificate.

Detective control   A control that warns that physical security measures are being violated.

Deterrent control   A control that is intended to discourage individuals from intentionally violating information security policies or procedures.

Development and Operations (DevOps)   A software development practice focused on culture, automation, and iterative development of software.

Differential backup   A backup that provides only the data that has changed since the last full backup. It is incomplete without the last full backup.

Diffie-Hellman (D-H) key exchange   An early key exchange design in which two parties, without prior arrangement, can agree on a secret key that is known only to them.

Digital certificate   An electronic document that includes the user's public key and the digital signature of the certificate authority (CA) that has authenticated the user. The digital certificate can also contain information about the user, the CA, and attributes that define what users are allowed to do with systems they access using the digital certificate.

Digital Signature Algorithm (DSA)   A U.S. standard for the generation and verification of digital signatures to ensure authenticity.

Disaster recovery plan (DRP)   Actions to be taken in case a business is hit with a natural or man-made disaster.

Discretionary access control (DAC)   Access control method in which access rights are configured at the discretion of accounts with authority over each resource, including the capability to extend administrative rights through the same mechanism.

Distributed denial of service (DDoS)   Attack that originates from multiple systems simultaneously, causing even more extreme consumption of bandwidth and other resources than a DoS attack.

Domain Name Service (DNS)   The service responsible for translation of hierarchical human-readable named addresses into their numeric IP equivalents.

E

EC2 Elastic Compute Cloud; the VM instance-running service in AWS.

Edge computing Computing that happens near the edge of a network closer to where it's used or needed.

e-discovery The discovery process for electronically stored information.

Elasticity The capability to expand and reduce cloud resources as needed at any given point in time.

Electromagnetic interference (EMI) Electronic device interference that occurs when the device is in the area of another device. EMI affects the performance of a device.

Encapsulating Security Payload (ESP) Method to provide confidentiality, data origin authentication, connectionless integrity, an antireplay service, and traffic flow confidentiality.

Encryption The process of turning plain text into cipher text.

Encryption algorithm A mathematical formula or method used to scramble information before it is transmitted over unsecure media. Examples include RSA, DH, IDEA, Blowfish, MD5, and DSS/DSA.

End-of-life (EOL) Software that is unsupported because the vendor has retired it.

Endpoint detection and response (EDR) Software that offers protection from malware for endpoints.

Escalation of privilege An exploitation technique that gives an attacker or tester access at a higher authorization and also provides the capability to conduct more advanced commands and routines.

F

Federation A way to connect identity management systems by allowing identities to cross multiple jurisdictions.

File Transfer Protocol (FTP) A client/server data file transfer service for TCP networks that are capable of anonymous or authenticated access.

Firewall A network system that monitors incoming and outgoing traffic and makes determinations to allow or deny the traffic based upon policy.

Framework A structure that generally includes more components than a guide and is used as a basis for implementing and managing security controls.

Full backup A complete backup of all data. This is the most time- and resource-intensive form of backup, requiring the largest amount of data storage.

G

General Data Protection Regulation (GDPR)   A regulation intended to strengthen data protection for all individuals within the European Union (EU).

Gray box   A testing method that combines white box and black box techniques. It can be more easily thought of as being translucent. Specifically, the tester has some understanding of or limited knowledge of the inner workings.

grep   A command-line file manipulation command to search files for patterns.

Group   A group of users that can be grouped as per common attributes.

Guide   Specific information about how standards should be implemented. A guide or guideline is generally not mandatory and provides recommendations or good practices.

H

HA   High availability; the capability to withstand failure and adhere to availability as defined in an SLA.

Hardware Security Module (HSM)   A dedicated crypto-processor that is specifically designed for the protection of transactions, identities, and applications by securing cryptographic keys.

Hash value   The resultant output or data generated from an encryption hash when applied to a specific set of data. If it is computed and passed as part of an incoming message and then is recomputed upon message receipt, such a hash value can be used to verify the received data when the two hash values match.

Hash-based Message Authentication Code (HMAC)   Additional security provided to MAC by adding another integrity check to the data being transmitted.

Hashing   A methodology used to calculate a short, secret value from a data set of any size (usually for an entire message or for individual transmission units). This secret value is recalculated independently on the receiving end and is compared to the submitted value to verify the sender's identity.

Health Insurance Portability and Accountability Act (HIPAA)   U.S. legislation that provides data privacy and security provisions for protecting medical information.

Honeypot   A decoy system designed to attract hackers. A honeypot usually has all its logging and tracing enabled, and its security level is lowered on purpose. Such systems often include deliberate lures or bait, in hopes of attracting would-be attackers who think they can obtain valuable items on these systems.

Host-based IDS (HIDS)   Systems that monitor communications on a host-by-host basis and try to filter malicious data. These types of IDSs are good at detecting unauthorized file modifications and user activity.

Host-based IPS (HIPS)   A software intrusion prevention system capable of reacting to and preventing or terminating unauthorized access within a single host system.

Hot site   A site that is immediately available for continuing computer operations if an emergency arises. It typically has all the necessary hardware and software loaded and configured, and it is available continuously. Compare this with warm and cold sites.

Hybrid cloud   A cloud deployment model in which an organization provides and manages some resources in-house and has other resources provided externally via a public cloud.

Hypertext Transfer Protocol (HTTP)   A client/server protocol for network transfer of information between a web server and a client browser over the World Wide Web (WWW).

Hypertext Transfer Protocol over Secure Sockets Layer (HTTPS)   A protocol used in a secured connection that encapsulates data transferred between the client and web server. It occurs on port 443.

Hypervisor   A virtualization platform that provides more than one operating system to run on a host computer at the same time. It controls how access to a computer's processors and memory is shared. A Type I native or bare-metal hypervisor

is software that runs directly on a hardware platform. A Type II or hosted hypervisor is software that runs within an operating system environment.

I

IaaS   Infrastructure as a Service; a service that makes it possible to provision and use infrastructure components such as compute units, disk, and network from the cloud.

IAM   Identity and Access Management; the identity service that cloud providers offer with which you provide access control for users, group, and roles.

IDE   Integrated development environment; a software application that provides comprehensive facilities to computer programmers for software development.

Identification   A process of presenting information such as a username, a process ID, a smart card, or another unique identifier, claiming an identity.

Identity   An attribute that identifies an individual in the cloud.

IdP   Identity provider; a directory that can authenticate a user when federated with IAM.

Incremental backup   Backup that includes only the data that has changed since the last incremental backup. It resets the archive bit.

Infrastructure as Code (IaC)   A term meaning that infrastructure configuration can be incorporated into application code. Also known as the programmable infrastructure.

International Organization for Standardization (ISO) A body that provides best practice recommendations on information security management.

Internet Control Message Protocol (ICMP) A transport protocol within the TCP/IP suite that operates separately from TCP or UDP transfer. ICMP is intended for passing error messages and is used for services such as **ping** and **traceroute**.

Internet of Things (IoT) Connected everyday devices performing specific functions using embedded systems and sensors.

Internet Protocol Security (IPsec) A mechanism used for the encryption of TCP/IP traffic. IPsec provides security extensions to IPv4. It manages special relationships between pairs of machines, called security associations.

Intranet A portion of the information technology infrastructure that belongs to and is controlled by the company in question.

Intrusion detection system (IDS) A sophisticated network protection system designed to detect attacks in progress but not to prevent potential attacks from occurring. Many IDSs actually can trace attacks back to an apparent source, and some can even automatically notify all hosts through which attack traffic passes that they are forwarding such traffic.

IOPS (input/output per second) A performance specification that defines the rate of input and output per second when storing and retrieving data.

IP spoofing An attack that seeks to bypass IP address filters by setting up a connection from a client and sourcing the packets with an IP address that is allowed through the filter.

ipconfig A command that displays network settings such as IP address, subnet mask, and default gateway.

J

JSON JavaScript Object Notation; a scripting language used widely in the cloud to define infrastructure characteristics, security, and so on.

K

Kerberos A set of authentication services, including the Authentication Service (AS) Exchange protocol, the Ticket-Granting Service (TGS) Exchange protocol, and the Client/Server (CS) Exchange protocol.

Key escrow Situation in which a CA or other entity maintains a copy of the private key associated with the public key signed by the CA.

Key exchange A technique in which a pair of keys is generated and then exchanged between two systems (typically, a client and a server) over a network connection to allow them to establish a secure connection.

Key management   The methods for creating and managing cryptographic keys and digital certificates.

KMS   Key Management Service; a cloud service that centrally manages customers' cryptographic keys and policies across the cloud services that require data encryption.

L

Layer 2 Tunneling Protocol (L2TP)   A protocol that performs tunneling at Layer 2 of the OSI model.

Least privilege   An access control practice in which a logon is given only minimal access to resources required to perform its tasks.

Lightweight Directory Access Protocol (LDAP)   A TCP/IP protocol that enables client systems to access directory services and related data. In most cases, LDAP is used as part of management or other applications, or in browsers to access directory services information.

Logger   A command-line tool used to add logs to the local syslog file or a remote syslog server.

M

Machine learning   Capability of software to gather information and make conclusions.

Malware   Malicious software used to cause damage or gain unauthorized access to systems.

Mandatory access control (MAC)   A centralized security method that does not allow users to change permissions on objects.

Man-in-the-middle   An attack in which a hacker attempts to intercept data in a network stream and then inserts his or her own data into the communication. The goal is to disrupt or take over communications.

Mean time between failures (MTBF)   The point in time at which a device will still be operational, denoting the average time a device will function before failing.

Mean time to failure (MTTF)   The expected time to failure for a nonrepairable system.

Mean time to recovery (MTTR)   The average time that a device will take to recover from any failure.

Message Authentication Code (MAC)   Way to authenticate a message. It works like a hash because it is used to detect tampering.

Message digest   The output of an encryption hash that is applied to some fixed-size chunk of data. A message digest provides a profound integrity check because even a change to 1 bit in the target data changes the resulting digest value. This explains why digests are included so often in network transmissions.

Message digest algorithm A hashing algorithm based on message digest.

Migration The process of moving an application to the cloud.

MITRE ATT&CK A knowledgebase and framework of different attack techniques to understand and defend against an attacker.

Monitoring Tracking performance, logs, and the state of an application.

Multifactor Authentication (MFA) Authentication that involves multiple factors, such as something you have and something you know.

N

National Institute of Standards and Technology (NIST) An agency within the U.S. Department of Commerce that is responsible for developing measurement standards, including standards for cybersecurity best practices, monitoring, and validation.

netcat A network utility for gathering information from TCP and UDP network connections.

Network access control list (NACL) A stateless subnet firewall that protects both inbound and outbound subnet traffic.

Network Address Translation (NAT) A service that provides indirect Internet access to cloud instances that are located on private subnets, hiding internal IPs.

Network Time Protocol (NTP) A UDP protocol used for device clock synchronization, providing a standard time base over variable-latency networks. This is critical for time-synchronized encryption and access protocols such as Kerberos.

Network-based IDS (NIDS) An IDS that monitors packet flow and tries to locate unauthorized packets that might have gotten through the firewall. An NIDS is best at detecting DoS attacks and unauthorized user access.

Network-based IPS (NIPS) A device or software program designed to sit inline with traffic flows and prevent attacks in real time.

Next-generation firewall (NGFW) Firewalls that go beyond traditional port and IP address examination to include application and user awareness.

nmap A network scanning tool used for locating network hosts, detecting operating systems, and identifying services.

Nondisclosure agreement (NDA) A legally binding document that organizations might require of their employees and other people who come into contact with confidential information.

Normalization The conversion of data to its anticipated, simplest known form.

NoSQL A type of database that does not follow SQL rules and architecture.

nslookup A command-line utility used for troubleshooting DNS.

O

OAuth (Open Authorization) A framework used for Internet token-based authorization. The main purpose of OAuth is API authorization between applications.

Object storage Data stored as a distinct object with associated metadata containing relevant information.

Onboarding A process used to create an identity profile and the necessary information required to describe the identity.

Online Certificate Status Protocol (OCSP) An Internet protocol defined by the IETF that is used to validate digital certificates issued by a CA. OCSP was created as an alternative to certificate revocation lists (CRLs) and overcomes certain limitations of CRLs.

Open Web Application Security Project (OWASP) A nonprofit organization that provides resources to improve the security of software.

OpenID Connect An identity layer based on OAuth 20 specifications used for consumer single sign-on.

Order of restoration The order in which backup tapes are restored.

P

Password attack Assaults on passwords using manual or automated techniques using methods such as dictionary, brute-force, spraying, and rainbow-table type attacks.

Password policy A policy containing global password settings for AWS account IAM users.

Payment Card Industry Data Security Standard (PCI DSS) A standard that governs the use and storage of credit card data.

Peering connection A private networking connection between two VPCs or two transit gateways.

PEM The most common format and extension for certificates.

Personal Health Information (PHI) Any medical data that can be used to identify an individual.

Personally Identifiable Information (PII) Broadly, any data that can be used to identify an individual.

ping A network tool to test the basic functions of a network commonly used to test whether a remote host is alive or responding.

Platform as a Service (PaaS) The delivery of a computing platform, often an operating system with associated services, over the Internet without downloads or installation.

Preventive control A control that attempts to avoid the occurrence of unwanted events by inhibiting the free use of computing resources.

Privacy A term that relates to rights to control the sharing and use of one's personal information.

Privacy Impact Assessment (PIA) An assessment needed for any organization that collects, uses, stores, or processes personal information such as PII or PHI.

Private cloud A cloud deployment model in which a private organization implements a cloud in its internal enterprise, and that cloud is used by the organization's employees and partners.

Private key A key that is maintained on the host system or application.

Privilege escalation A method of software exploitation that takes advantage of a program's flawed code. Usually, this crashes the system and leaves it in a state in which arbitrary code can be executed or an intruder can function as an administrator.

Protocol analyzer Tool that troubleshoots network issues by gathering packet-level information across the network. These applications capture packets and decode the information into readable data for analysis.

Public cloud A cloud deployment model in which a service provider makes resources available to the public over the Internet.

Public key A key that is made available to whoever is going to encrypt the data sent to the holder of a private key.

Public key infrastructure (PKI) A collection of systems, software, and communication protocols that distribute, manage, and control public key cryptography.

Python A popular and widely used general-purpose programming language.

R

RAID Redundant Array of Inexpensive (or Independent) Disks; the organization of multiple disks into a large, high-performance logical disk to provide redundancy in case of disk failure.

Ransomware A form of malware that attempts to hold a person or company ransom, often for monetary gain.

Read replica A read-only copy of a linked primary database.

Recovery point objective (RPO) The amount of time that can elapse during a disruption before the quantity of data lost during that period exceeds the BCP's maximum allowable threshold.

Recovery site The type of site an organization chooses for disaster recovery.

Recovery time objective (RTO) A measure of the time in which a service should be restored during disaster recovery operations.

Redundancy Replication of a component in identical copies to compensate for random hardware failures.

Refactoring   A practice for software developers that identifies ways to make code more efficient through better design.

Region   A set of cloud resources in a geographic area of the world. A region consists of two or more availability zones.

Relational database   A database that has the capability to perform complex queries over the data in a structured manner.

Representational state transfer (REST)   A client/server model for interacting with content on remote systems, typically using HTTP.

Reserved instance   A cloud instance for which you have prepaid.

risk acceptance   A process of recognizing a risk, identifying it, and then accepting that it is sufficiently unlikely or of such limited impact that corrective controls are not warranted.

Role-based access control (RBAC)   A security method that combines both MAC and DAC. RBAC uses profiles. Profiles are defined for specific roles within a company, and then users are assigned to such roles. This facilitates administration in a large group of users because when you modify a role and assign it new permissions, those settings are automatically conveyed to all users assigned to that role.

Router   A device that connects multiple network segments and routes packets between them. Routers split broadcast domains.

RSA algorithm   An asymmetric cryptography algorithm that allows anyone to create products that incorporate different implementations of the algorithm, without being subject to license and patent enforcement.

Rule-based access control (RBAC)   An extension of access control that includes stateful testing to determine whether a particular request for resource access may be granted. When a rule-based method is in force, access to resources might be granted or restricted, based on conditional testing.

S

Sandboxing   A method that enables programs and processes to be run in an isolated environment, to limit access to files and the host system.

Scalability   The capability to handle the changing needs of a system, process, or application within the confines of the current resources.

Scale up   To increase compute power automatically.

Scaling policy   A policy that describes the type of scaling of compute resources to be performed.

Scrum   A framework for managing application development as a team following three pillars: transparency, inspection, and adaptation.

Secure Hash Algorithm (SHA)   Hash algorithm pioneered by the

National Security Agency and widely used in the U.S. government.

Secure Hypertext Transfer Protocol (S-HTTP) An alternative to HTTPS. The Secure Hypertext Transfer Protocol was developed to support connectivity for banking transactions and other secure web communications.

Secure Shell (SSH) A protocol designed to support secure remote login, along with secure access to other services across an unsecure network. SSH includes a secure transport layer protocol that provides server authentication, confidentiality (encryption), and integrity (message digest functions), along with a user authentication protocol and a connection protocol that runs on top of the user authentication protocol.

Secure Sockets Layer (SSL) An Internet protocol that uses connection-oriented, end-to-end encryption to ensure that client/server communications are confidential (encrypted) and meet integrity constraints (message digests). Because SSL is independent of the application layer, any application protocol can work with SSL transparently. SSL can also work with a secure transport layer protocol, which is why the term *SSL/TLS* appears frequently. See also *Transport Layer Security*.

Secure/Multipurpose Internet Mail Extensions (S/MIME) An Internet protocol governed by RFC 2633 and used to secure email communications through encryption and digital signatures

for authentication. It generally works with PKI to validate digital signatures and related digital certificates.

Security Assertion Markup Language (SAML) An open standards protocol that uses Extensible Markup Language (XML) formatted messages for authentication and authorization.

Security group A stateful firewall protecting EC2 instances' network traffic.

Server Message Block (SMB) A network protocol used by Windows systems on the same network to store files.

Serverless A type of computing in which compute servers and integrated services are fully managed by the cloud provider.

Server-Side Encryption (SSE) Encryption of data records at rest by an application or a service.

Service-level agreement (SLA) A contract between two companies or a company and an individual that specifies, by contract, a level of service to be provided. Supplying replacement equipment within 24 hours of loss is a simple example of an SLA.

Session keys Randomly generated keys that perform both encryption and decryption during the communication of a session between two parties.

Simple Network Management Protocol (SNMP) UDP-based application layer Internet protocol used for network management. SNMP is governed by RFCs

2570 and 2574. In converting management information between management consoles (managers) and managed nodes (agents), SNMP implements configuration and event databases on managed nodes that can be configured to respond to interesting events by notifying network managers.

Single loss expectancy (SLE) The expected cost per instance arising from a risk's occurrence. The SLE is calculated as the product of the asset value and the risk's exposure factor (a percentage of loss if a risk occurs).

Snapshot An image of the file system that preserves the entire state and data of the virtual machine at the time it is taken.

Software as a Service (SaaS) A cloud computing model in which software applications are virtualized and provided by an outsourced service provider.

Software-defined networking (SDN) A method by which organizations can manage network services through a decoupled underlying infrastructure, enabling quick adjustments to changing business requirements.

Staging environment An SDLC environment that is primarily used to unit test the actual deployment of code before it is put into production.

Standard Specific mandatory controls based on policies.

Stateful A type of service that requires knowledge of all internal functions.

Stateless A type of self-contained redundant service that has no knowledge of its place in the application stack.

Structured Query Language (SQL) The de facto programming language used in relational databases.

Subnet A defined IP address range hosted within a VPC/VNet.

Symmetric key A single encryption key that is generated and used to encrypt data. This data is then passed across a network. After that data arrives at the recipient device, the same key used to encrypt that data is used to decrypt it. This technique requires a secure way to share keys because both the sender and the receiver use the same key (it is also called a shared secret because that key should be unknown to third parties).

Syslog A system logging protocol used to send logs or messaging events to a server.

System logging The process of collecting system data to be used for monitoring and auditing purposes.

T

Tag A metadata description for types of resources.

tcpdump A command-line packet analyzer tool that captures packets sent and received on an interface.

Transport Layer Security (TLS)
An end-to-end encryption protocol originally specified in ISO Standard 10736 that provides security services as part of the transport layer in a protocol stack.

Tunneling The process of transporting data securely over a network via an encrypted connection.

Type 1 hypervisor Virtualization software that is installed on hardware directly, which is why it is commonly called a bare metal hypervisor. A guest operating system runs on another level above the hypervisor. Examples include Citrix XenServer, Microsoft Hyper-V, and VMware vSphere.

Type 2 hypervisor A hypervisor installed over an existing operating system. Examples include VMware Workstation and Oracle VM VirtualBox.

U–V

User state Data that identifies an end user and the established session between the end user and a hosted application.

Versioning A process in which multiple copies of S3 objects, including the original object, are saved.

Virtual desktop infrastructure (VDI) The server-based virtualization technology that hosts and manages virtual desktops.

Virtual local-area network (VLAN)
A software technology that facilitates the grouping of network nodes connected to one or more network switches into a single logical network. By permitting logical aggregation of devices into virtual network segments, VLANs offer simplified user management and network resource access controls for switched networks.

Virtual machine (VM) An emulation that virtualizes a complete operating system and can be used as a substitute for a physical machine.

Virtual private cloud (VPC)
A logically isolated virtual network in the AWS cloud.

Virtual private network (VPN) A popular technology that supports reasonably secure, logical, private network links across some unsecure public network infrastructure, such as the Internet. VPNs are more secure than traditional remote access because they can be encrypted and because VPNs support tunneling (hiding numerous types of protocols and sessions within a single host-to-host connection).

Virtualization technology A technology developed to allow a guest operating system to run along with a host operating system with one set of hardware.

Virus A piece of malicious code that spreads to other computers by design, although some viruses also damage the systems on which they reside. Viruses can spread immediately upon reception or implement other unwanted actions, or they can lie dormant until a trigger in their code causes them to become active. The hidden code a virus executes is called its payload.

Voice over IP (VoIP) Network communications that are subject to the same attacks as other Internet communication methods.

Vulnerability scan A scanning method that identifies vulnerabilities, misconfigurations, and lack of security controls.

Vulnerability scanner A software utility that scans a range of IP addresses, testing for the presence of known vulnerabilities in software configuration and accessible services.

W

Warm site/Warm standby A backup site that has some of the equipment and infrastructure necessary for a business to begin operating at that location. Typically, organizations bring their own server systems and hardware to a warm site, but that site usually already includes a ready-to-use networking infrastructure. It also might include reliable power, climate controls, lighting, and Internet access points. Compare with hot and cold sites.

Waterfall A traditional SDLC model that starts with a defined set of requirements and a well-developed plan. Adjustments

are confined to the current development stage.

Web application firewall (WAF) Software or a hardware appliance used to protect the organization's web server from attack. A WAF is leveraged specifically for HTTP/HTTPS traffic at the application layer of the OSI model.

Web identity An identity provider that offers authentication of users from the web.

Web server A service hosting a website that is accessible via HTTP or HTTPS.

White box A testing method that provides some transparency. The assessor has knowledge about the inner workings of the system or knowledge of the source code. Also called clear box or glass box testing.

Wireshark A well-known packet analyzer.

Workflow orchestration Sequencing of events based on certain parameters by using scripting and scripting tools.

Worm A type of virus designed primarily to reproduce and replicate itself on as many computer systems as possible. A worm does not normally alter files; instead, it remains resident in a computer's memory. Worms typically rely on access to operating system capabilities that are invisible to users.

X, Y, Z

X509   A digital certificate that
uniquely identifies a potential
communications party or
participant. An X509 digital
certificate includes a party's name
and public key, among other
pieces, but it can also include
organizational affiliation, service or
access restrictions, and other access-
and security-related information.

**Yet Another Markup Language
(YAML)**   A language that is used
widely in the cloud to define
infrastructure characteristics,
security, and so on.

Index

Numbers

A

S

To receive your 10% off Exam Voucher, register your product at:

www.pearsonitcertification.com/register

and follow the instructions.